Shortlist

New York

WHAT'S NEW | WHAT'S ON | WHAT'S BEST

www.timeout.com/newyork

Contents

New York by Area

Essentials

Editorial Director Sarah Guy
Group Finance Manager Margaret Wright

Time Out Guides is a wholly owned subsidiary of Time Out Group Ltd.

© **Time Out Group Ltd**
Chairman & Founder Tony Elliott
Chief Executive Officer Tim Arthur
Chief Financial Officer Matt White
Publisher Alex Batho

Time Out and the Time Out logo are trademarks of Time Out Group Ltd.

This edition first published in Great Britain in 2014 by Ebury Publishing
A Random House Group Company
Company information can be found on www.randomhouse.co.uk
Random House UK Limited Reg. No. 954009
10 9 8 7 6 5 4 3 2 1

Distributed in the US and Latin America by Publishers Group West (1-510-809-3700)

For further distribution details, see www.timeout.com

ISBN: 978-1-84670-338-6

A CIP catalogue record for this book is available from the British Library.

Printed and bound in Germany by Appl.

While every effort has been made by the author(s) and the publisher to ensure that the information contained in this guide is accurate and up to date as at the date of publication, they accept no responsibility or liability in contract, tort, negligence, breach of statutory duty or otherwise for any inconvenience, loss, damage, costs or expenses of any nature whatsoever incurred or suffered by anyone as a result of any advice or information contained in this guide (except to the extent that such liability may not be excluded or limited as a matter of law). Before travelling, it is advisable to check all information locally, including without limitation, information on transport, accommodation, shopping and eating out. Anyone using this publication is entirely responsible for their own health, well-being and belongings and care should always be exercised while travelling.

MIX
Paper from
responsible sources
FSC
www.fsc.org   FSC® C004592

Penguin Random House is committed to a sustainable future for our business, our readers and our planet. This book is made from Forest Stewardship Council® certified paper.

New York Shortlist

The **Time Out New York Shortlist** is one of a series of guides that draws on Time Out's background as a magazine publisher to keep you current with everything that's going on in town. As well as New York's key sights and the best of its eating, drinking and leisure options, it picks out the most exciting venues to have opened in the last year and gives a full calendar of annual events. It also includes features on the important news, trends and openings, all compiled by locally based editors and writers. Whether you're visiting for the first time in your life or the first time this year, you'll find the *Time Out New York Shortlist* contains all you need to know, in a portable and easy-to-use format.

The guide divides Manhattan into three areas, each containing listings for Sights & Museums, Eating & Drinking, Shopping, Nightlife and Arts & Leisure, and maps pinpointing their locations; a further chapter rounds up the best of Outer Boroughs. At the front of the book are chapters rounding up these scenes city-wide, and giving a shortlist of our overall picks. We also include itineraries for days out, plus essentials such as transport information and hotels.

Our listings give phone numbers as dialled within the US. Within New York you need to use the initial 1 and the three-digit area code even if you're calling from within that area code. From abroad, use your country's exit code followed by the number (the initial 1 is the US country code.

We have noted price categories by using one to four dollar signs (**$-$$$$**), representing budget, moderate, expensive and luxury.

Major credit cards are accepted unless otherwise stated. We also indicate when a venue is NEW.

All our listings are double-checked, but places do sometimes close or change their hours or prices, so it's a good idea to call a venue before visiting. While every effort has been made to ensure accuracy, the publishers cannot accept responsibility for any errors that this guide may contain.

Venues are marked on the maps using symbols numbered according to their order within the chapter and colour-coded as follows:

❶ Sights & Museums
❶ Eating & Drinking
❶ Shopping
❶ Nightlife
❶ Arts & Leisure

Map Key

Major sight or landmark	▮
Hospital or college	▮
Railway station	▮
Park	▮
River	▮
Freeway	478
Main road	▮
Main road tunnel	▮
Pedestrian road	▮
Airport	✈
Church	✚
Subway station	Ⓜ
Area name	SOHO

Time Out **New York** Shortlist

EDITORIAL
Editor Lisa Ritchie
Proofreader Marion Moisy

DESIGN
Senior Designer Kei Ishimaru
Picture Editor Jael Marschner
Deputy Picture Editor Ben Rowe
Freelance Picture Researchers
   Lizzy Owen, Julie Turley

ADVERTISING
Advertising Sales Christy Stewart,
   Deborah Maclaren

MARKETING
Senior Publishing Brand Manager
   Luthfa Begum
Head of Circulation Dan Collins

PRODUCTION
Production Controller
   Katie Mulhern-Bhudia

CONTRIBUTORS
This guide was researched and written by Cristina Alonso, David Cote, Rebecca Dalzell,
Adam Feldman, Sophie Harris, Christina Izzo, Gia Kourlas, Ethan LaCroix, Matthew Love,
Marley Lynch, Lisa Ritchie, Steve Smith, Bruce Tantum, Mari Uyehara, and the writers of
Time Out New York.

PHOTOGRAPHY
Pages 2 (top left), 32 Atisha Paulson; 2 (top right), 44 T photography/Shutterstock.com;
2 (bottom left), 16, 69, 83 (top left) Virginia Rollison; 2 (bottom right), 47 M. Shcherbyna/
Shutterstock.com; 3 (top left), 62, 90 stockelements/Shutterstock.com; 3 (top right), 173,
174 Annie Schlechter; 3 (bottom left), 126 (top) Sean Pavone/Shutterstock.com; 3 (bottom
right), 179 Adrian Gaut; 9 Evan Lee/Courtesy The Metropolitan Museum of Art; 14, 73, 83
(top right and bottom), 152 Paul Wagtouicz; 17 Daniel Krieger Photography; 22, 141, 159
Filip Wolak Photography; 25 Liz Clayman; 27 Iñaki Vinaixa; 28, 154 littleny/Shutterstock.
com; 30 Francis Dzikowski/ESTO/Courtesy of H3 Hardy Collaboration Architecture; 31 Jeff
Schultes/Shutterstock.com; 35 Joseph Moran; 38 Jordan Loyd; 39 dibrova/Shutterstock.
com; 40/41 elissa1000/Shutterstock.com; 43, 57 (top) Christopher Penler/Shutterstock.
com; 46 LehaKoK/Shutterstock.com; 49 Pigprox/Shutterstock.com; 50 Ritu Manoj Jethani/
Shutterstock.com; 57 (bottom) Leonard Zhukovsky/Shutterstock.com; 58 (left) Joe
Woolhead; 58 (right) Amy Dreher; 76 KathyHyde/Shutterstock.com; 87 Timothy Schenck;
97 photo.ua/Shutterstock.com; 104 Jessica Lin; 109 Jacob Cohl; 121 Melissa Hom; 126
(bottom left) Tupungato/Shutterstock.com; 126 (bottom right) Pola Damonte/Shutterstock.
com; 130, 144 (top right and bottom) Marco Prati/Shutterstock.com; 136 Thinc; 144 (top
left) Jorg Hackemann/Shutterstock.com; 162 Jennifer Arnow; 167 (top left and bottom)
David Sundberg; 167 (top right) Scott Rudd; 181 Matthew Williams

The following images were supplied by the featured establishments: 7, 18, 37, 112,
169, 170

Cover photograph: Alan Copson/AWL-Images

MAPS
JS Graphics (john@jsgraphics.co.uk).

About **Time Out**

Founded in 1968, Time Out has expanded from humble London beginnings into the
leading resource for those wanting to know what's happening in the world's greatest
cities. As well as our influential what's-on weeklies in London and New York, we publish
nearly 30 other listings magazines in cities as varied as Beijing and Mumbai. The
magazines established Time Out's trademark style: sharp writing, informed reviewing
and bang up-to-date inside knowledge of every scene.

   Time Out made the natural leap into travel guides in the 1980s with the City Guide
series, which now extends to over 50 destinations around the world. Written and
researched by expert local writers and generously illustrated with original photography,
the full-size guides cover a larger area than our Shortlist guides and include many more
venue reviews, along with additional background features and a full set of maps.

   Throughout this rapid growth, the company has remained proudly independent, still
owned by Tony Elliott four decades after he started Time Out London as a single fold-
out sheet of A5 paper. This independence extends to the editorial content of all our
publications, this Shortlist included. No establishment has been featured because it
has advertised, and no payment has influenced any of our reviews. And, for our critics,
there's definitely no such thing as a free lunch: all restaurants and bars are visited and
reviewed anonymously, and Time Out always picks up the bill.
For more about the company, see www.timeout.com.

Don't Miss

NEW YORK CityPASS.

SAVE 41%
6 famous attractions

Empire State Building Observatory

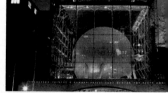

American Museum of Natural Histor

The Metropolitan Museum of Art

The Museum of Modern Art (MoMA

Your choice of Top of the Rock®
OR Guggenheim Museum

Your choice of Statue of Liberty & Elli
Island OR Circle Line Sightseeing Cruis

Buy at these attractions

- **Good for 9 days**
- **Skip most ticket lines**

Connect for current pricing
citypass.com or (888) 330-5008

ATLANTA | BOSTON | CHICAGO | HOUSTON | NEW YORK CITY | PHILADELPHIA

Metropolitan Museum of Art

WHAT'S BEST
Sights & Museums

Most visitors are aware of New York's massive **Metropolitan Museum of Art** (p137) – at two million square feet, it houses more than that number of objects. But you may not have heard about the city's smallest cultural institution. Launched by a trio of filmmakers, the 60-square-foot cabinet of curiosities known as **Mmuseumm** (p61) occupies an elevator shaft in Tribeca. In between, there are institutions devoted to just about everything you can think of, from **sex** (p107) to the country's first national **Museum of Mathematics** (p106). Spring 2014 saw an important debut: the long-anticipated **National September 11 Museum** (see box p58), which serves a threefold function as memorial tribute, historical record and mind-boggling evocation of the immense scale of the disaster.

Walking through the tree-shaded memorial plaza, with its monumental waterfalls, it's hard to believe that this area was a gaping hole, then a fenced-off construction site, for most of the previous decade. In addition to memorialising the tragedy, the rebuilt World Trade Center has more impressive visitor attractions than its previous incarnation. In spring 2015, **One World Observatory** (www. oneworldobservatory.com) opens on floors 100 to 102 of the 1,776-foot-high 1 World Trade Center, offering far-reaching vistas that give the Empire State Building some serious competition. Also on the horizon is a multilevel shopping and dining complex – larger than six football fields – operated by shopping-mall giant Westfield and spread across the towers and starchitect Santiago Calatrava's bird-like transit hub. On

lower Manhattan's east side, South Street Seaport's shuttered Pier 17 is slated to be transformed from a down-at-heel mall to a gleaming mixed-use complex including a marina and global food market, but the East River Esplanade and Piers Project has already transformed Pier 15 into a cool, bi-level leisure space comprising a contemporary glass-fronted bar and grassy patches above – both offering harbour panoramas.

Another long-term project that is transforming a section of the cityscape is the **High Line** (p92), a 1.5-mile defunct elevated train track on the West Side that's being converted into a stylish, slender park. The first two stretches (from Gansevoort Street in the Meatpacking District to 30th Street in Chelsea) debuted 2009 and 2011, respectively, and the park has already joined the ranks of the city's most popular attractions, drawing more than 4.5 million visitors in 2013. The High Line hopes to open the first phase of its final stretch shortly after publication of this guide. Eventually extending from 30th Street north to 34th Street and west to Twelfth Avenue, skirting around the under-construction mixed-use Hudson Yards development, it will feature a path through existing wild plant life, benches and picnic tables, plus a kids' play area incorporating the original sleepers. The elevated park-cum-promenade cuts through the city's prime gallery district, so it's fitting that the **Whitney Museum of American Art**, which hosts a high-profile biennial of current creative talent, is taking up residence at its southern foot (see box p87). After earlier plans to expand its Upper East Side building were scrapped in the face of local opposition, the museum broke ground on its High Line-hugging home in 2011 and the Renzo Piano-designed space opens in spring 2015. Together with the **New Museum**

SHORTLIST

Best new/revamped
- Cooper Hewitt, Smithsonian Design Museum (p136)
- National September 11 Memorial & Museum (p58)
- Whitney Museum of American Art (p87)

Best for local insight
- Lower East Side Tenement Museum (p70)
- Museum of the City of New York (p138)
- New-York Historical Society (p145)
- Queens Museum (p166)

New York icons
- Chrysler Building (p128)
- Empire State Building (p124)
- Statue of Liberty (p56)

Best free
- Governors Island (p51)
- Mmuseumm (p61)
- National Museum of the American Indian (p56)
- Staten Island Ferry (p56)

Best urban oases
- Central Park (p130)
- The Cloisters (p150)
- High Line (left)
- New York Botanical Garden (p155)

The 'big three' museums
- American Museum of Natural History (p143)
- Metropolitan Museum of Art (p137)
- Museum of Modern Art (p124)

Best museum buildings
- New Museum of Contemporary Art (p71)
- Solomon R Guggenheim Museum (p139)

of **Contemporary Art** (p71), a striking off-kilter structure built on the Bowery in 2007, it represents a considerable culture shift downtown.

Although many of the city's venerable institutions have been in place for decades, even the stateliest are moving with the times. On the Upper West Side, the city's oldest museum, the **New-York Historical Society** (p145), has embraced the digital age with a high-tech revamp that brings its extraordinary trove of artefacts, art and documents to vivid life. Across the park on Museum Mile, the **Cooper Hewitt, Smithsonian Design Museum**, housed in the elegant Carnegie mansion, reopens in December 2014 after a $64 million renovation and expansion (see box p136). Even the mighty Metropolitan Museum of Art isn't complacent; following the reopening of its revamped and renamed Anna Wintour Costume Center, it is wrapping up a redesign of its front plaza, offering spaces for visitors to congregate without clogging up its sweeping front steps.

Of course, a priority for first-time visitors will be to see some of the world-class collections for which the city is famous, and the Met is renowned for its European painting and sculpture, Islamic art, Greek and Roman collections and an ever-changing array of blockbuster travelling shows. The **Museum of Modern Art** (p124) contains some of the most famous artworks of the 19th century to the present; it's also worth trekking to Queens to check out its cutting-edge affiliate, **MoMA PS1** (p165) and the expanded **Queens Museum** (p166). The latter occupies a former World's Fair pavilion and contains the remarkable scale model of the metropolis, the Panorama of the City of New York.

The **Guggenheim** (p139), in Frank Lloyd Wright's Upper East Side landmark building, is another

New York essential. If you want a bit of background, then the **Museum of the City of New York** (see p138) provides fascinating insight, while the **Lower East Side Tenement Museum** (see p70) brings New York's immigrant history to life.

It may have been surpassed by 1 World Trade Center in height, but the **Empire State Building** (p124) is still New York's most famous skyscraper. There can be a long wait to ascend to the observation deck, but the building is now open until 2am and late-night viewings are usually less crowded – and the illuminated cityscape is spectacular. Another option for panoramas is the Top of the Rock observation deck, perched above midtown's **Rockefeller Center** (p125). The art deco tower gets one up on the Empire State by allowing a view of that iconic structure. And, on the subject of spectacular views, ascending to the crown of the **Statue of Liberty** (p56) is another exhilarating experience.

Slicing up the Apple

This book is divided by neighbourhood. Downtown is the oldest part of Manhattan and also the most happening. At the tip of the island, the **Financial District** contains the seat of local government and the epicentre of capitalism. Elsewhere, the character of many downtown neighbourhoods is in a state of continual evolution as the forces of gentrification take hold. Over the past decade, trendy bars, boutiques and galleries have been moving into erstwhile immigrant neighbourhood the **Lower East Side**. Former bohemian stomping ground **Greenwich Village** still resounds with cultural associations, but today is more moneyed and has the restaurants to prove it; to the west, leafy, winding streets give way to the **Meatpacking District**'s warehouses, now colonised by designer stores, eateries and nightspots. The once-radical **East Village** brims with bars and restaurants. Former art enclave **Soho** is now a prime shopping and dining destination, along with well-heeled neighbour **Tribeca**, while **Little Italy** is being crowded out by ever-expanding **Chinatown** and, to the north, boutique-riddled **Nolita**.

In midtown, **Chelsea** contains New York's main contemporary-gallery district, while rapidly gentrifying **Hell's Kitchen** to the north has overtaken it as the city's hottest gay enclave. The **Flatiron District** has evolved into a prime dining and shopping destination and nearby **Union Square** attracts foodies four days a week to New York's biggest farmers' market. Among the skyscrapers of midtown's prime commercial stretch are some of NYC's most iconic attractions. Here, **Fifth Avenue** is home to some of the city's poshest retail, while Broadway is the world's most famous theatreland. Love it or loathe it, garish **Times Square** (p117) is a must-gawp spectacle.

Uptown, bucolic **Central Park** (p130), with its picturesque lakes, expansive lawns and famous zoo, is the green divider between the affluent **Upper East Side** and the equally well-heeled **Upper West Side**. Between them, these wealthy locales contain the lion's share of the city's cultural institutions: most museums are on the UES – the Metropolitan Museum of Art and others on Fifth Avenue's Museum Mile, in the stately former mansions of the early 20th-century elite – but the UWS has the Metropolitan Opera, the New York Philharmonic and the New York City Ballet at **Lincoln Center** (see p149). Further

north, regenerated **Harlem** offers vibrant nightlife, soul food and plenty of cultural history.

Making the most of it

First, accept that you can never see it all. A week's visit to the city will involve some tough choices. And it's self-defeating to attempt to hit all the major collections in one visit to an institution as large as the Met or the American Museum of Natural History. So plan, pace yourself and take time to enjoy aimless wandering in picturesque areas like the West Village or Central Park.

Because the city's museums are privately funded, admission prices can be steep. However, these usually include entry to temporary shows as well as the permanent collections, and many institutions offer one day or evening a week when admission fees are either waived or switched to a voluntary donation (and remember, 'suggested donation' prices are just that). Be warned that many museums are closed on Mondays – except on some holidays, such as Columbus Day and Presidents' Day.

Despite recent budget cuts, the **subway** (p184) is still highly efficient and runs 24 hours a day. It is generally well populated, clean and relatively easy to navigate. It will often get you from one end of the city to another more quickly (not to mention more cheaply) than a cab. Charge up a MetroCard and you can travel seamlessly by subway and bus. Of course, you should keep your wits about you and take basic precautions, but New York these days is a pretty safe place. However, the very best way to get to know the city is by walking. Manhattan is a mere 13.4 miles long and 2.3 miles across at its widest point, and once you've mastered the grid, it's easy to find your way (although it gets a little trickier downtown).

Mission Cantina

WHAT'S BEST
Eating & Drinking

In Gotham, where apartments are as tight as sardine cans, restaurants serve as vibrant second living rooms and top chefs are elevated to rock-star status. For visitors, there's no better way to tap into the city's zeitgeist than soaking up the scene at its most beloved culinary destinations. Among the heavyweights who are defining the flavour of the rapidly changing culinary scene are fine-dining vets Mario Carbone and Rich Torrisi. Their game-changing hotspots **Torrisi Italian Specialties** and **Parm** (p68) rejuvenated Italian-American cuisine, paving the way for the duo's next venture, **Carbone** (see p88), a souped-up version of Godfather-esque supper clubs. Together with Jeff 'ZZ' Zalaznick, they followed it up with raw bar-and-cocktail den ZZ's Clam Bar, and the

trio's first foray into Gallic fare, Dirty French in the Ludlow hotel, was poised to open as this guide went to press. Summer 2014 saw the culinary comeback of ground-breaking chef David Waltuck, who teamed up with former Chanterelle manager George Stinson to open French-American knockout **élan** (43 East 20th Street, 1-646 682 7105, www.elannyc.com) in the Flatiron District.

There was a time, in the early 20th century, when grand hotels were the place to find the best restaurants in New York. You'll find a return to form at the **NoMad** (p108), an opulent throwback from chef Daniel Humm and Will Guidara of **Eleven Madison Park** (p107) renown. No meal is complete without the show-stopping chicken for two – amber-hued, with foie gras, brioche and black truffle stuffing under its skin.

Boutique hotels – and their restaurants – have also arrived in Williamsburg, Brooklyn, where Andrew Tarlow, empire builder behind fan favourites **Diner** and **Marlow & Sons** (p158), opened seasonal brasserie **Reynard** in the Wythe Hotel (p182), and haute technician Paul Liebrandt turned to more casual eats with the Elm at **McCarren Hotel & Pool** (p182).

The East Village and Lower East Side tend to sprout reasonably priced eateries that draw big followings – tuck into superlative smoked meats at **Mighty Quinn's** (p81), a standout in the latest wave of barbecue joints to hit town. While San Francisco transplant Danny Bowien's revelatory Szechuan spot, Mission Chinese Food, is on hiatus, he has followed up with popular **Mission Cantina** (p72). The East Village is also the location of **Lafayette** (p80), the French café from Andrew Carmellini of boisterous Italian tavern Locanda Verde in the **Greenwich Hotel** (p172) and cross-cultural American canteen the **Dutch** (p63).

While gastronomes take pride in haute cuisine temples like **Per Se** (p147) and **Daniel** (p140), you'll find equal devotion to more humble classics. The city's best burger is a source of constant debate, with many critics giving their budget-patty nod to celebrated restaurateur Danny Meyer's **Shake Shack** chain (p147). The Neapolitan pizza craze has shown no sign of flagging, either, though another trend to take hold is the *montanara* – a puffy, golden-crusted pie that's flash-fried before hitting the oven. Find standout examples at **Don Antonio by Starita** (p118). Ramen is also a local obsession; Tokyo noodle guru Ivan Orkin has returned to home soil with a Lower East Side *ramen-ya* **Ivan Ramen** (p71) and a Slurp Shop at **Gotham West Market** (p118) in

SHORTLIST

Best new
- Betony (p127)
- élan (p14)
- Empire Diner (p102)
- Estela (p67)
- The Gilroy (p140)
- Ivan Ramen (p71)
- Mission Cantina (p72)
- M Wells Steakhouse (p166)
- Tørst (p160)

Best cheap eats
- Cafe Edison (p118)
- Dos Toros (p79)
- Gotham West Market (p118)
- Pok Pok NY (p158)
- Shake Shack (p147)

Where to blow the budget
- Carbone (p88)
- The NoMad (p108)

The classics
- Bemelmans Bar (p139)
- Grand Central Oyster Bar & Restaurant (p129)
- Katz's Delicatessen (p72)

New twists on NYC faves
- Black Seed (bagels) (p67)
- Dominique Ansel Bakery (doughnuts) (p64)
- Don Antonio by Starita (pizza) (p118)
- RedFarm (dim sum) (p94)

Best seasonal fare
- Blue Hill (p88)
- Roberta's (p158)

Best for carnivores
- The Breslin Bar & Dining Room (p107)
- BrisketTown (p157)
- The Cannibal (p113)

Best cocktails
- Attaboy (p71)
- Pegu Club (p63)

DON'T MISS

Hell's Kitchen. The latter, along with **Hudson Eats** (p59) in the Financial District, is an example of the recent reinvention of that shopping-mall standby, the food court. Both offer a cluster of cult purveyors of inexpensive snacks and meals such as tapas, barbecue and bagels. NYC's diners may be a dying breed, but one iconic chrome-plated gem was recently saved when celebrity chef Amanda Freitag took over Chelsea's **Empire Diner** (p102), giving the interior a subtle update and the menu a contemporary locavore slant.

New York's farm-to-table movement is perhaps most robust in Brooklyn, where cheaper rents and a DIY spirit have made the borough a refuge for young, risk-taking chefs. The nerve centre of the movement is **Roberta's** (see p158), which grows some of its own produce and spun off a tasting-menu spot, Blanca, spotlighting chef Carlo Mirarchi's exceptional talents, in the back. In 2012, Andy Ricker turned Cobble Hill into a Thai food destination with **Pok Pok NY** (p158); the following year, the insanely popular eaterie moved a block away and opened a separate South-east Asian-style drinkery, Whiskey Soda Lounge, picking up spillover crowds across the street.

Elsewhere, there are cheek-by-jowl Asian restaurants in **Chinatown**, while **Koreatown**, the stretch of West 32nd Street between Fifth and Sixth Avenues, is lined with Korean barbecue joints and other eateries. Further afield, **Harlem** is in the midst of a restaurant-and-bar renaissance (see box p152), while the most diverse borough, **Queens**, counts Greek (in Astoria), Thai (in Elmhurst) and Indian (in Jackson Heights) among its globe-spanning cuisines.

Some of these further-flung locales are now attracting big-name chefs. Quebecois toque Hugue

Dufour put Queens on the food map a few years ago with his snout-to-tail cooking at the short-lived M Wells, which he followed up with museum eaterie **M Wells Dinette** at MoMA PS1 (p165) and, more recently, **M Wells Steakhouse** (p166).

Veg out

In spite of the city's obsession with locally sourced produce, new vegetarian restaurants are few and far between. **Dirt Candy**, from talented chef Amanda Cohen, serves sometimes sinful, always sophisticated meat-free eats, but at time of writing was planning to relocate from the East Village to the Lower East Side; visit www. dirtcandynyc.com for updates. **Kajitsu** (p113) draws reverent devotees for *shojin* cuisine, a type of hyperseasonal vegan cooking that originated in Zen Buddhism.

Empire Diner

Dead Rabbit

Sweet spots

If something sweet is what you're after, look no further than Soho's **Dominique Ansel Bakery** (p64), which launched international phenom the Cronut, a doughnut-croissant hybrid. At another cultishly beloved bakeshop, **Momofuku Milk Bar** (p81), which has several locations in the city, you can sate your sweet tooth with Christina Tosi's madcap creations, such as Cereal Milk soft-serve ice-cream and the addictively creamy Crack Pie.

The big tipple

New York continues to be a cradle of cocktail culture. Standard bearers like Audrey Saunders' renowned **Pegu Club** (p63) still offer fine drinks, but new life is brought to the scene by newcomers, including **Attaboy** (p71), a sultry den in the former Milk and Honey space from two of its longtime bartenders, and the **Dead Rabbit** (p59), a Financial District barroom with a sprawling historical menu. Thoughtful drinking also thrives in Brooklyn, most notably in Williamsburg at spots such as **Maison Premiere** (p158) – a throwback New Orleans-Style *boîte* specialising in absinthe-based tipples.

The craft-beer revolution that's swept the country has a firm foothold in NYC, too, with producers like Brooklyn Brewery, Sixpoint and SingleCut Beersmiths. The most dependable spots to sample the local offerings are hops-head havens like **Jimmy's No. 43** (p80) and **Blind Tiger Ale House** (p92), while the pint-size den **Proletariat** (p82) and rare-brew taproom **Tørst** (p160) in Greenpoint, Brooklyn offer a more sophisticated beer-geek experience.

While wine doesn't drive the boozing scene like cocktails and beer, a new breed of vino bars is tossing out the pretence and putting an emphasis on well-chosen but affordable lists. The poster child of this movement is **Terroir** (p82), which has locations in the East Village, Tribeca and Murray Hill.

Where there's smoke…

The only legal places to smoke indoors are venues that cater largely to cigar smokers (and sell tobacco products) and those that have created areas for smokers. Try **Circa Tabac** (32 Watts Street, between Sixth Avenue & Thompson Street, Soho, 1-212 941 1781) or **Hudson Bar & Books** (636 Hudson Street, at Horatio Street, 1-212 229 2642).

Dover Street Market New York

WHAT'S BEST

Shopping

One of the best cities in the world in which to drop some of your hard-earned cash, New York offers anything you could possibly want to buy, and – as long as you're prepared to shop around or hit some sample sales – at the best prices. Locals may complain about the 'mallification' of certain neighbourhoods such as Soho, but for visitors (and, if they're honest, many New Yorkers), these retail-rich areas are intoxicating consumer playgrounds. As America's fashion capital, and the site of the prestigious Fashion Institute of Technology and other high-profile art colleges, the metropolis is a magnet for creative young designers from around the country. This ensures that the shops and markets are stuffed with unique finds, and it also means that the Garment District

is a hotbed of open-to-the-public showroom sales (p21).

In the post-recession retail landscape, shopkeepers have become more creative in order to survive, launching pop-up shops that in some cases take root in permanent digs, such as Hell's Kitchen men's accessories trove **Fine and Dandy** (p119). Others hedge their bets with mixed-use businesses, such as the **Dressing Room** (p75), which combines a bar and a boutique. Increasingly, small shops are selling a combination of goods, and on a larger scale, there has been a resurgence in concept stores that incorporate art and food into the shopping experience – Rei Kawakubo has brought her kooky-chic **Dover Street Market** mega-boutique to NYC (p114) and lifestyle chain Urban Outfitters opened eclectic five-floor emporium **Space Ninety 8** (www.spaceninety8.com) in trendy Williamsburg, Brooklyn. The vintage trend, appealing to the environmentally aware and budget-conscious alike, is stronger than ever. Good hunting grounds include the East Village, the Lower East Side and Williamsburg, where stock is skewed towards a young, hip customer base. Under-the-radar troves include **David Owens Vintage** (p74) and **Grand Street Bakery** (p161).

Retail hotspots

Although many of the city's retail-rich districts are within walking distance of one another, and you can zip quickly between others on the subway, because of the dense concentration of shops in some areas (for example, the Lower East Side or Madison Avenue), you might want to limit yourself to a couple of areas in a day out. Generally speaking, you'll find the most unusual shops downtown and in parts of Brooklyn.

Soho has been heavily commercialised, especially the main thoroughfares, but this once edgy, arty enclave still has some idiosyncratic survivors and numerous top-notch shops. Urban fashion abounds on Lafayette Street, while Broome Street is becoming an enclave for chic home design. To the east, Nolita has been colonised by indie designers, especially along Mott and Mulberry Streets. Once the centre of the 'rag' trade, the Lower East Side used to be associated with bargain outlets and bagels. Now a bar- and boutique-laden patch, it's especially good for vintage, streetwear and local designers, such as secretive sneaker store **Alife Rivington Club** (p74) and Chuck Guarino's rockin' clothing label the **Cast** (p74). Orchard, Ludlow and Rivington Streets are hotspots. North of here, in the

SHORTLIST

Best new
- Dover Street Market New York (p114)
- Rough Trade (p161)
- Will Leather Goods (p70)

Best vintage and antiques
- Doyle & Doyle (p95)
- Grand Street Bakery (p161)
- Mantiques Modern (p103)
- Obscura Antiques & Oddities (p84)
- Screaming Mimi's (p85)
- What Goes Around Comes Around (p65)

Taste of New York
- Russ & Daughters (p75)
- Smorgasburg (p32)
- Zabar's (p149)

Best books and music
- Downtown Music Gallery (p70)
- Other Music (p84)
- Rough Trade (p161)
- Strand Book Store (p85)

Local lines
- The Cast (p74)
- Erica Weiner (p70)
- In God We Trust (p65)
- Obsessive Compulsive Cosmetics (p75

Best for gifts
- Bond Street Chocolate (p82)
- By Brooklyn (p160)
- Kiosk (p110)
- Magpie (p148)

Best home goods
- ABC Carpet & Home (p110)
- The Future Perfect (p84)
- Modern Anthology (p161)

Best for designer labels
- Barneys New York (p142)
- Fivestory (p142)
- Kirna Zabete (p65)
- Opening Ceremony (p65)

East Village, you'll find a highly browsable mix of vintage clothing, streetwear and records alongside stylish home and kids' goods, but shops are more scattered than on the Lower East Side.

Over on the other side of the island, the one-time wholesale meat market, stretching south from 14th Street, has become a high-end consumer playground; the warehouses of the Meatpacking District are now populated by a clutch of upscale stores, including **Owen** (p96), which was launched by a FIT graduate and showcases both established and emerging labels. Meanwhile, the western strip of Bleecker Street is lined with a further cache of designer boutiques.

Most of the city's department stores can be found on Fifth Avenue between 38th and 59th Streets, in the company of chain stores and designer flagships (the parade of lofty names continues east on 57th Street). The exceptions are Macy's, in Herald Square, and Bloomingdale's and Barneys, which are both on the Upper East Side. The Uptown stretch of Madison Avenue has long been synonymous with the crème de la crème of international fashion.

It's also well worth venturing across the East River. Williamsburg abounds with idiosyncratic shops and one-off buys. As well as the main drag, Bedford Avenue, hit North 6th and Grand Streets for shops selling vintage clothes, arty housewares and records. There are further treasures in Cobble Hill, Carroll Gardens and Boerum Hill, especially on Court and Smith Streets and Atlantic Avenue; the latter has been known mainly for antiques, but cool clothiers have moved in.

Keep it local

Of course, many of the country's most popular designers are based in

New York, from long-established names like Diane von Furstenberg and Marc Jacobs to newer contemporary stars such as Phillip Lim, Thakoon Panichgul, and Marcus Wainwright and David Neville of **Rag & Bone** (p96). Made-in-NYC items – jewellery by **Erica Weiner** (p70), make-up from **Obsessive Compulsive Cosmetics** (p75), accessories from **In God We Trust** (p65) or cards printed at **Bowne & Co Stationers** (p60) – are chic souvenirs. Stores that stock local designs among their wares include **Spiritual America** (p75), **Opening Ceremony** (p65) and the **Future Perfect** (p84) for interior items. There are also opportunities to buy goods direct from emerging designers at popular weekend markets such as the **Brooklyn Flea** (see box p32).

Famous names

Of course, many visitors to New York will simply be looking to make the most of the incredible variety of big brands on offer in the city. For young, casual and streetwear labels, head to Broadway in Soho. Fifth Avenue heaves with a mix of designer showcases and mall-level megastores. Madison Avenue is more consistently posh, though contemporary designers (Helmut Lang, Maje, Rebecca Taylor, Alice + Olivia and more) have joined the line-up of deluxe labels like Alexander McQueen, Givenchy and Lanvin.

If you prefer to do all your shopping under one roof, famous department stores Macy's (good for mid-range brands), Bloomingdale's (a mix of mid-range and designer), Barneys (cutting-edge and high-fashion) and Bergdorf Goodman (luxury goods and international designer) are all stuffed with desirable items.

Sniffing out sales

New York is fertile bargain-hunting territory. The traditional post-season sales (which usually start just after Christmas and in early to mid June) have given way to frequent markdowns throughout the year: look for sale racks in boutiques, chain and department stores.

Of course, as New York is home to numerous designer studios and showrooms, there is a weekly spate of sample sales. The best are listed in the Shopping & Style section of *Time Out New York* magazine and www.timeout.com/newyork. Other terrific resources are **Racked** (www. ny.racked.com), **Top Button** (www. topbutton.com) and **Clothing Line** (1-212 947 8748, www.clothingline. com), which holds sales for a variety of labels – from J Crew and Theory to Helmut Lang and Rag & Bone, at its Garment District showroom.

Chief among the permanent sale stores is the famous **Century 21** (p61) – it's beloved of rummagers, but detested by those with little patience for sifting through less than fabulous merchandise for the prize finds. There is now a second Manhattan location on the Upper West Side, but we recommend braving the original for breadth of stock and, sometimes, deeper discounts. Union Square's **Nordstrom Rack** (60 E 14th Street, between Broadway & Fourth Avenue, 1-212 220 2080, www. nordstromrack.com), the discount arm of the department store, is worth checking out too.

Have a rummage

Flea market browsing is a popular weekend pastime among New Yorkers. Outdoor markets selling antiques and bric-a-brac operate in Chelsea (West 25th Street, between Broadway & Sixth Avenues) and Hell's Kitchen (West 39th Street, between Ninth & Tenth Avenues, www.hellskitchenfleamarket.com) on Saturday and Sunday. In the Flatiron District, the sprawling **Showplace Antique & Design Center** (p111) is home to more than 200 dealers. Make the pilgrimage to one of the deservedly popular **Brooklyn Flea** (see box p32) to browse everything from vintage jewellery and crafts to salvage and locally made foodstuffs.

Consumer culture

Despite recent closures, chain retailer **Barnes & Noble** (www.barnesand noble.com) still dominates the book scene, but well-loved independents, such as the **Strand Book Store** (p85), have been holding their own for years. **Housing Works Bookstore Café** (p64) doubles as a popular Soho hangout. For art books, as well as cool souvenirs, don't forget museum shops – MoMA Design & Book Store, attached to the **Museum of Modern Art** (p124) and the **New Museum of Contemporary Art** store (p71) are both excellent.

When **Other Music** (p84) opened opposite Tower Records in the East Village in the mid 1990s, it boldly stood as a small pocket of resistance to corporate music. Its Goliath now shuttered, Other Music rolls on, offering a well-curated selection of indie-rock, world music and experimental sounds. Tucked away in a Chinatown basement, the **Downtown Music Gallery** (p70) is an essential stop for seekers of avant-garde jazz and new classical. Across the East River, the recently opened flagship of UK indie retailer Rough Trade and several smaller record stores within walking distance have made North Brooklyn a prime place for casual music lovers and serious vinyl collectors to spend an afternoon (see box p162).

Output

WHAT'S BEST
Nightlife

The discotheque may have had its
origins in occupied Paris during
World War II – apparently, the Nazis
weren't too keen on jazz, dancing
and high times, driving such
pursuits underground – but it was
in New York City that the modern
concept of clubbing came into
being. Hallowed halls such as
the Loft, Studio 54, the Paradise
Garage and Area are imbedded in
nightlife's collective consciousness
as near-mythic ideals. But in this
millennium? Well, the city can no
longer claim to be the world's
clubbing capital; the balance of
power has shifted eastward to cities
like London and Berlin. Still, with
this much history (not to mention
eight million people ready to party),
New York nightlife can never be
counted out – and the scene today
is as strong as it's been in years.

This is largely thanks to a burst of
roving shindigs, often held in out-of-
the-way warehouses and lofts. Some
of the best – particularly if you're a
fan of underground house, techno
or bass music – are run by the teams
at Blkmarket Membership (www.
facebook.com/blkmarket), ReSolute
(www.resolutenyc.com), Rinsed
(www.rinsed.it) and Mister Saturday
Night (www.mistersaturdaynight.
com); a visit to www.timeout.com/
newyork should help to clue you in.

Don't rule out the clubs themselves,
though, as there are still plenty of
fabulous DJs playing music of all
persuasions. **Cielo** (p96), an intimate
and beautiful Meatpacking District
venue, boasts underground jocks
playing over one of the city's best
sound systems. At the other end of
the spectrum, **Pacha** (p122) is the
club of choice for followers of

big-name superstars, with the likes of Afrojack and Fedde Le Grand regularly presiding over the dance floor. **Santos Party House** (p65) is another good bet, particularly when Danny Krivit takes the spot over for the soulful house and classics-oriented 718 Sessions (www.dannykrivit.net). But nightlife's nerve centre has moved across the East River. Since **Output** (p161) opened in 2013, it has attracted the underground scene's best jocks to Williamsburg, Brooklyn, to play outer-limits house, techno and bass music over its monster of a sound system. The following year, the techno-happy Verboten gang opened their long-awaited permanent digs around the corner, cementing the 'Burg as New York's clubland paradise.

Some of the city's best parties take place only occasionally or are seasonal. **Warm Up**, a summertime soirée held every Saturday during July and August in the courtyard at **MoMA PS1** (see p165) in Queens, attracts kids who like to boogie down to some pretty twisted DJs and bands. The **Bunker** bash, usually held three times a month and one of New York's top techno get-togethers, has been nomadic of late, but you can follow the party at www.thebunkerny.com. And, of course, there's the Sunday-night tea dance **Body & Soul** (www.bodyandsoul-nyc.com), helmed by the DJ holy trinity of Danny Krivit, Joe Claussell and François K. The formerly weekly affair now pops up only a few times each year – but it's still a spectacle, with a few thousand sweaty revellers dancing their hearts out from start till finish.

For those who like a bit of bump-and-grind in their after-dark activities, the city's burlesque scene is as strong as it's ever been. Some of the best producers and performers – they often cross over – are Doc

SHORTLIST

Best new/revamped
- Atlas Social Club (p120)
- Madison Square Garden (p116)
- Verboten (p163)

Best for indie bands
- Bowery Ballroom (p75)
- Cake Shop (p75)
- Mercury Lounge (p75)

Hottest dancefloors
- Cielo (p96)
- Output (p161)
- Santos Party House (p65)

Best jazz joints
- Jazz at Lincoln Center (p149)
- Smalls (p96)
- Village Vanguard (p96)

Most storied venues
- Apollo Theater (p153)
- Carnegie Hall (p122)
- Radio City Music Hall (p128)

Best for rising stars
- Joe's Pub (p85)
- Le Poisson Rouge (p91)
- Rockwood Music Hall (p77)

Best gay spots
- Atlas Social Club (p120)
- Fairytail Lounge (p120)
- BPM At The Out NYC (p178)

Best for laughs
- Carolines on Broadway (p120)
- Comedy Cellar (p91)
- Upright Citizens Brigade Theatre (p105)

Best dance parties
- 718 Sessions (left)
- The Bunker (left)
- Mister Saturday Night/ Mister Sunday (p22)
- Warm Up (p165)

Wasabassco (www.wasabassco.com), Shien Lee (www.dancesofvice.com), Jen Gapay's Thirsty Girl Productions (www.thirstygirl productions.com), Angie Pontani of the World Famous Pontani Sisters (www.angiepontani.com) and Calamity Chang, 'the Asian Sexation' (www.calamitychang.com). The **Slipper Room** (p77) on the Lower East Side and **Duane Park** (p85) on the Bowery are prime places to watch the tassle-twirling action.

Live from New York

New York is among the greatest cities in the world in which to see live music. Manhattan and Brooklyn are packed with venues, from hole-in-the-wall dives to resplendent concert halls. Plan accordingly and you can catch more than one world-class show on any given night.

For larger seated shows, try the posh theatres in midtown and further north. The palatial art deco **Radio City Music Hall** (p128) gives grandeur to pop performances, while Harlem's **Apollo Theater** (p153) still hosts its legendary Amateur Night competition. In addition to classical performances, **Carnegie Hall** (p122) welcomes jazz mavericks like Keith Jarrett, and Jazz at Lincoln Center's **Allen Room** (p149) has a million-dollar view that threatens to upstage even the good shows.

Some of music's biggest acts – Bruno Mars, Lady Gaga, Arctic Monkeys – play at **Madison Square Garden** (p116), which recently wrapped up a complete renovation. But after 45 years, Manhattan's legendary music and sports hub got some serious competition – from a Brooklyn contender. Since the **Barclays Center** (p163) opened in 2012, it's been attracting global megastars and local luminaries alike.

The rock scene's heart is in downtown Manhattan and Brooklyn. Numerous clubs dot the East Village and Lower East Side, but don't miss the **Mercury Lounge** (p75), the no-nonsense spot that launched the career of the Strokes, among others; **Rockwood Music Hall** (p77), a small storefront venue showcasing up-and-comers; and **Joe's Pub** (p85), the classy cabaret room tucked inside the Public Theater that continues to present great acts of all genres.

For medium-size gigs, **Bowery Ballroom** (p75) is Manhattan's hub, while its sister venue in Brooklyn, **Music Hall of Williamsburg** (p161), hosts the likes of Delta Spirit and Bernhoft, often a few days after they've played the Bowery. Also based in Brooklyn's indie-rock epicentre are downtown Manhattan migrant the **Knitting Factory** (361 Metropolitan Avenue, at Havemeyer Street, 1-347 529 6696, www.knittingfactory.com) and **Glasslands** (289 Kent Avenue, between South 1st & 2nd Steets, www.theglasslands.com), a hip warehouse-space that's popular with touring bands looking to escape the corporate atmosphere of a mainstream club. On the quieter front, cute local spot **Pete's Candy Store** (p163) offers everything from whimsical folk music to poetry readings.

Working the room

Few cities in the world, if any, offer a cabaret scene as varied as New York's. The genre offers a confluence of opposites: the heights of polish and the depths of amateurism; intense honesty and airy pretence; earnestness and camp. At its best, it can provide a uniquely intimate experience of musical communication. For a classic, high-end New York cabaret experience, visit the speakeasy-style **54 Below**

Atlas Social Club p23

(p120), whose line-up of performers leans towards A-list Broadway stars, or the elegant but pricey **Café Carlyle** in the plush Upper East Side hotel (35 E 76th Street, at Madison Avenue, 1-212 744 1600, www.thecarlyle.com); the Flatiron District venue **Metropolitan Room** (p111) is easier on the wallet. In recent years, an edgier alt-cabaret scene – with a more subversive style – has sprouted up in spots such as Joe's Pub.

If it's laughs you're after, the city's myriad comedy clubs serve both as platforms for big names and as launchpads for stars of tomorrow. The looming presence of TV sketch giant *Saturday Night Live,* which has been filmed at Rockefeller Center since 1975, helps to ensure the continued presence of theatrical comedy; more influential in the day-to-day landscape, however, is the improv and sketch troupe **Upright Citizens Brigade**. Its theatre (p105) has been the most visible catalyst in New York's current alternative comedy boom, and it expanded with a second space in the East Village in 2011. The **Comedy Cellar** (p91), another popular venue,

spread out with a spin-off space nearby in summer 2013.

Out and about

Offering much more than drag and piano bars (though, delightfully, they still thrive), today's LGBT New York has popular venues devoted to rock and country music and an abundance of arty, pan-queer parties and events (you'll find the best at www.timeout.com/newyork). Each June, NYC Pride brings a whirl of parties and performances. The weekend-capping event, the **NYC LGBT Pride March** (p36), draws millions of spectators and participants. The Black Party Weekend in March and the Urban Bear Weekend in May also draw hordes to NYC, visibly upping the gay quotient around town. While there are good LGBT bars across the city in areas including the Village, Chelsea and Williamsburg, Hell's Kitchen has emerged as Gotham's gayest gaybourhood. With a relaxed, straight-friendly scene, HK is the location of New York's first gay luxury hotel, the **Out NYC** (p178), which contains one of surprisingly few all-gay megaclubs in the city.

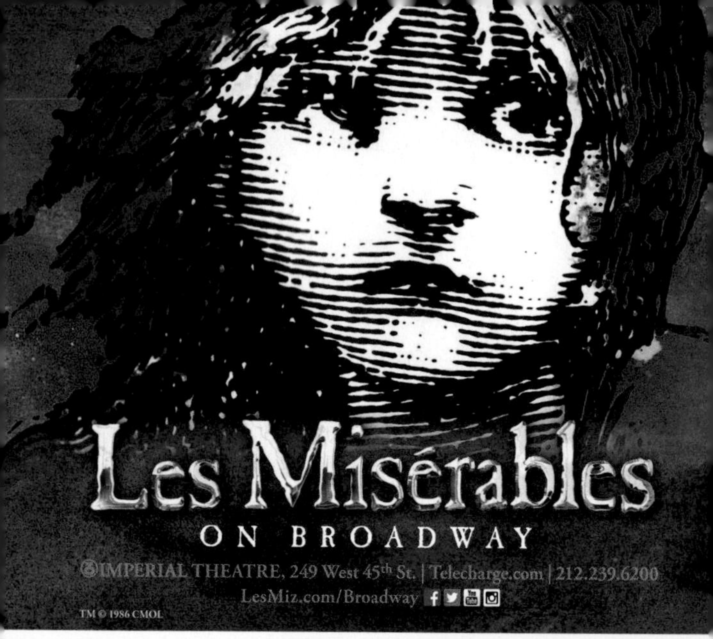
Les Misérables
ON BROADWAY
IMPERIAL THEATRE, 249 West 45th St. | Telecharge.com | 212.239.6200
LesMiz.com/Broadway
TM © 1986 CMOL

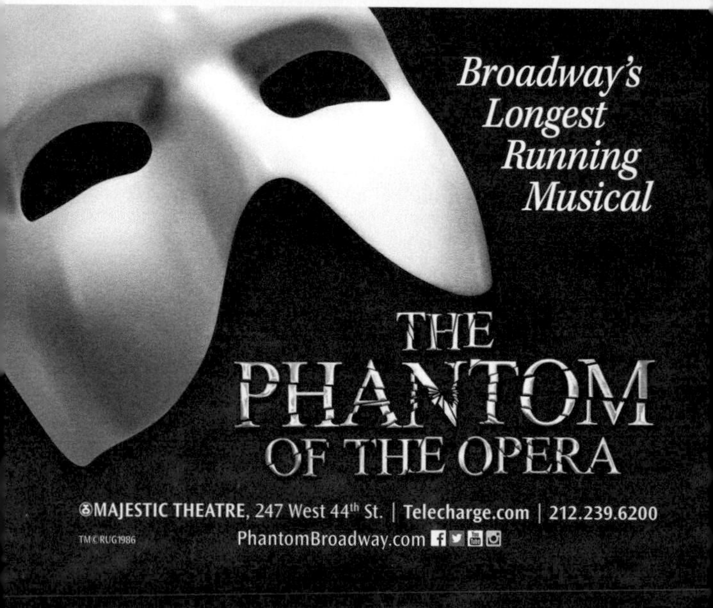
Broadway's
Longest
Running
Musical
THE
PHANTOM
OF THE OPERA
MAJESTIC THEATRE, 247 West 44th St. | Telecharge.com | 212.239.6200
PhantomBroadway.com
TM©RUG1986

Lincoln Center

WHAT'S BEST
Arts & Leisure

Given the impressive sweep of New York's cultural life, it's easy to be overwhelmed by the number of events on offer. From enormous stadiums to tiny Off Broadway stages, from revival cinemas to avant-garde dance venues, the choices are endless. With a little planning, however, you can take in that game, concert or show that will make your visit more memorable. Consult *Time Out New York* magazine or www.timeout.com/newyork for the latest listings.

Classical music & opera

In recent years, the primary story of New York's classical music scene has been the advent of musical entrepreneurs such as the International Contemporary Ensemble (ICE), New Amsterdam Records and Gotham Chamber Opera, among others. It's been interesting to observe how mainstay institutions have adapted – and in some ways adopted – lessons taught by those grassroots upstarts.

Lincoln Center (p149), for example, has been enriched and enlivened with the kind of ground-breaking, genre-flouting programming that was once the exclusive province of fledgling institutions – not least the White Light Festival, an ongoing autumn exploration of spiritual dimensions in art. At the **Metropolitan Opera**, fresh productions and up-to-date technologies continue to lure newcomers while also giving long-time admirers fresh notions to mull over. And the esteemed **New York Philharmonic**, based in Avery Fisher Hall, continues its steady

Museum of Modern Art

march forward under the leadership of music director Alan Gilbert, who introduced the orchestra's inaugural NY Phil Biennial in 2014.

The venerable **Carnegie Hall** (p122) continues to live up to its legendary status as the world's most prestigious concert hall. The **Brooklyn Academy of Music** (p163) is another invaluable player, hosting the perennially popular multidiscipline **Next Wave Festival** (p31). The area around BAM has evolved into the Downtown Brooklyn Cultural District, which includes the relocated bastion of experimental music, **Roulette** (509 Atlantic Avenue, at Third Avenue, Boerum Hill, 1-917 267 0363, www.roulette. org). Chic Greenwich Village nightclub **Le Poisson Rouge** (p91) is another place to catch the latest musical innovators in their native habitats.

Dance

With its uptown and downtown divide, New York dance includes both luminous tradition and daring experimentation. For classical dance,

Lincoln Center is home to both the **New York City Ballet** and **American Ballet Theatre**. NYCB is known for staging works by George Balanchine and Jerome Robbins, while ABT is the spot for story ballets, international guest artists and, if you're lucky, a new piece by the extraordinary Russian choreographer Alexei Ratmansky, who is also the company's artist in residence.

While Lincoln Center's David H Koch Theater is officially NYCB's home, during its off seasons it hosts other big-name dance companies too, including the **Paul Taylor Dance Company**. The **Alvin Ailey American Dance Theater**, which has been infused with new life by artistic director Robert Battle, is in residence at **New York City Center** (p123) each December.

Yet there's a world beyond traditional modern dance. Throughout New York, but especially in parts of Brooklyn and Queens, choreographers are intent on exploring the more complex notions of performance and the body; the internationally admired laboratory **Movement Research** (www.movementresearch.org) is devoted to the investigation of dance and movement-based forms and showcases works-in-progress at Greenwich Village's historic Judson Church. The art-world's continuing obsession with dance is reflected in programming at the **Museum of Modern Art** (p124) and the **Whitney Museum of American Art**, which has started to give performing arts a prominent place in the Whitney Biennial. The museum's new building (see box p87) has two flexible performance spaces.

Film

Every corner of NYC has been immortalised in celluloid, so it's not surprising that the city has a special relationship with the movies. The calendar is packed with festivals, including **Tribeca** (p34), the New York Film Festival and several others organised by the excellent **Film Society of Lincoln Center** (p150), which a few years ago opened its new Elinor Bunin Monroe Film Center. Summer brings the great tradition of free outdoor screenings in midtown's **Bryant Park** and other green spaces (see box p37). Cinephiles love **Film Forum** (p66) for its wide range of revivals and new indie features, while **Anthology Film Archives** (p85) specialises in experimental programming.

Sports

NYC's professional sports teams have upped their game with new stadiums and improved amenities in an effort to tempt fans away from their HD TVs. First it was baseball's turn with the 2009 openings of **Citi Field** in Queens and **Yankee Stadium** in the Bronx, the respective homes of the Mets (newyork.mets.mlb.com) and the Yankees (newyork.yankees.mlb.com). The Giants and

---

SHORTLIST

Best new/revamped
- Luna Park, Coney Island (p164)
- Madison Square Garden (p116)
- Polonsky Shakespeare Center (p164)

Most experimental
- Anthology Film Archives (p85)
- The Kitchen (p105)

Best for unwinding
- Cornelia Spa (p142)
- Great Jones Spa (p86)
- Juvenex (p116)

Best for cinephiles
- Film Forum (p66)
- Film Society of Lincoln Center (p150)

Best long-running shows
- Book of Mormon (p122)
- Fuerza Bruta: Wayra (p111)
- Sleep No More (p106)

Best Off Broadway
- New York Theatre Workshop (p86)
- Playwrights Horizons (p123)
- Public Theater (p86)

Best free outdoor arts
- River to River Festival (p37)
- Shakespeare in the Park (p37)
- SummerStage (p37)

Essential high culture
- Carnegie Hall (p122)
- Metropolitan Opera House (p149)
- New York City Center (p123)

Best cheap tickets
- Lincoln Center Theater's Claire Tow Theater (p149)
- Soho Rep (p66)
- TKTS (p118)

DON'T MISS

Jets now kick off football season at the **MetLife Stadium** (www.metlifestadium.com) across the river in New Jersey. Basketball scored the new **Barclays Center** (p163) for the rebranded Brooklyn Nets, and formerly musty **Madison Square Garden** (p116), home to basketball's Knicks and hockey's Rangers, finally wrapped up a three-year multi-million-dollar revamp.

Theatre

Broadway theatre is one of New York's crowning attractions. The oldest venues, such as the New Amsterdam and the Belasco, date back to the early 20th century, and unique architectural features enhance the experience. Musicals continue to be the big crowd-pullers. Straight plays tend to have shorter runs but can generate considerable excitement, especially when they include big stars. And serious theatre fans will want to visit the more intimate world of Off Broadway. You don't have to leave midtown to find **Playwrights Horizons** (p123) or the Frank Gehry-designed **Pershing Square Signature Center** (p123).

You can also find strong Off Broadway work at **New York Theatre Workshop** (p86) and the **Public Theater** (p86), which mounts two free **Shakespeare in the Park** (p37) shows each summer. Brooklyn Academy of Music stages first-rate productions from around the world at its **Harvey Theater** (p163). In autumn 2013, Theatre for a New Audience premiered new Brooklyn headquarters, the **Polonsky Shakespeare Center** (p164).

It can be tough to score tickets for popular shows, so check www.theatermania.com and www.playbill.com for advance information. Nearly all Broadway and Off Broadway shows are served by big ticketing agencies, but for cheap seats to shows that aren't sold out, your best bet is the **TKTS** (p118).

For theatre that is edgier and more adventurous – and less expensive – explore the Off-Off Broadway scene downtown and in Brooklyn, where the experimental impulse is alive and well, with troupes such as Elevator Repair Service (www.elevator.org), Radiohole (www.radiohole.com) and the Civilians (www.thecivilians.org), and venues like **HERE** (p66).

Polonsky Shakespeare Center

Calendar

Rockefeller Center Christmas tree

Plan ahead with our pick of the best annual events in New York. Pick up the weekly *Time Out New York* magazine or visit www.timeout.com/newyork for updates and one-off events, and be sure to confirm any dates before making plans.

Autumn

mid Sept **Feast of San Gennaro**
Little Italy, p66
www.sangennaro.org
Celebrate the martyred third-century bishop and patron saint of Naples at this 11-day festival. After dark, sparkling lights arch over Mulberry Street and the smells of sausages and frying *zeppole* (custard- or jam-filled fritters) hang in the air. On the final Saturday in September, a statue of San Gennaro is carried in a Grand Procession outside the Most Precious Blood Church (109 Mulberry Street, between Canal & Hester Streets).

Sept-Dec **Next Wave Festival**
Brooklyn Academy of Music, p163
www.bam.org

Among the most highly anticipated of the city's autumn culture offerings, this festival showcases only the very best in avant-garde music, dance, theatre and opera over more than three months.

late Sept **Dumbo Arts Festival**
Dumbo, Brooklyn
www.dumboartsfestival.com
Dumbo has been an artists' enclave for decades, and this weekend of art appreciation is hugely popular. Expect gallery shows, installations, open studios, concerts and other arts events.

late Sept **New York Film Festival**
Film Society of Lincoln Center, p150
www.filmlinc.com
For more than two weeks, Alice Tully Hall and Lincoln Center's two cinemas host premieres, features and short flicks from around the globe.

mid Oct **Open House New York Weekend**
Various venues
www.ohny.org
More than 150 architectural sites, private homes and landmarks open their

Flea season

Shop and nosh at cool markets throughout the year.

Rummaging in the city's flea markets has long been a favourite New York weekend pastime, but the past several years have seen the emergence of a more sophisticated breed of bazaar, offering high-quality crafts, gourmet snacks and even entertainment, alongside vintage wares and bric-a-brac. Launched in 2008 by Jonathan Butler, founder of real-estate blog Brownstoner.com, and Eric Demby, former PR man for the Brooklyn borough president, the hugely popular **Brooklyn Flea** (176 Lafayette Avenue, between Clermont & Vanderbilt Avenues, Fort Greene, www.brooklynflea.com) operates outdoors from April until the third week of November on Saturdays. Around 150 vendors sell a mix of vintage clothing, records, furnishings, locally designed fashion and crafts. Several spin-offs include the nosh-only Smorgasburg, and in winter the market moves to an indoor space (see website for addresses and hours).

On weekends from late April through October, you can sample everything from locally made ice-cream to tacos as you browse vintage fashion, handmade jewellery, skincare and more at **Hester Street Fair** (Hester Street, at Essex Street, Lower East Side, www.hesterstreetfair.com). Located on the site of a former pushcart market, it has around 60 vendors. And on Friday and Saturday nights year round, **Brooklyn Night Bazaar** (165 Banker Street, at Norman Avenue, Greenpoint, www.bkbazaar. com) features a locally focused line-up of art, crafts and food in a 24,000-square-foot warehouse. It

Hester Street Fair

also adds a beer garden and music to the mix – four to five bands, curated by a record label or publication, play each night.

In winter, several holiday markets set up shop. From late October until early January, 125 glassed-in shoplets operate in Bryant Park (between Fifth & Sixth Avenues and 40th & 42nd Streets), forming a festive microcosm, the **Holiday Shops at Bryant Park** (www.winter village.org/holidayshops), clustered around a seasonal skating rink. Although some of the wares skirt tourist-craft-shop territory, there are plenty of unusual finds, including jewellery and accessories, toys and foodstuffs. You'll find a similar mix at the **Union Square Holiday Market** at the south-west corner of Union Square, at 14th Street, Flatiron District (www.urbanspace nyc.com), open mid/late November to late December.

doors during a weekend of urban exploration. Behind-the-scenes tours and educational programmes are also on offer.

mid Oct **New York City Wine & Food Festival**
Various venues
www.nycwff.org
The Food Network's epicurean blow-out offers four belt-busting days of tasting events and celeb-chef demos.

late Oct **CMJ Music Marathon**
Various venues
www.cmj.com
The annual *College Music Journal* schmooze-fest draws fans and music-industry folks to one of the best show-cases for new rock, indie, hip hop and electronica acts.

31 Oct **Village Halloween Parade**
Sixth Avenue, Greenwich Village
www.halloween-nyc.com
The sidewalks at this iconic Village shindig are always packed. For the best vantage point, don a costume and watch from inside the parade.

Winter

early Nov **New York Comedy Festival**
Various venues
www.nycomedyfestival.com
This five-day laugh fest features both big names (Bill Cosby, Jerry Seinfeld and Louis CK in recent years) and up-and-comers.

early Nov **New York City Marathon**
Staten Island to Central Park
www.tcsnycmarathon.org
Around 45,000 runners hotfoot it through all five boroughs over a 26.2-mile course.

late Nov **Macy's Thanksgiving Day Parade & Balloon Inflation**
Upper West Side to Macy's
www.macys.com/parade

At 9am on Thanksgiving Day, the stars of this nationally televised parade are the gigantic balloons, the elaborate floats and good ol' Santa Claus. The evening before, New Yorkers brave the cold night air to watch the rubbery colossi take shape outside the American Museum of Natural History.

late Nov/early Dec **Rockefeller Center Tree-Lighting Ceremony**
Rockefeller Center, p125
www.rockefellercenter.com
Proceedings start at 7pm, but this festive celebration is always mobbed, so get there early. Most of the two-hour event is devoted to celebrity performances, then the 30,000 LEDs covering the massive evergreen are switched on.

mid Dec **Unsilent Night**
Greenwich Village to East Village
www.unsilentnight.com
Downtown's arty, secular answer to Christmas carolling: participants gather under the Washington Square Arch to pick up a cassette or CD of one of four different atmospheric tracks, or sync up via smartphone app. Everyone then presses play at the same time and marches through the streets, filling the air with a 45-minute piece.

31 Dec **New Year's Eve celebrations**
Times Square, p117
www.timessquarenyc.org
Join a million others and watch the giant illuminated Waterford Crystal ball descend amid confetti and cheering. Arrive by 3pm or earlier to stake out a spot in the Broadway-Seventh Avenue bowtie and be prepared to stay put. There are no public restrooms or food vendors, and leaving means giving up your spot. Celebrity performances are held across two stages, from 6pm.

1 Jan **New Year's Day Marathon Benefit Reading**
St Mark's Church, East Village
www.poetryproject.org

Around 140 of the city's best poets, artists and performers gather at St Mark's Church in-the-Bowery and recite their work to a hall full of listeners.

late Jan/early Feb **Winter Restaurant Week**
Various venues
www.nycgo.com/restaurantweek
Twice a year, for two weeks or more at a stretch, some of the city's finest restaurants dish out three-course prix-fixe lunches for $25; some places also offer dinner for $38. For the full list of participating restaurants, visit the website, and make reservations well in advance.

Feb **Chinese New Year**
Around Mott Street, Chinatown
www.betterchinatown.com
Chinatown is charged with energy during the two weeks of the Lunar New Year. The firecracker ceremony and parade are key events.

Spring

early Mar **Armory Show**
Piers 92 & 94, Twelfth Avenue, at 55th Street, Hell's Kitchen
www.thearmoryshow.com
Though its name pays homage to the 1913 show that introduced avant-garde European art to an American audience, this contemporary international art mart debuted in 1999. It's now held on the Hudson River.

17 Mar **St Patrick's Day Parade**
Fifth Avenue, from 44th to 86th Streets
www.nycstpatricksparade.org
This massive march is even older than the United States – it was started by a group of homesick Irish conscripts from the British army in 1762. Today, thousands of green-clad merrymakers strut to the sounds of pipe bands.

late Mar/early Apr **Easter Parade**
Fifth Avenue, from 49th to 57th Streets

Starting at 10am on Easter Sunday, Fifth Avenue becomes a car-free promenade of gussied-up crowds milling around and showing off their extravagant Easter bonnets.

Apr **Tribeca Film Festival**
Various venues
www.tribecafilmfestival.org
Launched in 2002, Robert De Niro's downtown festival draws more than 400,000 indie fans to screenings of independent movies and other events.

late Apr **Sakura Matsuri (Cherry Blossom Festival)**
Brooklyn Botanic Garden, p156
www.bbg.org
The annual Sakura Matsuri celebrates both the blooms and Japanese culture with concerts, traditional dance, manga exhibitions, cosplay fashion shows and tea ceremonies.

early May **TD Five Boro Bike Tour**
Lower Manhattan to Staten Island
www.bikenewyork.org
Thousands of cyclists take over the city for a 40-mile, car-free Tour de New York. The route begins near Battery Park, moves up through Manhattan and makes a circuit of the boroughs before winding up at Staten Island's Fort Wadsworth for a festival.

mid May **Frieze Art Fair New York**
Randalls Island Park
www.friezenewyork.com
The New York edition of the tent-tastic London art fair first arrived on Randalls Island in 2011. A global array of around 190 galleries set up shop under a temporary structure overlooking the East River.

late May/early June **Washington Square Outdoor Art Exhibit**
Various streets surrounding Washington Square Park, p86
www.wsoae.org
In 1931, Jackson Pollock and Willem de Kooning propped up a few of

Shakespeare in the Park

their paintings on the sidewalk near Washington Square Park and called it a show. A lot has changed since then: now, more than 125 artists and artisans participate in the Washington Square Outdoor Art Exhibit.

Summer

June-Aug **SummerStage**
Rumsey Playfield, Central Park
www.summerstage.org
Rockers, world music stars, orchestras and performers in various disciplines take over the main stage in Central Park – and green spaces across the five boroughs – for this very popular and mostly free annual series. Show up early or listen from outside the enclosure gates.

June-Aug **Shakespeare in the Park**
Delacorte Theater, Central Park, p131
www.publictheater.org
The Public Theater offers the best of the Bard outdoors. Free tickets (two per person) are distributed at the Delacorte at noon on the day of the performance. Around 8am is usually a good time to begin waiting, although the queue can start forming as early as 6am when big-name stars are on the bill.

June-Aug **Celebrate Brooklyn!**
Prospect Park Bandshell, Prospect Park, Brooklyn
www.bricartsmedia.org
Since community arts organisation BRIC launched this series of outdoor performances to revitalise Prospect Park, it's become Brooklyn's premier summer fête, featuring music, dance, film and spoken word acts.

early June **National Puerto Rican Day Parade**
Fifth Avenue, from 44th to 79th Streets
www.nprdpinc.org
A whopping 80,000 Nuyoricans take part in the march, including *vejigantes* (carnival dancers). There are also colourful floats and live salsa and reggaetón bands at this freewheeling celebration of the city's largest Hispanic community and its culture.

early June **Egg Rolls & Egg Creams Festival**
Museum at Eldridge Street, p71
www.eldridgestreet.org
This block party celebrates the convergence of Jewish and Chinese traditions on the Lower East Side, with klezmer music, acrobats, Chinese opera and, of course, plenty of the titular treats.

early June **Governors Ball Music Festival**
Randalls Island Park
www.governorsballmusicfestival.com
Catch big names in rock, pop and hip hop at this three-day outdoor festival.

early June **Big Apple Barbecue Block Party**
Madison Square Park, p106
www.bigapplebbq.org
Get your fill of the best 'cue around as the country's top pit masters come together for this two-day outdoor carnivore's paradise. Music and chefs' demos and tips are also on the menu.

early June **Museum Mile Festival**
Fifth Avenue, from 82nd to 105th Streets, Upper East Side
www.museummilefestival.org
Eight of the city's most prestigious art institutions – including the Met and the Guggenheim – open their doors to the public free of charge. Music, dance and children's activities turn this into a 23-block-long celebration, but you'll have to arrive early to stand a chance of getting into the museums themselves.

mid/late June **River to River Festival**
Various venues
www.rivertorivernyc.com
Lower Manhattan organisations present dozens of free events – from visual art to all sorts of performances – at various venues. Past performers have included Patti Smith, Laurie Anderson, DJ Nickodemus and Angélique Kidjo.

late June **Mermaid Parade**
Coney Island, Brooklyn, p164
www.coneyisland.com
Glitter-covered semi-nude revellers, aquatically adorned floats and classic cruisers fill Surf Avenue for this annual art parade.

late June **Midsummer Night Swing**
Lincoln Center, p149
www.midsummernightswing.org

Lincoln Center's Damrosch Park is turned into a giant dancefloor as bands play salsa, Cajun, swing and other music. For three weeks (Tue-Sat), each night's party is devoted to a different dance style, and is preceded by lessons. Beginners are, of course, welcome.

late June **NYC LGBT Pride March**
Fifth Avenue, from 36th Street to the West Village
www.nycpride.org
Downtown Manhattan becomes a sea of rainbow flags as lesbian, gay, bisexual and transgendered people from the city and beyond parade down Fifth Avenue in commemoration of the 1969 Stonewall Riots. After the march, there's a massive street fair and a dance on the West Side piers.

July-Aug **Warm Up**
MoMA PS1, p165
www.momaps1.org/warmup
Since 1997, PS1's courtyard has played host to one of the most anticipated, resolutely underground clubbing events in the city. Thousands of dance-music fanatics and alt-rock enthusiasts make the pilgrimage to Long Island City on summer Saturdays to drink and dance. The sounds range from spiritually inclined soul to full-bore techno.

4 July **Macy's Fourth of July Fireworks**
Various East River locations
www.macys.com/fireworks
After a few years on the Hudson, NYC's main Independence Day attraction moved back to the East River – where fireworks are launched from barges and the Brooklyn Bridge – in 2014. The pyrotechnics start at around 9pm, but you'll need to scope out your vantage point much earlier. Spectators are packed like sardines at prime spots.

late July-early Aug **Lincoln Center Out of Doors**
Lincoln Center, p149
www.lcoutofdoors.org

Summer in the city

Get outside and soak up some free culture.

SummerStage

While many New Yorkers escape to the coast for summer weekends, there are many advantages to visiting NYC in July and August. For one thing, hotel rates are at their lowest, apart from chilly January-March. Yes, it will be hot and humid, but there is less competition for tickets to Broadway shows and tables at hyped restaurants. Summer Streets (www.nyc.gov/summerstreets) – which creates a car-free route from Brooklyn Bridge to Central Park for three Saturdays in August – offers a rare opportunity to stroll along Park Avenue sans traffic. But best of all, summer brings a roster of standout free events.

Shakespeare in the Park (p35)

Droves of theatre-lovers line up for hours in Central Park for open-air performances. Free tickets (two per person) are distributed at the park's Delacorte Theater at noon on the day of the show. The queue can start forming as early as 6am when big-name stars are on the bill. Bring a blanket and provisions (though many local eateries distribute menus and deliver to your spot).

SummerStage (p35)

This annual cultural behemoth brings more than 100 free shows to parks in all five boroughs, from concerts and DJ events to theatre, comedy and dance performances.

River to River (p36)

Though it has shrunk from a month to two weeks in June, this festival showcases dozens of free concerts, art installations, dance and theatrical performances in waterside spots and lower Manhattan venues.

Lincoln Center Out of Doors (p36)

The sprawling campus comes alive with dozens of gratis shows by musicians, dancers and other artists from all over the world.

Outdoor movie festivals

Alfresco film series in city parks, including Bryant Park (www.bryantpark.org) and Central Park (www.centralparknyc.org) are a summer tradition. Arrive early to claim a prime patch of grass in front of the big screen.

Free dance, music, theatre, opera and more make up the programme over the course of three weeks at this family-friendly and ambitious festival run by the Lincoln Center.

late July-late Aug **Harlem Week**
Various venues in Harlem
www.harlemweek.com
Get into the groove at this massive culture fest, which began in 1974 as a one-day event. Harlem Day is still the centrepiece of the event, but 'Week' is now a misnomer; besides the street fair serving up music, art and food along 135th Street, a wealth of concerts, films, dance performances, fashion and sports events are on tap for about a month.

late July-early Aug **Summer Restaurant Week**
Various venues
www.nycgo.com/restaurantweek
See Winter.

Aug **New York International Fringe Festival**
Various venues
www.fringenyc.org

Wacky and sometimes wonderful, downtown's Fringe Festival – inspired by the Edinburgh original – shoehorns hundreds of arts performances into 17 theatre-crammed days.

late Aug-early **Sept US Open**
USTA Billie Jean King National Tennis Center, Flushing Meadows Corona Park, Queens
www.usopen.org
Flushing, Queens, becomes the centre of the tennis universe when it hosts the final Grand Slam event of the year.

late Aug-early Sept **Washington Square Outdoor Art Exhibit**
Various streets surrounding Washington Square Park, p85
www.wsoae.org
See Spring.

early Sept **Electric Zoo**
Randall's Island
www.electriczoofestival.com
Don your Day-Glo shades and head for this three-day outdoor EDM rager. The line-up is heavy on superstar DJs such as Armin Van Buuren, David Guetta and Dimitri Vegas & Like Mike.

Electric Zoo

Itineraries

Elevated Pursuits

A disused freight train track reborn as a public park-cum-promenade, the **High Line** has existed in its current incarnation for only half a decade, but it is already one of the most popular spots with visitors and locals alike. The lush, landscaped green strip provides a verdant pathway between the somewhat hedonistic Meatpacking District and the still-evolving neighbourhood of Hell's Kitchen, cutting through the city's main gallery district in Chelsea. You could easily spend an entire day traversing its length, disembarking to enjoy attractions, eateries and bars along the way.

The urban sanctuary has a less-than-serene history. Back in the early days of the 20th century, the West Side had something in common with the Wild West. When freight-bearing trains competed with horses, carts and pedestrians on Tenth Avenue, the thoroughfare was so treacherous

it earned the moniker 'Death Avenue'. In an attempt to counteract the carnage, mounted men known as 'West Side Cowboys' would ride in front of the train, waving red flags to warn of its imminent approach. These urban cowboys lost their jobs when the West Side Improvement Project finally raised the railway off street level and put it up on to an overhead trestle – the High Line – in 1934. Originally stretching from 34th Street to Spring Street, the line fell into disuse after World War II as trucks replaced trains. A southern chunk was torn down in the 1960s, and, after the last train ground to a halt in 1980, local property owners lobbied for its destruction. However, thanks to the efforts of railroad enthusiast Peter Obletz and, later, the Friends of the High Line, which was founded by local residents Joshua David and Robert Hammond, the industrial relic was saved. A decade

High Line

The new home of the **Whitney Museum of American Art** (see box p87) opens in spring 2015, so if you're reading this after that date you can pop into the free ground-floor gallery for a taster. In celebration of the museum's new digs, the façade of the building opposite the High Line across Gansevoort Street will feature changing artists' installations over the next five years.

As you stroll north alongside trees, flowers and landscaped greenery, keep an eye out for several interesting features along the way. Commanding an expansive river view, the 'sun deck' between 14th and 15th Streets has wooden deck chairs that can be rolled along the original tracks, plus a water feature for cooling your feet. Just past 15th Street, the High Line cuts through the old loading dock of the former Nabisco factory, where the first Oreo cookie was made in 1912. This conglomeration of 18 structures, built between the 1890s and the 1930s, now houses **Chelsea Market** (75 Ninth Avenue, between 15th & 16th Streets, www.chelseamarket. com). Alight here if you want to shop in the ground-floor food arcade for artisanal bread, wine, baked goods and freshly made ice-cream, among other treats. From around late April until late October, however, food vendors set up on the High Line itself, and you can stop for a tipple at seasonal open-air café, the Porch, at 15th Street, which serves local wine and beer from cult vino spot **Terroir** (p82).

At 17th Street, steps descend into a sunken amphitheatre with a glassed-over 'window' in the steel structure overlooking the avenue. The elevated walkway provides a great vantage point for viewing the surrounding architecture; you will see not only iconic structures like the Statue of Liberty and the Empire State Building during your stroll, but

after the group began advocating for its reuse as a public space, the first phase of New York's first elevated public park opened in summer 2009 (the second leg followed in 2011).

Start your expedition in the Meatpacking District, where upscale shops include designer department store **Jeffrey New York** (p95), new independent boutique **Owen** (p95), relocated antique jewellery trove **Doyle & Doyle** (p95) and longtime local fixture **Diane von Furstenberg** (874 Washington Street, at W 14th Street, 1-646 486 4800, www.dvf.com). Combine retail therapy with a jolt of caffeine at the **Rag & Bone General Store** (p95). The latest location of the rapidly growing New York-born boutique chain has an on-site cult coffee bar courtesy of **Jack's Stir Brew Coffee** (p60).

From here, it's just a couple of blocks to the southernmost entrance to the High Line, on Washington Street, at Gansevoort Street. As you mount the stairs, you'll notice a dramatic building to your left.

also newer buildings such as Frank Gehry's 2007 headquarters for Barry Diller's InterActiveCorp (555 W 18th Street, at West Side Highway), which comprises tilting glass volumes that resemble a fully rigged tall ship.

By now it's probably time for brunch. Descend the stairs at 20th Street for **Cookshop** (p102), which serves eggs with applewood bacon and seasonal variations on French toast. Or try the pancakes at rebooted New York icon the **Empire Diner** (p102), which has been given an up-to-date seasonal spin by celebrity chef Amanda Freitag.

Fortified, you're ready for some cultural sustenance. Before you embark on a contemporary art crawl, note the block-long campus of the General Theological Seminary of the Episcopal Church across 20th Street. The land was once part of the estate known as Chelsea, owned by poet Clement Clarke Moore, author of 'A Visit from St Nicholas' (more commonly known as "Twas the Night Before Christmas'). The seminary's former guest wing is now the **High Line Hotel** (p176).

In the 1980s, many of New York's galleries left Soho for what was then an industrial wasteland on the western edge of Chelsea. Today, blue-chip spaces and numerous less exalted ones attract swarms of art aficionados to the area between Tenth and Eleventh Avenues from 19th to 29th Streets. If you have limited time, hit **24th Street**, where high-profile spaces include Gagosian Gallery, Mary Boone Gallery, Gladstone Gallery, Luhring Augustine and Matthew Marks Gallery. At the street's western corner, check out the 19-storey apartment building at **200 Eleventh Avenue**. Designed by Annabelle Selldorf, it has a car elevator, allowing residents to bring their prized motor up to their door. A couple of blocks north is a notable example of industrial architecture, the 1929 Starrett-Lehigh

Building (601 W 26th Street, at Eleventh Avenue).

It's also worth swinging by 22nd Street, between Tenth and Eleventh Avenues, to see the outdoor art installation *7000 Oaks* by German artist Joseph Beuys: 18 pairings of basalt stones and trees. Maintained by Dia Art Foundation (diaart.org), the piece is a spin-off of a five-year international effort, begun in 1982 at Germany's Documenta 7 exhibition, to enact social and environmental change by planting 7,000 trees. If you want a souvenir, stop by arty bookshop **Printed Matter** (p103).

Your art tour isn't over when you resume your High Line perambulation (there are stairs at 23rd and 26th Street). Befitting its location, the park itself is a platform for creativity and has a dedicated curator of temporary site-specific installations. Unless you're reading this in early 2015 or beyond, chances are you'll reach the end of the line at 30th Street; the final section of the park, skirting the under-construction mixed-use complex of Hudson Yards, will open in stages, featuring a kids' play area incorporating the original sleepers and, eventually, the Spur – a bowl-like structure lined with lush greenery and seating steps, hovering over the intersection of 30th Street and Tenth Avenue.

From here, you can walk or take a taxi to Hell's Kitchen. At **Gotham West Market** (p119), a modern take on a food court, cult eateries include new arrival from Tokyo, Ivan Ramen. Otherwise, Ninth Avenue in the 40s and 50s is packed with inexpensive restaurants serving just about any ethnic cuisine you can think of. Afterwards, the bright lights of **Broadway** (and Off Broadway), a few blocks away, beckon. Score cut-price Broadway tickets at **TKTS** (p119), or see high-level cabaret at **54 Below** (p121), located in the bowels of legendary nightspot Studio 54.

Brooklyn Bridge

A Bridge Not Too Far

Not long ago, many Manhattanites baulked at the idea of crossing the East River for a day or night out in Brooklyn. Times sure have changed. Not only is the second borough a destination in its own right, with a thriving cultural and food scene, but it has also become shorthand for a particular brand of indie cool recognised from Peoria to Paris. Now it's an essential stop on many visitors' itineraries, and newcomers are discovering it's not as far from Manhattan as they thought – one of the nicest ways to get there is on foot. This full-day, two-borough itinerary links two historic, art-rich and fashionable neighbourhoods – with some staggering views in the middle.

New York's character has been shaped by successive waves of immigrants, from the Dutch settlers who invaded the domain of the Lenape Indians in the 16th century to more recent Asian and Latino arrivals. But between the late 19th century and the mid-1950s, more than 12 million hopefuls sailed into New York Harbor from Europe. Many of these newcomers crowded into the dark, squalid tenements of the Lower East Side, which by 1900 was the most populous neighbourhood in the US. While it may still feel overpopulated when you're waiting for a table at a hot restaurant like **Mission Cantina** (p72), nowadays the streets are packed with trendy young things flitting from boutiques to cocktail bars. But remnants of the past remain. You can still get a taste of the Lower East Side's largely Jewish legacy at **Russ & Daughters**, the iconic smoked fish shop that opened a nearby café on Orchard Street (p74) to celebrate its 100th birthday. In homage to the old country, order the Shtetl: smoked sable and goat's milk cream cheese on a bialy. Cross

Jane's Carousel

Delancey Street for the **Lower East Side Tenement Museum** (p71), which offers a window into how locals lived – and worked – in the 19th and early 20th centuries through tours of apartments once occupied by documented residents, some of whom operated businesses on the site. If you'd rather contemplate the provenance of impeccably selected vintage wares, boutiques include **Edith Machinist** (104 Rivington Street, 1-212 979 9992, www.edith machinist.com), **David Owens Vintage** (p74) and the **Dressing Room** (p75). But it's not all about history in the locale, which is home to some of the most cutting-edge boutiques and galleries in the city along with the **New Museum of Contemporary Art** (p71).

Once you've had enough art and commerce, pick up the J or Z train at the Bowery or Delancey-Essex Streets station and get off at Chambers Street, near City Hall. Every day, more than 6,500 people walk or bike across the wide, wood-planked promenade of the Brooklyn Bridge, and it's easy to see why: the structure itself is gorgeous, and so are the views of New York Harbor, the Statue of Liberty and the skyscrapers

of lower Manhattan. Crowds have always been part of the scene here. Six days after the bridge opened on 24 May 1883, a stampede on a stairway crushed 12 people to death and injured 35. A scream sparked hysteria that the structure was collapsing, and people surged down the steps. They were understandably wary: it was the longest suspension bridge in the world at the time.

When you reach the halfway mark, pause to take in the view but also to marvel at the bridge's construction, which began on the Brooklyn side. To lay the foundation on bedrock 44 feet below, workers in airtight containers chipped away at the riverbed. More than 100 were paralysed with the bends, caused by the change in air pressure when they surfaced. When the Manhattan side was built, chief engineer Washington Roebling got the bends as well. Washington spent the next decade watching the bridge's progress through a telescope and relaying directions through his wife, Emily. Fearing more deaths on the Manhattan tower, he stopped construction before it reached the 100-foot-deep bedrock. To this day, that tower rests on sand and hardpan.

Bear left to take the first exit off the bridge, which brings you to the top of Washington Street in Dumbo – but the neighbourhood actually takes its name from the neighbouring span (Down Under the Manhattan Bridge Overpass). As you cross York Street, take note of the handsome 1889 brick structure on your right, which once housed Thomson Meter Company, one of many businesses, including Brillo and Benjamin Moore, that were based in the erstwhile industrial hub. Now the old factory buildings have been converted into high-end apartments, eateries and shops – retail highlights include designer boutique **Zoe** (68 Washington Street, between Front & York Streets, 1-718 237 4002, www.shopzoeonline.com), bookstore-cum-event-space the **powerHouse Arena** (37 Main Street, between Front & Water Streets, 1-718 666 3049, www.powerhouse arena.com) and men's concept store **Modern Anthology** (p161). If you need a pick-me-up, swing by **Brooklyn Roasting Company** (25 Jay Street, between John & Plymouth Streets, 1-718 522 2664, www.brooklynroasting.com), which has revived the local tradition – the Arbuckle Bros coffee roasting plant was established in Dumbo in 1891 – and has an airy, industrial-chic café.

Head back up Jay Street then right on Water Street to the Pearl Street Triangle, which often spotlights temporary art installations. Cut under the Manhattan Bridge through the dramatic, 45-foot-high erstwhile storage facility, the Archway. Shuttered for 17 years, it now functions as an event space as well as an atmospheric passageway. Take a right on to Washington Street and down to **Brooklyn Bridge Park**. On both sides of the bridge, the park has been undergoing a rolling renovation over several years. Walk alongside the post-Civil War coffee warehouses, Empire Stores, to the park's jewel, **Jane's Carousel**, a restored 1922 merry-go-round in its Jean Nouvel-designed pavilion.

On the other side of the Brooklyn Bridge, you'll arrive at Fulton Ferry Landing. It was here that General George Washington and his troops beat a hasty retreat by boat from the Battle of Brooklyn in 1776. If you want to head back to Manhattan by water, board the East River Ferry (www.nywaterway.com), which connects Dumbo to six points in Manhattan, Brooklyn and Queens. Take a turn around the park's **Pier One** for expansive Manhattan-skyline views and a snack – food stands include cult sandwich shop No. 7 Sub (it closes at 4pm) and Luke's Lobster for superior seafood rolls. Or relax with a glass of wine or locally brewed beer at the park's outdoor **Brooklyn Bridge Garden Bar** (brooklynbridgegardenbar.com) or take in some chamber music at floating venue **Bargemusic** (p163).

When you're ready for dinner, head east on Water or Front Street to discover one of Brooklyn's forgotten neighbourhoods. Once a rough and bawdy patch dotted with bars and brothels frequented by sailors and dockworkers, Vinegar Hill, between Bridge Street and the Navy Yard, earned the moniker 'Hell's Half Acre' in the 19th century. Only fragments of the enclave remain (parts of it were designated a historic district in the late 1990s), and it's considerably quieter today. Although inhabited, the isolated strips of early-19th-century row houses and defunct storefronts on Bridge, Hudson and Plymouth Streets, and a stretch of Front Street, have a ghost-town quality, heightened by their juxtaposition with a Con Edison generating station. The enclave's tavern-like **Vinegar Hill House** (p160), which also has an enclosed back patio, is a lovely tucked-away spot for a meal.

ITINERARIES

1 World Trade Center

High Points

In *Here is New York*, EB White wrote that the city 'is to the nation what the white church spire is to the village – the visible symbol of aspiration and faith, the white plume saying that the way is up.' Despite the irrevocable damage to the skyline from the 9/11 attacks, that comment still resonates – New York is constantly rebuilding itself and adding to its cache of cloudbusters.

The logical starting point for an architectural tour is a visit to the **Skyscraper Museum** (p56) in the Financial District. Here you can see large-scale photographs of lower Manhattan's skyscrapers from 1956, 1976 and 2004, and a 1931 silent film documenting the construction of the Empire State Building. You can also see various models and documentation related to the construction of the original Twin Towers and the World Trade

Center's new centrepiece skyscraper, in preparation for a subsequent stop.

Head out of the door, make a left and follow Battery Place across West Street and along the northern edge of Battery Park. Turn left up Greenwich Street, and at Morris Street walk along Trinity Place to make a brief stop at **Trinity Wall Street** (p59). In stark contrast to the skyscrapers that surround it, Trinity – designed by Richard Upjohn, it's the third church to stand on this spot – remains frozen in Gothic Revival style, but it was the island's tallest structure when it was completed in 1846, thanks to its 281-foot spire. The churchyard, which dates back to 1697, is one of New York's oldest cemeteries. Alexander Hamilton (the nation's first secretary of the treasury – you can check out his mug on the $10 bill) is buried here.

Afterwards, it's time to visit one of the most powerfully moving sites in

Trinity Wall Street

at Barclay Street). Note the flamboyant Gothic terracotta cladding designed by Cass Gilbert in 1913. The 55-storey, 793-foot 'Cathedral of Commerce' was the world's tallest structure for 16 years until it was topped by 40 Wall Street. Nearby is the curled and warped stainless-steel façade of the audaciously named, 870-foot **New York** by Gehry (8 Spruce Street, between Gold & Nassau Streets). To get a better view of the Manhattan skyline, consider walking part or all the way across the **Brooklyn Bridge** (see p43).

Back to the current plan: once you've passed through the park (bordered to the east by Park Row), look for a subway entrance to your left. Board the Uptown 4 or 5 train to Grand Central-42nd Street. On the subway, consider this: it took ten years of unflagging effort for Jacqueline Kennedy Onassis and others to save **Grand Central Terminal** (p128), your next destination. After the original Pennsylvania Station was demolished in 1963, developers unveiled plans to wreck the magnificent Beaux Arts edifice and erect an office tower in its place. Jackie O rallied politicians and celebrities to her cause. In 1978, her committee won a Supreme Court decision affirming landmark status for the beloved building, which celebrated its centennial in 2013.

By now you'll likely be famished. Head back downstairs to one of the city's most famous eateries, the **Grand Central Oyster Bar & Restaurant** (lower concourse, p129), for a late lunch. Before heading inside, linger a moment under the low ceramic arches, dubbed the 'whispering gallery'. Instruct a friend to stand in an opposite, diagonal corner from you and whisper to each other – they'll sound as clear as if you were face to face.

recent history: the spot where the mighty Twin Towers once stood. From the church, continue to walk up Trinity Place for two more blocks and cross over Liberty Street. The World Trade Center is to your left. The awe-inspiring **National September 11 Memorial**, comprising two 30-foot-deep waterfalls in the footprints of the towers, opened on the ten-year anniversary of the attacks, and you can now descend to their foundations in the **9/11 Memorial Museum** (box p58). One of three completed skyscrapers on the site at time of writing, **1 World Trade Center** is now the country's tallest building. If you're reading this in spring 2015 or beyond, you can zip up to the One World Observatory on the 100th to 102nd floors – the city's highest lookout point.

From the place where New York's tallest towers fell, it's onwards and upwards to the spot where the race to the heavens began. Walk up Vesey Street, then north on Broadway to the **Woolworth Building** (no.233,

Revitalised, you're ready for the next stop: **Columbus Circle**. Either hop back on the subway (S to Times Square, transfer to the Uptown 1 train and get off at 59th Street-Columbus Circle) or, preferably, you can hoof it there in about 30 minutes. Exit Grand Central on 42nd Street and head west. At Fifth Avenue, you'll pass another Beaux Arts treasure from the city's grand metropolitan era, the **New York Public Library** (p125) with its sumptuous white-marble façade. Completed in 1911, the library now sits on the greensward known as Bryant Park. When you get to Broadway, make a right and head north into Times Square. Imposing, sentinel-like skyscrapers mark the southern entry to the electric carnival here; the 2000 **Condé Nast Building** (no.4) and the 2001 **Reuters Building** (no.3), both by Fox & Fowle, complement Kohn Pedersen Fox's 2002 postmodern **5 Times Square** and David Childs' 2004 **Times Square Tower** (no.7). Originally Longacre Square, the 'Crossroads of the World' was renamed after the *New York Times* moved here in the early 1900s; beneath its sheath of billboards and snaking news zipper, the broadsheet's old HQ, **1 Times Square**, is an elegant 1904 structure. Take a detour if you want to see the paper's current home base, Renzo Piano's 2007 **New York Times Building** (620 Eighth Avenue, between W 40th & 41st Streets), one block west and a couple of blocks south. The glass-walled design represents the newspaper's desire for transparency in its reporting.

Back on Broadway, walk north on the pedestrian-packed sidewalks until you spot Christopher gazing out from his perch in the centre of Columbus Circle at 59th Street.

The renovated traffic circle, with its ring of fountains and benches, is the perfect place to contemplate another set of twin towers, the 2003 **Time Warner Center**, also designed by David Childs.

Increasingly, skyscrapers are incorporating green design. Norman Foster's extraordinary 2006 **Hearst Magazine Building** (959 Eighth Avenue, at W 57th Street) is a shining example. Look south-west and you can't miss it; it's the one that resembles a giant greenhouse.

At this point you have two options. The first is to end the day at the Time Warner Center and enjoy the staggering view from the Mandarin Oriental Hotel's Lobby Lounge, perched 35 floors up. The drinks prices here are equally staggering, but the Fifth Avenue and Central Park South skylines make it worth the splurge. Or, you can hail a cab and top off a day of skyscraper gazing with a panoramic view from either New York's most iconic tower, the **Empire State Building** (p124), or the Top of the Rock observation deck at **Rockefeller Center** (p125). The latter has an edge as it affords a great view of the former. Also look out for William Van Alen's silver-hooded **Chrysler Building** (p128). The acme of art deco design, it was part of a madcap three-way race to become the world's tallest building. The competitors were 40 Wall Street (now the Trump Building) and the Empire State Building. Van Alen waited for the first to top out at 927 feet before unveiling his secret weapon – a spire assembled inside the Chrysler's dome and raised from within to bring the height to 1,046 feet. At 102 storeys and 1,250 feet, the Empire State Building surpassed it only 11 months later.

New York by Area

Pier 15, South
Street Seaport

Downtown

NEW YORK BY AREA

Lower Manhattan has always
been the city's financial, legal and
political powerhouse. It's where New
York began as a Dutch colony, and
where the 19th-century influx of
immigrants infused the city with new
energy. Much of this part of the city
is off the Big Apple's orderly grid,
|and the landscape shifts from block
to block. In the Financial District,
gleaming skyscrapers rub shoulders
with 18th-century landmarks;
Tribeca's top dining spots are only
a short hop from Chinatown's
frenetic food markets; and the quiet
brownstone-lined streets of the West
Village are just around the corner
from the flashy nightspots of the
Meatpacking District.

Financial District

Commerce has been the backbone of
New York's prosperity since its earliest
days. The southern tip of the island
quickly evolved into the Financial

District because, in the days before
telecommunications, banks established
their headquarters near the port. As the
arrival point for the 19th-century influx
of immigrants, it played another vital
role in the city's evolution. This part of
town is still in transition, as more than a
decade of construction moves towards
completion. The new World Trade
Center is finally taking shape and in
the wake of Hurricane Sandy's damage,
the South Street Seaport is being
transformed from a touristy eyesore
into a waterfront destination where
locals will want to stroll, shop and relax.

Sights & museums

City Hall

*City Hall Park, from Vesey to Chambers
Streets, between Broadway & Park Row
(1-212 788 2656, www.nyc.gov/design
commission). Subway J, Z to Chambers
Street; R to City Hall; 2, 3 to Park Place;
4, 5, 6 to Brooklyn Bridge-City Hall.*
Open *Tours* (individuals) noon Wed,

10am Thur; (groups) 10.30am Mon, Tue (advance reservations required). **Admission** free. **Map** p52 C2 ❶

Designed by French émigré Joseph François Mangin and John McComb Jr, the fine, Federal-style City Hall was completed in 1812. Tours take in the City Council Chamber and the Governor's Room, with its collection of American 19th-century political portraits and historic furnishings (including George Washington's desk). Individuals can book (at least two days in advance) for the Thursday morning tour; alternatively, sign up between 10am and 11.30am on Wednesday at the NYC tourism kiosk at the southern end of City Hall Park on the east side of Broadway, at Barclay Street, for the first-come, first-served tour at noon.

Fraunces Tavern Museum

2nd & 3rd Floors, 54 Pearl Street, at Broad Street (1-212 425 1778, www.frauncestavernmuseum.org). Subway J, Z to Broad Street; 4, 5 to Bowling Green. **Open** noon-5pm daily. **Admission** $7; free-$4 reductions. **Map** p52 C4 ❷

True, George Washington slept here, but there's little left of the original 18th-century tavern that was favoured by Washington during the Revolution. Fire-damaged and rebuilt in the 19th century, it was reconstructed in its current Colonial Revival style in 1907. The museum itself features period rooms, a collection of 800 Revolutionary flags and such Washington relics as a lock of his hair. It was here, after the British had finally been defeated in 1783, that Washington took tearful farewell of his troops and vowed to retire from public life. Luckily, he had a change of heart six years later and became the country's first president. You can still raise a pint in the bar, run by Dublin's Porterhouse Brewing Company.

Governors Island

www.govisland.com. Subway R to Whitehall Street-South Ferry; 1 to South Ferry; 4, 5 to Bowling Green; then take ferry from Battery Maritime Building at Slip no.7. **Open** Late May-late Sept 10am-6pm Mon-Fri; 10am-7pm Sat, Sun (see website for hours and ferry schedule). **Admission** *Ferry* $2 round trip; free under-12s; free 10-11.30am Sat, Sun. **Map** p52 C5 ❸

A seven-minute ferry ride takes you to this seasonal island sanctuary, a scant 800 yards from lower Manhattan. Because of its strategic position in the middle of New York Harbor, Governors Island was a military outpost and off-limits to the public for 200 years. It finally opened to summer visitors in 2006. The verdant, 172-acre isle still retains a significant chunk of its military-era architecture, including Fort Jay, started in 1776, and Castle Williams, completed in 1812 and for years used as a prison. Today, as well as providing a peaceful setting for cycling (bring a bike, or rent one on arrival), the island hosts a programme of events, and 30 acres of new green space opened to the public for the 2014 season. The Hammock Grove, with hammocks set among 1,500 trees, offers shady reclining, and 14 acres of lawn include two ball fields. Eventually, new hills constructed from the debris of demolished buildings will provide even more spectacular viewpoints for harbour panoramas.

Museum of American Finance

48 Wall Street, at William Street (1-212 908 4110, www.moaf.org). Subway 2, 3, 4, 5 to Wall Street; R, 1 to Rector Street. **Open** 10am-4pm Tue-Sat. **Admission** $8; free-$5 reductions; free Sat through 2014. **Map** p52 C4 ❹

Situated in the old headquarters of the Bank of New York, the Museum of American Finance's permanent collection traces the history of Wall Street and America's financial markets. Displays in the stately banking hall include a bearer bond made out to President George Washington and ticker tape from the morning of the stock market crash of 1929.

THE BOWERY

D

ELDRIDGE ST
ALLEN ST
ORCHARD ST
LUDLOW ST
ESSEX ST

See
p55
Seward
Park

E

EAST BROADWAY

F

East
River
Park

1

CHRYSTIE ST
FORSYTH ST
HESTER ST

CANAL ST

50 Eldridge St
Synagogue

M

JEFFERSON ST
CLINTON ST

HENRY ST
MONTGOMERY ST
GOUVERNEUR ST

MADISON ST

WATER ST

Confucius
Plaza

DIVISION ST

RUTGERS ST

MADISON ST

PIKE ST

CHERRY ST

PELL ST

49

47
CHATHAM
SQ

K ROW

HENRY ST

MARKET ST

Rutgers
Park

OLIVER ST

51 MONROE ST

CATHERINE ST

First Shearith
Israel Graveyard

WATER ST

2

MANHATTAN BRIDGE

ST JAMES PL

SOUTH ST

ROOSEVELT DR

D

WAGNER PL

PEARL ST
DOVER ST
PECK SLIP

FRANKLIN

BROOKLYN BRIDGE

3

WATER ST

BEEKMAN ST

13

16

19

South Street
Seaport

18

TON ST

17

R ST

16

15
15

BROOKLYN

PEYSTER ST

14

4

13

URR LN

11

0   200 m

9

0   200 yds

© Copyright Time Out Group 2014

5

❶ Sights & museums
❶ Eating & drinking
❶ Shopping
❶ Nightlife
❶ Arts & leisure

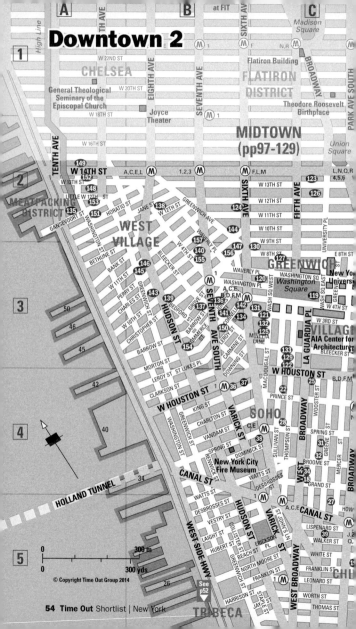

Downtown 2

A — TH AVE
B — at FIT
C — Madison Square

High Line

1

CHELSEA
W 22ND ST

Flatiron Building

General Theological
Seminary of the
Episcopal Church
W 20TH ST

FLATIRON
DISTRICT

EIGHTH AVE

SEVENTH AVE

BROADWAY

PARK AVE SOUTH

W 18TH ST

Theodore Roosevelt
Birthplace

Joyce
Theater
W 16TH ST

MIDTOWN
(pp97-129)

Union
Square

TENTH AVE

149 W 14TH ST   A,C,E,L Ⓜ   1,2,3 Ⓜ   Ⓜ F,L,M   123   L,N,Q,R,6
152   126   4,5,6
148 W 13TH ST   W 13TH ST
153 LITTLE W 12TH ST   W 12TH ST
135 151 HORATIO ST   138 W 12TH ST 124   W 11TH ST

FIFTH AVE

SIXTH AVE

GANSEVOORT ST   GREENWICH AVE

MEATPACKING
DISTRICT

2

WEST
VILLAGE

JANE ST   157   144   W 10TH ST
140 155 147   W 9TH ST
156   W 8TH ST
130

GREENWICH
New York
University

WASHINGTON ST

BETHUNE ST

BANK ST
146
145   W 11TH ST

WAVERLY PL

WAVERLY PL   120
WASHINGTON SQ   WASHINGTON SQ WEST
A,C,E,F,M
Washington
Square   116
WASH SQ SOUTH
W 4TH ST

E 8TH ST

GREENE ST

3

50

46

45

42

40

34

PERRY ST
CHARLES ST
143 139
CHRISTOPHER ST
BARROW ST
MORTON ST
154
LEROY ST ST LUKES PL
CLARKSON ST

GREENWICH ST
W 10TH ST

BLEECKER ST

HUDSON ST

BEDFORD ST
GROVE ST
137
BARROW ST
COMMERCE ST
LEROY ST
CARMINE ST
DOWNING ST

SEVENTH AVE SOUTH

142 131
141 134 121
125
132

W 3RD ST

VILLAGE
AIA Center for
Architecture
BLEECKER ST

LA GUARDIA PL

MINETTA LANE

133 129
128

MACDOUGAL ST

W HOUSTON ST   Ⓜ 36 37
22 25

B,D,F,M

50

46

45

42

40

HOLLAND TUNNEL

PRINCE ST

SOHO
C,E

28

38

SULLIVAN ST

THOMPSON ST

WEST BROADWAY

WOOSTER ST

GREENE ST

MERCER ST

BROADWAY

SPRING ST
31
34
18

BROOME ST

27

4

W HOUSTON ST
KING ST
CHARLTON ST
VANDAM ST
SPRING ST
DOMINICK ST
New York City
Fire Museum
WATTS ST
CANAL ST   DESBROSSES ST
Ⓜ A,C,E CANAL ST

WASHINGTON ST

GREENWICH ST

RENWICK ST

VARICK ST

HUDSON ST

HOW

LISPENARD ST

J,Z

WALKER ST

WHITE ST

FRANKLIN ST

LEONARD ST

WORTH ST

THOMAS ST

5

WEST SIDE HWY

300 m
300 yds

© Copyright Time Out Group 2014

WATTS ST
DESBROSSES ST
VESTRY ST
LAIGHT ST
HUBERT ST
BEACH ST
NORTH MOORE ST
FRANKLIN ST

HUDSON ST

COLLISTER ST

GREENWICH ST

ERICSSON PL

VARICK ST

WEST BROADWAY

26

See
p52

TRIBECA

National Museum of the American Indian

George Gustav Heye Center, Alexander Hamilton US Custom House, 1 Bowling Green, between State & Whitehall Streets (1-212 514 3700, www.nmai.si.edu). Subway R to Whitehall Street-South Ferry; 1 to South Ferry; 4, 5 to Bowling Green. Open 10am-5pm Mon-Wed, Fri-Sun; 10am-8pm Thur. Admission free. Map p52 C4 **⑤**

The National Museum of the American Indian's George Gustav Heye Center, a branch of the Smithsonian Institution, displays its collection on the first two floors of Cass Gilbert's grand 1907 Custom House, one of the finest Beaux-Arts buildings in the city. On the second level, the life and culture of Native Americans is illuminated in three galleries radiating out from the rotunda. A permanent exhibition, 'Infinity of Nations', displays 700 items from the museum's wide-ranging collection of Native American art and objects, from decorated baskets to elaborate ceremonial headdresses, organised by region. On the ground floor, the Diker Pavilion for Native Arts & Culture is the city's only dedicated showcase for Native American performing arts.

National September 11 Memorial & Museum

NEW *Enter on Liberty Street at Greenwich or West Street, or on West Street at Fulton Street (1-212 312 8800, www.911memorial.org). Subway A, C, J, Z, 2, 3, 4, 5 to Fulton Street; E to World Trade Center; R, 1 to Rector Street. Open Memorial plaza 7.30am-9pm daily. Museum 9am-7pm daily (hours vary seasonally; see website for updates). Admission Memorial plaza free. Museum $24; free-$18 reductions; free 5-7pm Tue (advance reservations required). Map p52 B3* **⑥**
See box p58.

Skyscraper Museum

39 Battery Place, between Little West Street & 1st Place (1-212 968 1961, www.skyscraper.org). Subway 4, 5 to Bowling Green. Open noon-6pm Wed-Sun. Admission $5; $2.50 reductions. Map p52 B4 **⑦**

The only institution of its kind in the world, this intimate space explores high-rise buildings as objects of design, products of technology, real-estate investments and places of work and residence. A large part of the single gallery (a mirrored ceiling gives the illusion of height) is devoted to temporary exhibitions. A substantial chunk of the permanent collection relates to the Word Trade Center, including original models of the Twin Towers and the new 1 World Trade Center. Other highlights of the display are large-scale photographs of lower Manhattan's skyscrapers from 1956, 1976 and 2004, and a 1931 silent film documenting the Empire State Building's construction.

Staten Island Ferry

Battery Park, South Street, at Whitehall Street (1-718 727 2508, www.siferry.com). Subway R to Whitehall Street-South Ferry; 1 to South Ferry; 4, 5 to Bowling Green. Open ferry runs 24hrs daily. Tickets free. Map p52 C5 **⑧**

During this commuter ferry's 25-minute crossing, you'll see superb panoramas of lower Manhattan and the Statue of Liberty.

Statue of Liberty & Ellis Island Immigration Museum

Liberty Island (1-212 363 3200, www.nps.gov/stli). Subway R to Whitehall Street-South Ferry; 1 to South Ferry; 4, 5 to Bowling Green; then take Statue of Liberty ferry (1-201 604 2800, 1-877 523 9849, www.statuecruises.com), departing roughly every 30mins from gangway 4 or 5 in southernmost Battery Park. Open ferry runs 9.30am-3.30pm daily. Purchase tickets online, by phone or at Castle Clinton in Battery Park. Admission $18; free-$14 reductions. Map p52 B5 **⑨**

Staten Island Ferry

Remembering 9/11

A new national museum covers the worst attack on US soil.

In a city known for its sky-high aspirations, Ground Zero was a potent symbol of grief, and for most of the decade following 9/11, it felt as if the gaping wound in the middle of downtown Manhattan would never be healed. More than a decade on, however, the new World Trade Center has taken shape. The National September 11 Memorial opened on the tenth anniversary of the attacks and the centrepiece tower – one of three completed skyscrapers on the site – is now America's tallest building. In spring 2014, the long-awaited 9/11 Memorial Museum opened to the public.

Surrounded by a tree-shaded plaza, the memorial itself, Reflecting Absence, created by architects Michael Arad and Peter Walker, comprises two one-acre 'footprints' of the destroyed towers, with 30-foot man-made waterfalls cascading down their sides. Bronze parapets around the edges are inscribed with the names of the 2,983 victims of the 2001 attacks at the World Trade Center, the Pentagon and the passengers of United Flight 93, as well as those who lost their lives in the bombing on 26 February 1993.

The museum pavilion, designed by Oslo-based firm Snøhetta, rises between the pools. Its web-like glass atrium houses two steel trident-shaped columns salvaged from the base of the Twin Towers. Visitors descend to the vast spaces of the WTC's original foundations alongside a remnant of the Vesey Street staircase known as the 'Survivors' Stairs', which was used by hundreds of people escaping the carnage. Massive pieces of twisted metal and a fallen segment of the North Tower's radio/TV antenna bring home the enormous scale of the disaster.

Around 1,000 artefacts, plus images, documents and oral histories chronicle events leading up to the attacks, commemorate the victims and document how the world changed after 9/11. Items vividly evoke individual stories, from private voicemails left by people in the towers to the East Village's Ladder Company 3 fire truck, dispatched with 11 firefighters who died during the rescue effort. The In Memoriam exhibition pays tribute to each victim with a portrait, bio and audio remembrances.

The sole occupant of Liberty Island, *Liberty Enlightening the World* stands 305ft tall from the bottom of her base to the tip of her gold-leaf torch. Intended as a gift from France on America's 100th birthday, the statue was designed by Frédéric Auguste Bartholdi (1834-1904). Construction began in Paris in 1874, her skeletal iron framework crafted by Gustave Eiffel (the man behind the Tower), but only the arm with the torch was finished in time for the centennial in 1876. In 1884, the statue was finally completed – only to be taken apart to be shipped to New York, where it was unveiled in 1886. It served as a lighthouse until 1902, and as a welcoming beacon for millions of immigrants. These 'tired…poor…huddled masses' were evoked in Emma Lazarus's poem 'The New Colossus', written in 1883 to raise funds for the pedestal and engraved inside the statue in 1903. With a free Monument Pass, available only with ferry tickets reserved in advance, you can enter the pedestal and view the interior through a glass ceiling. Access to the crown costs an extra $3 and must be reserved in advance with your ferry tickets.

A half-mile across the harbour from Liberty Island is the 32-acre Ellis Island, gateway for over 12 million people who entered the country between 1892 and 1954. In the Immigration Museum (a former check-in depot), three floors of photos, interactive displays and exhibits pay tribute to the hopeful souls who made the voyage.

Trinity Wall Street & St Paul's Chapel

Trinity Wall Street *89 Broadway, at Wall Street. Subway R, 1 to Rector Street; 2, 3, 4, 5 to Wall Street.* **Open** *7am-6pm Mon-Fri; 10am-4pm Sat; 7am-4pm Sun. See website for cemetery hours.*

St Paul's Chapel *209 Broadway, between Fulton & Vesey Streets. Subway A, C to Broadway-Nassau Street; J, Z, 2, 3, 4, 5 to Fulton Street.* **Open** *10am-6pm Mon-Sat; 7am-6pm Sun.*

Both *(1-212 602 0800, www.trinity wallstreet.org).* **Admission** free. **Map** p52 B3 ⓾

Trinity Church was the island's tallest structure when it was completed in 1846 (the original burned down in 1776; a second was demolished in 1839). A set of gates north of the church on Broadway allows access to the adjacent cemetery, where tombstones mark the final resting places of dozens of past city dwellers, including such notable New Yorkers as Founding Father Alexander Hamilton and steamboat inventor Robert Fulton. The church museum displays an assortment of historic diaries, photographs, sermons and burial records.

Six blocks north, Trinity's satellite, St Paul's Chapel (1766), is more important architecturally. The oldest building in New York still in continuous use, it is one of the nation's most valued Georgian structures.

Eating & drinking

The Dead Rabbit Grocery & Grog

30 Water Street, between Broad Street and Old Slip (1-646 422 7906, www. deadrabbitnyc.com). Subway R to Whitehall Street-South Ferry. **Open** *11am-4am daily.* **Bar.** **Map** p52 C4 ⓫
Belfast bar vets Sean Muldoon and Jack McGarry have conjured up a rough-and-tumble 19th-century tavern in a red-brick landmark. Resurrecting long-forgotten quaffs is nothing new in NYC, but the Dead Rabbit's sheer breadth of mid-19th-century libations eclipses the competition, spanning 100-odd bishops, fixes, nogs and smashes. The fruit-forward Byrrh Wine Daisy, era-appropriate in its china teacup with moustache guard, is particularly well wrought.

Hudson Eats

NEW *Brookfield Place , 225 Liberty Street, between South End Avenue & West Street (1-212 417 7000, www. brookfieldplaceny.com/hudsoneats).*

Subway A, C, J, Z, 2, 3, 4, 5 to Fulton Street; E to World Trade Center; R, 1 to Rector Street. **Open** 7am-10pm Mon-Fri; 10am-9pm Sat; 11am-7pm Sun (hours vary for individual eateries) **$-$$**.
Eclectic. Map p52 B3 ⑫

Carved out from the second floor of a monster retail complex, the glossy, 600-seat dining terrace upgrades food-court schlock with white-marble counters, 17-foot-high windows offering gobsmacking waterfront views and 14 chef-driven kiosks, including branches of Mighty Quinn (see p81) for Texas-meets-Carolina 'cue and lox-and-schmear outfit Black Seed (see p73).

Jack's Stir Brew Coffee

222 Front Street, between Beekman Street & Peck Slip (1-212 227 7631, www.jacksstirbrew.com). Subway A, C, J, Z, 2, 3, 4, 5 to Fulton Street. **Open** 7am-6pm Mon-Fri; 8am-6pm Sat, Sun. **$**.
Café. Map p53 D3 ⑬

Java fiends convene at this award-winning caffeine spot that offers organic, shade-grown beans and a homey vibe. Coffee is served by espresso artisans with a knack for oddball concoctions, such as the super-silky Mountie latte, infused with maple syrup.

North End Grill

104 North End Avenue, at Murray Street (1-646 747 1600, www.northendgrillnyc. com). Subway A, C to Chambers Street; E to World Trade Center; 2, 3 to Park Place. **Open** 11.30am-2pm Mon-Fri; 11am-10.30pm Sat; 11am-9pm Sun. **$$$**.
American. Map p52 A3 ⑭

Danny Meyer has brought his Midas touch to Battery Park City. The place has all the hallmarks of a Meyer joint: effortless, affable service; a warm, buzzy space; and cooking that's easy and accessible. Chef Floyd Cardoz puts his stamp on the seasonal menu, devoting an entire section to eggs and adding doses of fire and spice. We were impressed by composed plates such as wood-fired lamb loin shingled on a bed of green lentils seasoned with mint.

Watermark

NEW *Pier 15, between Fletcher Street & Maiden Lane (1-212 742 8200, www.watermarkny.com). Subway A, C, J, Z, 2, 3, 4, 5 to Fulton Street; 2, 3 to Wall Street.* **Open** Apr-Oct 11am-11.30pm daily. Nov-Mar 11am-6pm daily. **Bar**. Map p53 D3 ⑮

Sip local craft beers accompanied by sea-inspired bar bites like lobster rolls and crab cakes at this contemporary waterfront bar – the skyline views through the floor-to-ceiling windows are spectacular. In summer, the bar also doles out cones of Ben & Jerry's ice-cream, sorbets and frozen yoghurt, fit for indulging your inner kid as you soak up rays on the outdoor deck.

Shopping

Bowne Printers and Bowne & Co Stationers

209-211 Water Street, between Fulton & Beekman Streets (1-212 748 8681). Subway A, C, J, Z, 2, 3, 4, 5 to Fulton Street. **Open** 11am-7pm daily. Map p53 D3 ⑯

At time of writing, the South Street Seaport Museum (www.southstreet seaportmuseum.org) remained closed due to damage from 2012's Hurricane Sandy, but the museum shop, comprising Bowne Printers and Bowne & Co Stationers, was open. The re-creation of a 19th-century print shop doesn't just look the part: the platen presses – hand-set using antique letterpress and type from the museum's collection – also turn out custom and small-batch stationery and cards. Next door, Bowne & Co Stationers, founded in 1775, sells hand-printed cards, prints, journals and other gifts.

Century 21

22 Cortlandt Street, between Broadway & Church Street (1-212 227 9092, www. c21stores.com). Subway A, C, J, Z, 2, 3, 4, 5 to Fulton Street; E to World Trade Center; R to Cortlandt Street. **Open** 7.45am-9pm Mon-Wed; 7.45am-9.30pm Thur, Fri; 10am-9pm Sat; 11am-8pm Sun. Map p52 C3 ⑰

A Gucci men's suit for $300? A Marc Jacobs cashmere sweater for less than $200? No, you're not dreaming – you're shopping at Century 21. You may have to rummage around to unearth a treasure, but with savings of up to 65% off regular prices, it's often worth it.

Tribeca & Soho

A former industrial wasteland, Tribeca (the Triangle Below Canal Street) is now one of the city's most expensive areas. Likewise, Soho (the area South of Houston Street) was once a hardscrabble manufacturing zone. Earmarked for destruction in the 1960s by over-zealous urban planner Robert Moses, its signature cast-iron warehouses were saved by the artists who inhabited them as cheap live-work spaces. Although the chain stores and sidewalk-encroaching street vendors along Broadway create a crush at weekends, there are some fabulous shops, galleries and eateries in the locale.

Sights & museums

Drawing Center

35 Wooster Street, between Broome & Grand Streets (1-212 219 2166, www. drawingcenter.org). Subway A, C, E, 1 to Canal Street. **Open** noon-6pm Wed-Sun. **Admission** $5; free-$3 reductions; free 6-8pm Thur. **Map** p54 C4 ⑱
Established in 1977, this non-profit standout recently reopened after expanding its gallery space by 50%. Now comprising three galleries, the Center assembles shows of museum-calibre legends such as Philip Guston, James Ensor and Willem de Kooning, but also 'Selections' surveys of newcomers. Art stars such as Kara Walker, Chris Ofili and Julie Mehretu received some of their earliest NYC exposure here.

Mmuseumm

Cortlandt Alley, between Franklin & White Streets. Subway J, N, Q, R, Z, *6 to Canal Street (no phone, www. mmuseumm.com).* **Open** noon-6pm Sat, Sun. **Admission** free. **Map** p52 C1 ⑲
Founded by indie filmmakers Alex Kalman, Josh Safdie and Benny Safdie, this micro museum housed in a 60-square-foot freight elevator showcases a mishmash of found objects and artefacts donated by hobbyists. Mmuseumm is open only at weekends, but viewers can also get a peek at the space when it's closed – look for small peepholes in a metal door on the narrow throughway between Franklin and White Streets. Exhibits for each season, lasting roughly six months, have included such varied displays as a collection of fake vomit from around the world, memorabilia from one of Saddam Hussein's palaces, and part of a collection of 200 mosquitoes killed mid-bite amassed by a traveller in New Delhi.

Eating & drinking

Balthazar

80 Spring Street, between Broadway & Crosby Street (1-212 965 1414, www.balthazarny.com). Subway N, R to Prince Street; 6 to Spring Street. **Open** 7am-midnight daily. $$. **French**. **Map** p54 C4 ⑳
At dinner, this iconic eaterie is perennially packed with rail-thin lookers dressed to the nines. But it's more than simply fashionable – the kitchen rarely makes a false step and the service is surprisingly friendly. The three-tiered seafood platter casts an impressive shadow, and the roast chicken with garlic mashed potatoes for two is *délicieux*.

Brushstroke

30 Hudson Street, at Duane Street (1-212 791 3771, www.davidbouley. com). Subway 1, 2, 3 to Chambers Street. **Open** 5.30-10.30pm Mon; 11.30am-2.45pm, 5.30-10.30pm Tue-Thur; 11.30am-2.45pm, 5.30-11pm Fri, Sat. $$$. **Japanese**. **Map** p52 B2 ㉑
Prominent local chef David Bouley's name may be behind this venture, but

Soho

he's not in the kitchen, having handed the reins over to talented import Isao Yamada, who turns out some of the most accomplished Japanese food in the city. The ever-changing seasonal menu is best experienced as an intricate multicourse feast inspired by the Japanese *kaiseki*. A meal might start with crab *chawanmushi* (egg custard) with Oregon black truffles, before building slowly towards top-notch *chirashi* or seafood and rice cooked in a clay casserole, and delicate sweets such as creamy soy-milk panna cotta. The sushi bar is run by Tokyo-trained chef Eiji Ichimura, who serves a traditional Edomae-style *omakase*.

The Dutch

131 Sullivan Street, at Prince Street (1-212 677 6200, www.thedutchnyc. com). Subway C, E to Spring Street. **Open** 11.30am-3pm, 5.30-11pm Mon-Wed; 11.30am-3pm, 5.30pm-midnight Thur, Fri; 10am-3pm, 5.30pm-midnight Sat; 10am-3pm, 5.30-11pm Sun. **$$.** **American. Map** p54 C4 ㉒
Andrew Carmellini, Josh Pickard and Luke Ostrom – the white-hot team behind Italian hit Locanda Verde in the Greenwich Hotel (see p172) – turned to American eats for their sophomore effort. The Dutch boasts late-night hours and a freewheeling menu, reflecting Carmellini's progression from haute golden boy (Café Boulud, Lespinasse) to champion of lusty plates and raucous settings. Carmellini plays off the country's diverse influences with a broad spectrum of dishes. Mini fried-oyster sandwiches, dry-aged steaks and peel 'n' eat prawns all get their due. Drop by the airy oak bar, with its adjacent oyster room, to sip one of the extensive selection of American whiskies.

Jack's Wife Freda

224 Lafayette Street, between Kenmare & Spring Streets (1-212 510 8550, www. jackswifefreda.com). Subway 6 to Spring Street. **Open** 9am-midnight Mon-Sat; 9am-10pm Sun. **$$. Café. Map** p55 D4 ㉓

Keith McNally protégé Dean Jankelowitz is behind this charming café. The 45-seat spot – sporting dark-green leather banquettes, brass railings and marble counters – serves homey fare, like Jankelowitz's grandmother's matzo ball soup made with duck fat or a skirt steak sandwich accompanied by hand-cut fries. In a prime shopping area between Soho and Nolita, it's also a great brunch spot.

Osteria Morini

218 Lafayette Street, between Broome & Spring Streets (1-212 965 8777, www.osteriamorini.com). Subway 6 to Spring Street. **Open** 11.30am-11pm Mon-Thur; 11.30am-midnight Fri; 11am-11pm Sat; 11am-10pm Sun.
$$. Italian. Map p55 D4 ㉔
Michael White is one of New York's most successful Italian-American chefs, and this terrific homage to a classic Bolognese tavern is his most accessible restaurant. White spent seven years cooking in Italy's Emilia-Romagna region, and his connection to the area surfaces in the rustic food. Handmade pastas are fantastic across the board, while the frequently changing selection of superb meat dishes might include porchetta with crisp, crackling skin and potatoes bathed in pan drippings.

Pegu Club

2nd Floor, 77 W Houston Street, between West Broadway & Wooster Street (1-212 473 7348, www.peguclub.com). Subway B, D, F, M to Broadway-Lafayette Street; N, R to Prince Street. **Open** 5pm-2am Mon-Thur, Sun; 5pm-4am Fri, Sat. **Bar. Map** p54 C4 ㉕
Audrey Saunders, the drinks maven who turned Bemelmans Bar (see p139) into one of the city's most respected cocktail lounges, is behind this sleek destination. Tucked away on the second floor, the sophisticated spot was inspired by a British officers' club in Burma. The cocktail menu features classics culled from decades-old booze bibles, and gin is the key ingredient – these are serious drinks for grown-up tastes.

NEW YORK BY AREA

Weather Up Tribeca

159 Duane Street, between Hudson Street & West Broadway (1-212 766 3202, www.weatherupnyc.com). Subway 1, 2, 3 to Chambers Street. **Open** 5pm-midnight Mon-Thur; 5pm-2am Fri-Sun. **Bar**. **Map** p52 B2 ㉖

At Kathryn Weatherup's tiny Manhattan drinkery, a spin-off of her popular Brooklyn bar, the well-balanced cocktail list features a regularly rotating mix of classics and original quaffs. Pair the booze with smart snacks such as grilled cheese sandwiches and steak tartare.

Shopping

Soho's converted warehouses are packed with just about every major fashion brand you can think of, from budget and mid-priced international chains such as H&M and Topshop to contemporary stars Alexander Wang and Phillip Lim and A-list designer labels like Chanel and Prada, plus stores selling home goods, cosmetics, food and more. Listed below is a selection of our favourite independent shops.

(3x1)

15 Mercer Street, between Howard & Grand Streets (1-212 391 6969, www.3x1.us). Subway A, C, E, J, N, Q, R, Z, 1, 6 to Canal Street. **Open** 11am-7pm Mon-Sat; noon-6pm Sun. **Map** p54 C5 ㉗

Denim obsessives who are always looking for the next It jeans have another place to splurge: (3x1) creates entirely limited-edition styles sewn in the store. Designer Scott Morrison, who previously launched Paper Denim & Cloth and Earnest Sewn, fills the large, gallery-like space with a variety of jeans (prices start at $185 for women, $265 for men) and other denim pieces such as shorts or miniskirts. Watch the construction process take place in a glass-walled design studio, positioned in the middle of the boutique.

Dominique Ansel Bakery

189 Spring Street, between Sullivan & Thompson Streets (1-212 219 2773, www.dominiqueansel.com). Subway C, E to Spring Street. **Open** 8am-7pm Mon-Sat; 9am-7pm Sun. **Map** p54 C4 ㉘

Dominique Ansel honed his skills as executive pastry chef at Daniel for six years before opening this innovative patisserie. In 2013, his croissant-doughnut hybrid, the Cronut, created a frenzy in foodie circles and put his ingenious creations into the spotlight. If you can't get your hands on one, try the DKA – a caramelised, flaky take on the croissant-like Breton speciality *kouign amann*. And Ansel's cotton-soft mini cheesecake, an ethereally light gâteau with a brûléed top, leaves the dense old New York classic sputtering in its dust.

Housing Works Bookstore Café

126 Crosby Street, between Houston & Prince Streets (1-212 334 3324, www. housingworksbookstore.org). Subway B, D, F, M to Broadway-Lafayette Street; N, R to Prince Street; 6 to Bleecker Street. **Open** 10am-9pm Mon-Fri; 10am-5pm Sat, Sun. **Map** p54 C4 ㉙

This endearing two-level space – which stocks literary fiction, non-fiction, rare books and collectibles – is a peaceful spot to relax over coffee or wine. All proceeds go to providing support services for people living with HIV/AIDS. Both emerging writers and the literati take the mic at the store's readings.

In God We Trust

265 Lafayette Street, between Prince & Spring Streets (1-212 966 9010, www.ingodwetrustnyc.com). Subway N, R to Prince Street; 6 to Spring Street. **Open** noon-8pm Mon-Sat; noon-7pm Sun. **Map** p55 D4 ㉚

Designer Shana Tabor's cosy antique-furnished store caters to that ever-appealing vintage-intellectual aesthetic, offering locally crafted collections for men and women. The line of well-priced, cheeky accessories is a highlight – for example, gold heart-shaped pendants engraved with blunt sayings like 'Boring' or 'Blah, blah, blah', rifle-shaped tie bars, and a wide selection of retro sunglasses for only $20 a pair.

Kiki de Montparnasse

79 Greene Street, between Broome & Spring Streets (1-212 965 8150, www. kikidm.com). Subway N, R to Prince Street; 6 to Spring Street. **Open** 11am-7pm Mon, Sun; 11am-8pm Tue-Sat. **Map** p54 C4 ❸❶
This erotic luxury boutique channels the spirit of its namesake, a 1920s sexual icon and Man Ray muse, with a posh array of tastefully provocative contemporary lingerie in satin and French lace. Look out for novelties such as cotton tank tops with built-in garters, and panties embroidered with saucy legends.

Kirna Zabete

NEW *477 Broome Street, between Greene & Wooster Streets (1-212 941 9656, www.kirnazabete.com). Subway N, R to Prince Street; C, E, 6 to Spring Street.* **Open** 11am-7pm Mon-Sat; noon-6pm Sun. **Map** p54 C4 ❸❷
Since relocating a block from their original boutique, founders Beth Buccini and Sarah Easley have more space to display their edited collection of coveted designer clothing and accessories – more than 25 labels are new to the store, including Valentino, Nina Ricci and Roland Mouret. True to the duo's aesthetic, the 10,000sq ft space features black-and-white striped hardwood floors and neon signs displaying quirky mantras such as 'life is short, buy the shoes'.

Opening Ceremony

33-35 Howard Street, between Broadway & Crosby Street (1-212 219 2688, www.openingceremony.us). Subway J, N, Q, R, Z, 6 to Canal Street. **Open** 11am-8pm Mon-Sat; noon-7pm Sun. **Map** p54 C5 ❸❸
The name references the Olympic Games; each year the store assembles hip US designers (Band of Outsiders, Alexander Wang, Patrik Ervell, Rodarte and its own house label) and pits them against the competition from abroad. The store is so popular it has expanded, adding a book and music section upstairs and a men's shop next door. There's an additional OC outpost at the Ace Hotel (see p176).

What Goes Around Comes Around

351 West Broadway, between Broome & Grand Streets (1-212 343 1225, www. whatgoesaroundnyc.com). Subway A, C, E, 1 to Canal Street. **Open** 11am-8pm Mon-Sat; noon-7pm Sun. **Map** p54 C4 ❸❹
A favourite among the New York fashion cognoscenti, this vintage destination sells highly curated stock alongside its own retro label. Style mavens particularly recommend it for 1960s, '70s and '80s rock T-shirts, pristine Alaïa clothing and vintage furs.

Nightlife

Santos Party House

96 Lafayette Street, between Walker & White Streets (1-212 584 5492, www. santospartyhouse.com). Subway J, N, Q, R, Z, 6 to Canal Street. **Open** varies (see website for schedule). **Map** p52 C1 ❸❺
Launched by a team that includes rocker Andrew WK, Santos Party House – two black, square rooms done out in a bare-bones, generic club style – was initially hailed as a scene game-changer. While those high expectations didn't exactly pan out, it's still a solid choice, featuring everything from hip hop to underground house.

SOB's

204 Varick Street, at Houston Street (1-212 243 4940, www.sobs.com). Subway 1 to Houston Street. **Map** p54 B4 ❸❻
The titular Sounds of Brazil (SOB, geddit?) are just some of the many global genres that keep this spot

hopping. Hip hop, soul, reggae and Latin beats all figure in the mix, with Raphael Saadiq, Maceo Parker and Eddie Palmieri each appearing in recent years. The drinks are expensive, but the sharp-looking clientele doesn't seem to mind.

Arts & leisure

Film Forum

209 W Houston Street, between Sixth Avenue & Varick Street (1-212 727 8110, www.filmforum.org). Subway 1 to Houston Street. **Map** p54 B4 ③⑦

The city's leading revival and repertory cinema is programmed by fest-scouring staff who take their duties as seriously as a Kurosawa samurai. Born in 1970 as a makeshift screening space with folding chairs, it is one of the few non-profit cinemas in the United States – but thankfully its three screens are now furnished with comfortable seats.

HERE

145 Sixth Avenue, between Broome & Spring Streets (1-212 647 0202, TheaterMania 1-212 352 3101, www. here.org). Subway C, E to Spring Street. **Map** p54 C4 ③⑧

Dedicated to not-for-profit arts enterprises, this complex has been the launch pad for such well-known shows as Eve Ensler's *The Vagina Monologues*. More recently, HERE has showcased the talents of the brilliantly freaky playwright-performer Taylor Mac.

Soho Rep

46 Walker Street, between Broadway & Church Street (1-212 941 8632, www. sohorep.org). Subway A, C, E, J, N, Q, R, Z, 6 to Canal Street; 1 to Franklin Street. **Map** p52 C1/p58 C5 ③⑨

A few years ago, this Off-Off mainstay moved to an Off Broadway contract, but tickets for most shows have remained cheap. Artistic director Sarah Benson's programming is diverse and audacious: recent productions include works by Young Jean Lee, Sarah Kane and the Nature Theater of Oklahoma.

Chinatown, Little Italy & Nolita

Take a walk around the area south of Broome Street and east of Broadway, and you'll feel as though you've entered a different continent. New York's Chinatown is one of the largest Chinese communities outside Asia. Here, crowded Mott and Grand Streets are lined with fish-, fruit- and vegetable-stocked stands, and Canal Street glitters with cheap jewellery and gift shops, but beware furtive vendors of (undoubtedly fake) designer goods. The main attraction is the food: Mott Street, between Kenmare and Worth Streets, is packed with restaurants.

Little Italy once stretched from Canal to Houston Streets, between Lafayette Street and the Bowery, but these days a strong Italian presence can only truly be observed on the blocks immediately surrounding Mulberry Street. Ethnic pride remains, though: Italian-Americans flood in from across the city during the 11-day Feast of San Gennaro (see p31).

Nolita (North of Little Italy) became a magnet for pricey boutiques and trendy eateries in the 1990s. Elizabeth, Mott and Mulberry Streets, between Houston and Spring Streets, in particular, are home to hip designer shops.

Sights & museums

Museum of Chinese in America

215 Centre Street, between Grand & Howard Streets (1-212 619 4785, www.mocanyc.org). Subway J, N, Q, R, Z, 6 to Canal Street. **Open** 11am-6pm Tue, Wed, Fri-Sun; 11am-9pm Thur. **Admission** $10; free-$5 reductions; free Thur. **Map** p53 D1/p59 D5 ④⓪

Designed by prominent Chinese-American architect Maya Lin, MoCA reopened in an airy former machine shop in 2009. Its interior is loosely inspired by a traditional Chinese house, with rooms radiating off a central courtyard and areas defined by screens. The core exhibition traces the development of Chinese communities in the US from the 1850s to the present through objects, images and video. Innovative displays cover the development of industries such as laundries and restaurants in New York and Chinese stereotypes in pop culture. A mocked-up Chinese general store evokes the feel of the multi-purpose spaces that served as vital community lifelines for men severed from their families under the 1882 Exclusion Act, which restricted immigration. There's also a gallery for special exhibitions.

Eating & drinking

Baz Bagel & Restaurant

NEW *181 Grand Street, between Baxter & Mulberry Streets (1-212 335 0609, www.bazbagel.com).* **Open** 7am-4pm Mon-Sat; 8am-4pm Sun. **$**. **Café**. **Map** p55 D5 ④
See box p73.

Big Wing Wong

102 Mott Street, between Canal & Hester Streets (1-212 274 0696). Subway J, N, Q, R, Z, 6 to Canal Street. **Open** 9am-10.30pm daily. **$**. No credit cards.
Chinese. **Map** p55 D5 ②
You'll be confused when you show up to this old-school Cantonese joint – the outside inexplicably says 102 Noodles Town. But clarity hits when you taste a slice of the roasted duck, with its fatty, succulent meat and crackly, burnished mahogany skin. You can get the bird over rice or congee, but purists stick to a mere drizzle of hoisin.

Black Seed

NEW *170 Elizabeth Street, between Kenmare & Spring Streets (no phone, www.blackseedbagels.com). Subway J, Z to Bowery.* **Open** 7am-4pm daily. **$**.
Café. **Map** p55 D4 ④
See box p73.

Café Habana

17 Prince Street, at Elizabeth Street (1-212 625 2001, www.cafehabana.com). Subway N, R to Prince Street; 6 to Spring Street. **Open** 9am-midnight daily. **$**.
Cuban. **Map** p55 D4 ④
This chrome corner fixture is known for its addictive grilled corn: golden ears doused in fresh mayo, chargrilled, and generously sprinkled with chilli powder and grated *cotija* cheese. Other staples include a Cuban sandwich of roasted pork, ham, melted swiss and pickles, and beer-battered catfish with spicy mayo.

Estela

NEW *47 E Houston Street, between Mott & Mulberry Streets (1-212 219 7693, www.estelanyc.com). Subway B, D, F, M to Broadway-Lafayette Street; 6 to Bleecker Street.* **Open** 5.30-11pm Mon-Fri; 11am-2.30pm, 5.30-11pm Sat; 11am-2.30pm, 5.30-10.30pm Sun. **$$**.
American. **Map** p55 D4 ④
The fashionable cookie-cutter decor – exposed brick, globe lights, hulking marble bar – may suggest you've stumbled into yet another bustling rustic restaurant-cum-bar that's not worth the wait. But there is more to this Mediterranean-tinged spot than meets the eye: primarily, the talent of imaginative Uruguayan-born chef Ignacio Mattos. An ever-changing, mostly small-plates menu pivots from avant-garde towards intimate. Highlights might include beef tartare with tart pickled elderberries, a musty baseline note from fish sauce and crunchy sunchoke (Jerusalem artichoke) chips, egg with gigante beans and cured tuna, and a creamy panna cotta with honey.

Mother's Ruin

18 Spring Street, between Elizabeth & Mott Streets (no phone, www.mothers ruinnyc.com). Subway J, Z to Bowery; 6 to Spring Street. **Open** 11am-4am Mon-Fri; noon-4am Sat, Sun. **Bar**.
Map p55 D4 ④
At this airy Nolita drinkery, co-owners Timothy Lynch and Richard Knapp

bring in a rotating cast of star bartenders to sling classic and contemporary drinks. The laid-back space – done up with a cream tin ceiling, exposed brick and weathered-wood bar – also offers a full menu of globally inflected bites.

Nom Wah Tea Parlor

13 Doyers Street, between Bowery & Pell Street (1-212 962 6047, www.nomwah com). Subway J, N, Q, R, Z, 6 to Canal Street; J, Z to Chambers Street. **Open** 10.30am-9pm Mon-Thur, Sun; 10.30am-10pm Fri, Sat. **$. Chinese. Map** p53 D1 ㊼

New York's first dim sum house, Nom Wah opened in 1920 and was owned by the same family for more than three decades. The current owner, Wilson Tang, has revamped it in a vintage style true to the restaurant's archival photographs. The most important tweaks, though, were behind the scenes: Tang updated the kitchen and did away with the procedure of cooking dim sum en masse. Now, each plate (ultra-fluffy oversized roasted-pork buns, flaky fried crêpe egg rolls) is cooked to order.

Parm & Torrisi Italian Specialties

Parm *248 Mulberry Street, between Prince and Spring Streets (1-212 993 7189, www.parmnyc.com).* **Open** 11am-11pm Mon-Wed, Sun; 11am-midnight Thur-Sat. **$.**
Torrisi Italian Specialties *250 Mulberry Street, between Prince & Spring Streets (1-212 965 0955, www.torrisinyc.com).* **Open** 6-10.30pm Mon-Thur; noon-2pm, 6-10.30pm Fri-Sun. **$$.**
Both *Subway N, R to Prince Street; 6 to Spring Street.* **Italian. Map** p55 D4 ㊽

Young guns Mario Carbone and Rich Torrisi, two fine-dining vets, brought a cool-kid sheen to red-sauce plates in 2010, when they debuted Torrisi Italian Specialties, a deli by day and haute eaterie by night. People lined up for their buzzworthy sandwiches (outstanding herb-rubbed roasted turkey, classic cold cuts or chicken parmesan) and hard-to-score dinner seats, packing the joint until it outgrew the space. The pair smartly split the operations, devoting their original flagship to tasting menus and transplanting the sandwich offerings to fetching diner digs next door.

Xi'an Famous Foods

67 Bayard Street, between Elizabeth & Mott Streets (no phone, www.xianfoods.com). Subway J, N, Q, R, Z, 6 to Canal Street. **Open** 11.30am-9pm Mon-Thur, Sun; 11.30am-9.30pm Fri, Sat. No credit cards. **$. Chinese. Map** p53 D1 ㊾

This cheap Chinese chainlet, which got the seal of approval from celebrity chef Anthony Bourdain, highlights the mouth-tingling cuisine of Xi'an, an ancient capital along China's Silk Road. Claim one of the 35 stools and nosh on spicy noodles or a cumin-spiced burger for less than $5.

Shopping

Creatures of Comfort

205 Mulberry Street, between Kenmare & Spring Streets (1-212 925 1005, www.creaturesofcomfort.us). Subway 6 to Spring Street; N, R to Prince Street. **Open** 11am-7pm Mon-Sat; noon-6pm Sun. **Map** p55 D4 ㊿

Jade Lai opened Creatures of Comfort in Los Angeles in 2005 and brought her cool-girl aesthetic east five years later. In the former home of the 12th police precinct, the New York offshoot offers a similar mix of pricey but oh-so-cool pieces from various avant-garde lines, such as MM6 Maison Martin Margiela, Acne and Isabel Marant's Etoile, plus the store's own-label bohemian basics and a selection of shoes and accessories.

Downtown Music Gallery

13 Monroe Street, between Catherine & Market Streets (1-212 473 0043, www.downtownmusicgallery.com). Subway J, Z to Chambers Street; 4, 5, 6 to Brooklyn Bridge-City Hall. **Open** 1-6pm daily. **Map** p53 D2 (51)

Many landmarks of the so-called downtown music scene have closed,

Estela p67

but as long as DMG exists, the community will have a sturdy anchor. This basement shop stocks the city's finest selection of avant-garde jazz, contemporary classical, progressive rock and related styles.

Erica Weiner

173 Elizabeth Street, between Kenmare & Spring Streets (1-212 334 6383, www.ericaweiner.com). Subway 6 to Spring Street. **Open** noon-8pm daily. **Map** p55 D4 ㉒

Seamstress-turned-jewellery-designer Erica Weiner sells her own bronze, brass, silver and gold creations – many priced at under $100 – alongside vintage and reworked baubles. Old wooden cabinets and stacked crates showcase rings and charm-laden necklaces, the latter dangling the likes of tiny harmonicas and steel pen-knives. Other popular items include brass ginkgo-leaf earrings, and movable-type-letter necklaces for your favourite wordsmith.

Warm

181 Mott Street, between Broome & Kenmare Streets (1-212 925 1200, www.warmny.com). Subway J, Z to Bowery; 6 to Spring Street. **Open** noon-7pm Mon-Sat; noon-6pm Sun. **Map** p55 D4 ㉝

The husband-and-wife owners, Rob Magnotta and Winnie Beattie, curate an eclectic selection of women's threads, accessories and vintage books, influenced by their globe-trotting surfer lifestyle. The laid-back looks include urban boho-chic clothing from Vanessa Bruno, Giada Forte and Maison Olga, and handcrafted jewellery by artist Suzannah Wainhouse.

Will Leather Goods

NEW *29 Prince Street, at Mott Street (1-212 925 2824, www.willleathergoods.com). Subway 6 to Spring Street.* **Open** 10am-10pm daily. **Map** p55 D4 ㉞

Designer Will Adler debuts the first NYC brick-and-mortar store for his eponymous label, Will Leather Goods

(the brand's goods were previously sold only at high-end retailers such as Barney's and Saks Fifth Avenue). The shop carries the brand's full collection of rustic leather accessories for men and women, including wallets, belts and bags such as canvas-and-leather totes and vintage Mexican wool-and-leather duffle bags.

Lower East Side

Once better known for bagels and bargains, this area – formerly an immigrant enclave – is now brimming with vintage and indie-designer boutiques, fashionable bars and, since the New Museum of Contemporary Art opened a $50 million building on the Bowery in late 2007, dozens of storefront galleries.

Sights & museums

Lower East Side Tenement Museum

Visitors' Center, 103 Orchard Street, at Delancey Street (1-212 982 8420, www.tenement.org). Subway F to Delancey Street; J, M, Z to Delancey-Essex Streets. **Open** *Museum shop & ticketing* 10am-6.30pm Mon-Wed, Fri-Sun; 10am-8.30pm Thur. *Tours* 10.30am-5pm Mon-Wed, Fri-Sun; 10.30am-8pm Thur (see website for schedule). **Admission** $25; $20 reductions. **Map** p55 E4 ㉟

This fascinating museum – actually a series of restored tenement apartments at 97 Orchard Street – is accessible only by guided tour, which start at the visitors' centre at 103 Orchard Street. Tours often sell out, so it's wise to book ahead. 'Hard Times' visits the homes of an Italian and a German-Jewish clan; 'Sweatshop Workers' explores the apartments of two Eastern European Jewish families as well as a garment shop where many of the locals would have found employment; and 'Irish Outsiders' unfurls the life of the Moore family, who are coping with the loss of their child. The newest tour, 'Shop Life', explores the diverse retailers that occupied the building's storefronts, including a 19th-century German saloon.

Museum at Eldridge Street (Eldridge Street Synagogue)

12 Eldridge Street, between Canal & Division Streets (1-212 219 0302, www.eldridgestreet.org). Subway F to East Broadway. **Open** 10am-5pm Mon-Thur, Sun; 10am-3pm Fri. **Admission** $12; free-$8 reductions; free Mon. **Map** p53 D1/p61 E5 **56**

With an impressive façade that combines Romanesque, Moorish and Gothic elements, the first grand synagogue on the Lower East Side is now surrounded by dumpling shops and Chinese herb stores. As Jews left the area the building fell into disrepair. However, a 20-year, nearly $20 million facelift has restored its splendour; the soaring main sanctuary features hand-stencilled walls and a resplendent stained-glass rose window incorporating Star of David motifs. The renovations were completed in 2010, with the installation of a new stained-glass window designed by artist Kiki Smith and architect Deborah Gans. The admission price includes a guided tour (see website for schedule).

New Museum of Contemporary Art

235 Bowery, at Prince Street (1-212 219 1222, www.newmuseum.org). Subway N, R to Prince Street; 6 to Spring Street. **Open** 11am-6pm Wed, Fri-Sun; 11am-9pm Thur. **Admission** $16; free-$14 reductions; pay what you wish 7-9pm Thur. **Map** p55 D4 **57**

Having occupied various sites for 30 years, New York City's only contemporary art museum finally got its own purpose-built space in late 2007. Dedicated to emerging media and under-recognised artists, the seven-floor space is worth a look for the architecture alone – a striking, off-centre stack of aluminium-mesh-clad boxes designed by the cutting-edge Tokyo architectural firm Sejima + Nishizawa/SANAA. At weekends don't miss the fabulous views from the minimalist seventh-floor Sky Room.

Eating & drinking

Attaboy

134 Eldridge Street, between Broome & Delancey Streets (no phone). Subway F to Delancey Street; J, M, Z to Delancey-Essex Streets. **Open** 6.45pm-3.30am daily. **Bar**. **Map** p55 D4 **58**

Occupying the original Milk and Honey (see p108) digs and run by alums Sam Ross and Michael McIlroy, Attaboy has a livelier, lighter air than Sasha Petraske's big-league cocktail den. The tucked-away haunt has kept the same bespoke protocol as its forebear: at the brushed-steel bar, suspender-clad drinks slingers stir off-the-cuff riffs to suit each customer's preference. Wistful boozers can seek solace in Petraske-era standard-bearers, like Ross's signature Penicillin, a still-inspiring blend of Laphroaig ten-year, honey-ginger syrup and lemon.

Clinton Street Baking Company & Restaurant

4 Clinton Street, between E Houston & Stanton Streets (1-646 602 6263, www.clintonstreetbaking.com). Subway F to Lower East Side-Second Avenue; J, M, Z to Delancey-Essex Streets. **Open** 8am-4pm, 6-11pm Mon-Fri; 9am-4pm, 6-11pm Sat; 9am-6pm Sun. **$**. **American**. **Map** p55 E4 **59**

The warm buttermilk biscuits and fluffy pancakes at this pioneering little eaterie give you reason enough to face the guaranteed brunch-time crowds. If you want to avoid the onslaught, however, the homely spot is just as reliable at both lunch and dinner; drop in for the $15 beer-and-burger special (6-8pm Mon-Thur).

Ivan Ramen

NEW *25 Clinton Street, between E Houston & Stanton Streets (1-646 678 3859, www.ivanramen.com).*

NEW YORK BY AREA

Open noon-3.30pm, 5.30pm-midnight daily. $. **Japanese**. Map p55 E4 ⑥⓪

Ivan Orkin has never been one to play by the rulebook – the brash, Yiddish-tongued Long Islander first built his food-world fame 6,000 miles away in Tokyo, where he stirred up Japan's devout ramen congregation with his light, silky slurp bowls in 2007. Seven years later, he opened this narrow slip of a *ramen-ya* on the Lower East Side. The vibrant 60-seat parlour tangles together the noodle virtuoso's all-American roots and Japanophile leanings – a massive, papier-mâché mural in front features a kaleidoscope of Dolly Parton, John Wayne, waving lucky cats and Technicolor geishas. The menu follows culture-crossing suit: along with his seminal rye-flour noodles (in both shio and shoyu varieties), there's four-cheese mazemen, like ramen gone Kraft, and fried chicken hearts – double-dipped à la KFC – with ponzu honey mustard.

Katz's Delicatessen

205 E Houston Street, at Ludlow Street (1-212 254 2246, www.katzs delicatessen.com). Subway F to Lower East Side-Second Avenue. **Open** 8am-10pm Mon, Tue; 8am-11pm Wed; 8am-3am Thur; 24 hours Fri-Sun. $-$$. **Delicatessen**. Map p55 E4 ⑥①

A visit to Gotham isn't complete without a stop at a quintessential New York deli, and this Lower East Side survivor is the real deal. You might get a kick out of the famous faces (from Bill Clinton to Ben Stiller) plastered to the panelled walls, or the spot where Meg Ryan faked it in *When Harry Met Sally…*, but the real stars of this cafeteria are the thick-cut pastrami sandwiches and the crisp-skinned all-beef hot dogs – the latter are a mere $3.45.

Mission Cantina

NEW *172 Orchard Street, at Stanton Street (1-212 254 2233, www.mission cantinanyc.com). Subway F to Lower East Side-Second Avenue.* **Open** noon-5pm, 5.30pm-midnight daily. $-$$.
Mexican. Map p55 E4 ⑥②

Rock-star chef Danny Bowien has changed the tune for his sophomore act, turning from Szechuan eats to Mexican fare. At a 40-seat hangout down the block from Mission Chinese Food (currently closed), he reworks classic dishes like rotisserie chicken stuffed with rice. Tacos also get the Bowien touch: tortillas made with Anson Mills corn are topped with such rotating fillings as rotisserie pork and house-made Oaxacan-style cheese. Yet, where the cooking at his first NYC spot launched a Szechuan reformation, his creative Mexican plates are merely a slight evolution. It stands to reason: Bowien brought Mission Chinese Food east after years of experimentation in San Francisco; his latest venture has had a much shorter incubation period.

Russ & Daughters Café

NEW *127 Orchard Street, between Delancey & Rivington Streets (1-212 475 4881, www.russanddaughterscafe.com). Subway F to Delancey Street; J, M, Z to Delancey-Essex Streets.* **Open** 10am-10pm Mon, Wed-Sun. $-$$. **Café**. Map p55 E4 ⑥③
See box p73.

Spitzer's Corner

101 Rivington Street, at Ludlow Street (1-212 228 0027, www.spitzerscorner. com). Subway F to Delancey Street; J, M, Z to Delancey-Essex Streets. **Open** noon-2am Mon-Wed; noon-4am Thur, Fri; 10am-4am Sat, Sun. **Bar**. Map p55 E4 ⑥④

Referencing the Lower East Side's pickle-making heritage, the walls at this rustic gastropub are made from salvaged wooden barrels. Mull over the formidable beer list of 40 rotating draughts with the help of appetising tasting notes at one of the wide communal tables. The gastro end of things is manifest in the menu of quality pub grub – truffle mac and cheese, for example, or grilled fish sliders.

Bagel boom

Neo nosh spots bring the NYC staple back in the spotlight.

Baz Bagel & Restaurant

Don't call it a comeback – bagels, introduced by late-19th-century Polish Jewish immigrants, have long been a quintessential NYC food. Yet their handcrafted heyday ended in the 1960s with the advent of automated bagel-making machines. That spawned five decades of far too many steam-baked, dough-conditioned pucks, puffier than an ageing screen star's face and stripped of taste and tradition. Now the New York bagel is returning to form, with a fresh batch of downtown shops giving the icon its due.

At newfangled Nolita bagelry **Black Seed** (see p67), from Mile End's Noah Bernamoff and the Smile impresario Matt Kliegman, the ambitious, hand-rolled rounds merge two disciplines: they're honey-enhanced à la Bernamoff's native Montreal, but with an eggless, touch-of-salt bite to satisfy lifelong Gothamite Kliegman. Kettle-boiled and wood-fired, the small but mighty bagels are crowned with house-made toppings both classic (scallion cream cheese, silky cold-smoked salmon) and fanciful (salty tobiko caviar, crisp watermelon radishes).

Bari Musacchio – Rubirosa's longtime general manager – is also tackling the old-fashioned boil-and-bake technique at nearby diner upgrade **Baz Bagel & Restaurant** (see p67). Partnering with Barney Greengrass vet David Heffernan, Musacchio's operation is, as in the olden days, small-batch and labour-intensive: slow-rising dough rings are set on burlap-covered boards and given a spin in a rotating tray oven, resulting in springy-yet-crusty vehicles for the house nova (cold-smoked salmon) and chive spread.

Meanwhile, Lower East Side institution **Russ & Daughters** (see p75) debuted a café (see p72) in its centennial year, where open-faced sandwich boards let you sample some of the store's famous fish: melt-in-your-mouth sable meets decadent goat's-milk cream cheese on a bagel or bialy in the Shtetl, or go classic with silky, saline nova, piled high with tomatoes, capers and onions.

Yonah Schimmel Knish Bakery

137 E Houston Street, between Eldridge & Forsyth Streets (1-212 477 2858, www.knishery.com). Subway F to Lower East Side-Second Avenue. **Open** 9am-7pm Mon, Tue, Sun; 9am-7.30pm Wed, Thur; 9am-9pm Fri, Sat (extended hours in summer). **$**. **Café**. Map p55 D4 **65**

This neighbourhood stalwart has been doling out its carb-laden goodies since 1910. About 20 rotating varieties are available, including blueberry, chocolate-cheese and pizza flavour, but traditional potato, kasha and spinach knishes are the most popular.

Shopping

Alife Rivington Club

158 Rivington Street, between Clinton & Suffolk Streets (1-212 432 7200, www.alifenewyork.com). Subway F to Delancey Street; J, M, Z to Delancey-Essex Streets. **Open** noon-7pm Mon-Sat; noon-6pm Sun. Map p55 E4 **66**

Whether you're looking for a simple white trainer or a trendy graphic style, you'll want to gain entry to this 'club', which stocks a wide range of major brands such as Nike (including sought-after re-issues like Air Jordan), Adidas and New Balance. You'll also find lesser-known names including the shop's own label.

The Cast

71 Orchard Street, between Broome & Grand Streets (1-212 228 2020, www.thecast.com). Subway B, D to Grand Street; F to Delancey Street; J, M, Z to Delancey-Essex Streets. **Open** noon-7pm daily. Map p55 E4 **67**

At the core of Chuck Guarino's rock 'n' roll-inspired collection is the trinity of well-cut denim, superior leather jackets based on classic motorcycle styles, and the artful T-shirts that launched the label in 2004. The ladies have their own line covering similar ground.

David Owens Vintage

NEW *154 Orchard Street, between Rivington & Stanton Streets (1-212 677 3301). Subway F to Second Avenue.* **Open** noon-8pm Mon-Sat; 11am-7pm Sun. Map p55 E4 **68**

Unlike many vintage stores that traffic in '80s and '90s garb, David Owens's eponymous boutique carries items exclusively from the '30s to the '70s. The small space is stuffed to the gills with rare and unique pieces, such as a '30s printed dress with the original store tags attached and a '60s clutch made to look like a rolled-up Harper's Bazaar magazine. Men will find just as many interesting items, including pin-up girl ties from the '40s to the '70s and leather motorcycle jackets.

The Dressing Room

75A Orchard Street, between Broome & Grand Streets (1-212 966 7330, www.thedressingroomnyc.com). Subway B, D to Grand Street; F to Delancey Street; J, M, Z to Delancey-Essex Streets. **Open** 1pm-midnight Tue, Wed; 1pm-2am Thur-Sat; 1-8pm Sun. Map p55 E4 **69**

At first glance, the Dressing Room may look like any Lower East Side lounge, thanks to a handsome wood bar, but this quirky co-op cum watering hole rewards the curious. The adjoining room displays lines by indie designers alongside select vintage pieces, and there's also a second-hand clothing exchange downstairs.

Obsessive Compulsive Cosmetics

174 Ludlow Street, between E Houston & Stanton Streets (1-212 675 2404, www.occmakeup.com). Subway F to Lower East Side-Second Avenue. **Open** 11am-7pm Mon-Sat; noon-6pm Sun. Map p55 E4 **70**

Creator David Klasfeld founded OCC in the kitchen of his Lower East Side apartment in 2004. The make-up artist has since expanded his 100% vegan and cruelty-free cosmetics line from just two shades of lip balm to an extensive assortment of bang-for-your-buck beauty products. In his flagship, you can browse more than 40 shades of nail polish and nearly 40 loose eye-shadow powders, among other products, but we especially like the Lip Tars, which glide on like a gloss but have the matte finish and saturated pigmentation of a lipstick.

Reed Space

151 Orchard Street, between Rivington & Stanton Streets (1-212 253 0588, www. thereedspace.com). Subway F to Delancey Street; J, M, Z to Delancey-Essex Streets. **Open** 1-7pm Mon-Fri; noon-7pm Sat, Sun. **Map** p55 D4 **71**

Reed Space is the brainchild of Jeff Ng (AKA Jeff Staple), who has worked on product design and branding with the likes of Nike and Timberland. It stocks local and international urban menswear brands – such as 10.Deep and Undefeated – and footwear, including exclusive Staple collaborations. Art books and culture mags are shelved on an eye-popping installation of four stacked rows of white chairs fixed to one wall.

Russ & Daughters

179 E Houston Street, between Allen & Orchard Streets (1-212 475 4880, www.russanddaughters.com). Subway F to Lower East Side-Second Avenue. **Open** 8am-8pm Mon-Fri; 8am-7pm Sat; 8am-5.30pm Sun. **Map** p55 D4 **72**

The daughters in the name have given way to great-grandchildren, but this Lower East Side institution (established 1914) is still run by the same family. Specialising in smoked and cured fish and caviar, it sells about ten varieties of smoked salmon, eight types of herring and many other Jewish-inflected Eastern European delectables. Filled bagels are available to take away, but a new café (see p72) offers a more extensive menu and table service.

Spiritual America

NEW *5 Rivington Street, between Bowery & Chrystie Street (1-212 960 8564, www. spiritualameri.ca). Subway F to Lower East Side-Second Avenue; J, Z to Bowery; 6 to Spring Street.* **Open** noon-8pm Mon-Fri; 11am-7pm Sat, Sun. **Map** p55 D4 **73**

Housed in the same storefront (and operating under the same name) as artist Richard Prince's original pop-up exhibition in 1983, this minimalist shop stocks a mix of European and American labels (Vanessa Bruno, Damir Doma, Derek Lam) and wares by up-and-coming designers. We're especially taken with the boutique's selection of cool shoes and accessories.

Nightlife

Bowery Ballroom

6 Delancey Street, between Bowery & Chrystie Street (1-212 533 2111, www.boweryballroom.com). Subway B, D to Grand Street; J, Z to Bowery; 6 to Spring Street. **Map** p55 D4 **74**

Bowery Ballroom is probably the best venue in the city for seeing indie bands, either on the way up or holding their own, but it also brings in a diverse range of artists from home and abroad. Expect a clear view and bright sound from any spot. The spacious downstairs lounge is a great place to hang out between sets.

Cake Shop

152 Ludlow Street, between Rivington & Stanton Streets (1-212 253 0036, www. cake-shop.com). Subway F to Lower East Side-Second Avenue. **Map** p55 E4 **75**

It can be hard to see the stage in this narrow, stuffy basement, but Cake Shop gets big points for its keen indie and underground-rock bookings, among the most adventurous in town. True to its name, the venue sells vegan pastries and coffee upstairs, and record-store ephemera in the street-level back room.

Mercury Lounge

217 E Houston Street, between Essex & Ludlow Streets (1-212 260 4700, www.mercuryloungenyc.com). Subway F to Lower East Side-Second Avenue. **Map** p55 E4 **76**

NEW YORK BY AREA

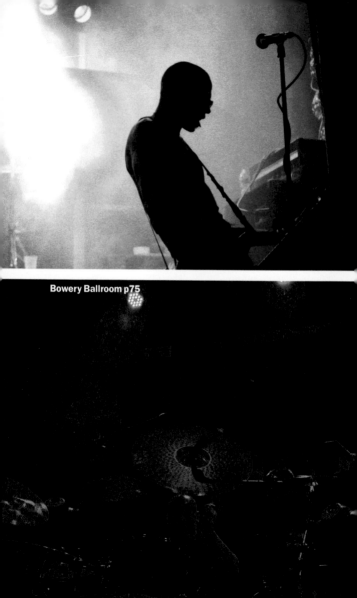
Bowery Ballroom p75

The unassuming, boxy Mercury Lounge is an old standby, with solid sound and sight lines (and a cramped bar in the front room). There are four-band bills most nights, though they can seem stylistically haphazard and set times are often later than advertised. It's a good idea to book bigger shows in advance.

Rockwood Music Hall

196 Allen Street, between E Houston & Stanton Streets (1-212 477 4155, www.rockwoodmusichall.com). Subway F to Lower East Side-Second Avenue. **Map** p55 D4 ⓱

The cramped quarters are part of this club's appeal: there are no bad seats (or standing spots) in the house. You can catch multiple acts every night of the week on three separate stages, and it's likely that many of those performers will soon be appearing in much bigger halls. Multi-genre polymath Gabriel Kahane is a regular, as is bluegrass great Michael Daves.

The Slipper Room

167 Orchard Street, at Stanton Street, (1-212 253 7246, www.slipperroom. com). Subway F to Lower East Side-Second Avenue. **Map** p55 D4 ⓲

After being rebuilt from the ground up (which took a little more than two years), the Slipper Room reopened with a better sound system, new lighting and a mezzanine, among other swank touches, and reclaimed its place as the city's premier burlesque venue. Many of the shows that once called it home, including Mr. Choade's Upstairs Downstairs (which began in 1999), have returned, and the setting is as intimate and fun as ever – but with upgrades that make the experience better than before.

Arts & leisure

Abrons Arts Center

466 Grand Street, at Pitt Street (1-212 598 0400, www.henrystreet.org/arts). Subway B, D to Grand Street; F to Delancey Street; J, M, Z to Delancey-Essex Streets. **Map** p55 E4 ⓳

This multidisciplinary arts venue, which features a beautiful proscenium theatre, focuses on a wealth of contemporary dance, courtesy of artistic director Jay Wegman. It's worth a look, especially in January when the American Realness festival fills the space's three theatres with experimental work.

East Village

The area east of Broadway between Houston and 14th Streets has a long history as a countercultural hotbed. From the 1950s to the '70s, St Marks Place (8th Street, between Lafayette Street & Avenue A) was a hangout for artists, writers, radicals and musicians. It's still packed until the wee hours, but these days it's with crowds of college students and tourists browsing for bargain T-shirts, used CDs and pot paraphernalia. While legendary music venues such as CBGB are no more, a few bohemian hangouts endure, and the East Village has also evolved into a superior cheap-eats hotspot. In the neighbourhood's renovated green space, Tompkins Square Park, bongo beaters, guitarists, yuppies, local families and the homeless all mingle.

Sights & museums

Merchant's House Museum

29 E 4th Street, between Lafayette Street & Bowery (1-212 777 1089, www.merchantshouse.org). Subway B, D, F, M to Broadway-Lafayette Street; 6 to Bleecker Street. **Open** noon-5pm Mon, Thur-Sun. **Admission** $10; $5 reductions; free under-12s. **Map** p55 D3 ⓰

Merchant's House Museum, the city's only fully preserved 19th-century family home, is an elegant, late Federal-Greek Revival property kitted out with the same furnishings and decorations it contained when it was inhabited from 1835 by hardware tycoon Seabury Tredwell and his family. Three years after Tredwell's eighth daughter died in 1933, it opened as a museum. You can peruse the house at your own pace, following along with the museum's printed guide, or opt for the 2pm guided tour. Be sure to ascend to the servants' quarters on the fourth floor.

Museum of Reclaimed Urban Space

155 Avenue C, between 9th & 10th Streets (1-646 833 7764, www. morusnyc.org). Subway L to First Avenue. **Open** 11am-7pm Tue, Thur-Sun. **Admission** free (donations appreciated). **Map** p55 E2 ③①

Co-founded by Bill Di Paola, director of advocacy group Time's Up!, this monument to local activism is housed in C-Squat, a five-floor walk-up that has sheltered activists, down-on-their-luck artists and members of several punk bands (including Leftover Crack, Old Skull and Nausea) from the 1970s through the present. Artefacts from Occupy Wall Street (including an energy bike that helped to power Zuccotti Park during its occupation in 2011) and earlier causes show how city residents, both past and present, created, protected and took back community spaces.

Eating & drinking

Acme

NEW *9 Great Jones Street, between Broadway & Lafayette Street (1-212 203 2121, www.acmenyc.com). Subway B, D, F, M to Broadway-Lafayette Street; 6 to Bleecker Street.* **Open** 6-11pm Mon-Wed; 6pm-midnight Thur, Fri; 11am-3pm, 6pm-midnight Sat; 11am-3pm, 6-11pm Sun. **$$**.

Scandinavian. Map p54 C3 ③②

Danish chef Mads Refslund, who co-founded Copenhagen's Noma with superstar René Redzepi, is behind this chic bistro. The menu delivers an easy introduction to the avant-garde cuisine of Northern Europe, unpretentious and moderately priced. Even the most oddball combinations work. The chef's spin on steak tartare marries hand-cut raw bison with delicious sweet shrimp – an elemental surf-and-turf spooned like retro canapés into bitter endive and radicchio leaves. The big family-style portions of meat, fish and fowl that round out the collection of shareable plates are even more down-to-earth.

Alder

157 Second Avenue, between 9th & 10th Streets (1-212 539 1900, www.aldernyc. com). Subway L to Third Avenue; 6 to Astor Place. **Open** 6-11pm Mon-Sat; noon-3pm, 5.30-9pm Sun. **$$**.

Gastropub. Map p55 D2 ③③

James Beard Award-winning chef Wylie Dufresne cultivated his modernist, tongue-in-cheek approach at wd~50 (now closed), creating curiosities such as deep-fried mayonnaise and scrambled-egg ravioli. At his gastropub, Dufresne is still challenging the orthodoxy of serious cooking, presenting familiar flavours in new frameworks: the wrappers in a pigs-in-a-blanket riff are Pepperidge Farm hot-dog buns, flattened in a pasta machine and fried into crisp jackets as gratifying as any puff pastry. But you can also eat quite simply here if you want to, with a pub cheese platter or bowl of New England clam chowder. Intriguing tapped cocktails like the Dr Dave's 'Scrip Pad, made with rye, amaro, smoked maple and yuzu, are sold in full-size or short portions, so you can taste your way through the lot.

Back Forty

190 Avenue B, at 12th Street (1-212 388 1990, www.backfortynyc.com). Subway L to First Avenue. **Open** 6-11pm Mon-Thur; 6pm-midnight Fri; 11am-4pm, 6pm-midnight Sat; 11am-3.30pm, 6-10pm Sun. **$$. American. Map** p55 E2 ③④

Farm-to-table pioneer Peter Hoffman is behind this East Village seasonal-eats tavern, where pared-down rustic chic prevails in the decor and on the menu. House specialities include juicy grass-fed burgers and ice-cream floats made with small-batch root beer. The spacious back garden is a bonus during the warmer months.

Big Gay Ice Cream Shop

125 E 7th Street, between First Avenue & Avenue A (1-212 533 9333, www. biggayicecream.com). Subway L to First Avenue. **Open** *noon-10pm Mon-Wed, Sun; noon-midnight Thur-Sat.* **$.** **Ice-cream.** Map p55 E3 ⓺

Ice-cream truckers Doug Quint and Bryan Petroff now have two brick-and-mortar shops dispensing their quirky soft-serve creations (the second is in the West Village). Toppings run the gamut from cayenne pepper to bourbon-butterscotch sauce, or opt for one of the signature combos like the Salty Pimp (vanilla ice-cream, dulce de leche, sea salt and chocolate dip) or the Bea Arthur (vanilla ice-cream, dulce de leche and crushed Nilla wafers).

Crif Dogs

113 St Marks Place, between First Avenue & Avenue A (1-212 614 2728, www.crifdogs.com). Subway L to First Avenue; 6 to Astor Place. **Open** *noon-2am Mon-Thur, Sun; noon-1am Fri; noon-4am Sat.* **$.** **Hot dogs.** Map p55 D3 ⓺

You'll recognise this place by the giant hot dog outside, bearing the come-on 'Eat me'. Crif offers the best New Jersey-style dogs this side of the Hudson: handmade smoked-pork tube-steaks that are deep-fried until they're bursting out of their skins. While they're served in various guises, among them the Spicy Redneck (wrapped in bacon and covered in chilli, coleslaw and jalapeños), we're partial to the classic with mustard and kraut. If you're wondering why there are so

many people hanging around near the public phone booth at night, it's because there's a trendy cocktail bar, PDT (see p81), concealed behind it.

DBGB Kitchen & Bar

299 Bowery, at E Houston Street (1-212 933 5300, www.dbgb.com/nyc). Subway B, D, F, M to Broadway-Lafayette Street; 6 to Bleecker Street. **Open** *5-11pm Mon; 5pm-midnight Tue-Thur; noon-1am Fri; 11am-1am Sat; 11am-11pm Sun.* **$$.** **French.** Map p55 D3 ⓺

This big, buzzy brasserie – chef Daniel Boulud's most populist venture – stands out for its kitchen-sink scope. Around ten kinds of sausage, from Thai-accented to Tunisienne, are served alongside burgers, offal and haute bistro fare. The best way to get your head around the eclectic enterprise is to bring a large group and try to sample as much of the range as possible, including ice-cream sundaes or sumptuous cakes for dessert.

Dos Toros

137 Fourth Avenue, between 13th & 14th Streets (1-212 677 7300, www. dostoros.com). Subway L to Third Avenue; L, N, Q, R, 4, 5, 6 to 14th Street-Union Square. **Open** *11.30am-10.30pm Mon; 11.30am-11pm Tue-Fri; noon-11pm Sat; noon-10.30pm Sun.* **$.** **Mexican.** Map p54 C2 ⓺

When it hit NYC a few years ago, this bright little Cal-Mex taqueria was lauded by *Time Out New York* critics for its bangin' burritos, and, while it has expanded into a mini chain, it hasn't lost a step since. The fillings – juicy flap steak, moist grilled chicken, smooth guacamole – are among the best in town.

Il Buco Alimentari & Vineria

53 Great Jones Street, between Bowery and Lafayette Street (1-212 837 2622, www.ilbucovineria.com). Subway B, D, F, M to Broadway-Lafayette Street; 6 to Bleecker Street. **Open** *7am-midnight*

Mon-Thur; 7am-1am Fri; 9am-1am Sat; 9am-11pm Sun. $$. **Italian**. Map p55 D3 69

Il Buco has been a mainstay of the downtown dining scene since the '90s and a pioneer in the sort of rustic Italian food now consuming the city. Owner Donna Leonard took her sweet time (18 years, to be exact) to unveil her first offshoot, Il Buco Alimentari & Vineria. It was worth the wait: the hybrid bakery, food shop, café and trattoria is as confident as its decades-old sibling with sure-footed service, the familial bustle of a neighbourhood pillar, and heady aromas of wood-fired short ribs and salt-crusted fish drifting from an open kitchen.

Other location Il Buco, 47 Bond Street, between Bowery & Lafayette Street (1-212 533 1932).

Jimmy's No. 43

43 E 7th Street, between Second & Third Avenues (1-212 982 3006, www.jimmysno43.com). Subway F to Lower East Side-Second Avenue; 6 to Astor Place. **Open** noon-2am Mon-Thur; noon-4am Fri, Sat; 11.30am-2am Sun. No credit cards. **Bar**. Map p55 D3 90

You could easily miss this worthy subterranean spot if it weren't for the sign painted on a doorway over an inconspicuous set of stairs. Descend them and you'll encounter burnt-yellow walls displaying taxidermy, mismatched wooden tables and medieval-style arched passageways that lead to different rooms. Beer is a star here, with about a dozen quality selections on tap (and more in the bottle), many of which also make it into the slow-food dishes filled with organic ingredients.

Kyo Ya

94 E 7th Street, between First Avenue & Avenue A (1-212 982 4140). Subway 6 to Astor Place. **Open** 5.30-11.30pm Mon-Sat; 5.30-10.30pm Sun (closed Mondays in summer). $$$. **Japanese**. Map p55 D3 91

The city's most ambitious Japanese speakeasy is marked only by an 'Open' sign, but in-the-know diners still find their way inside. The food, presented on beautiful handmade plates, is gorgeous: maitake mushrooms are fried in the lightest tempura batter and delivered on a polished stone bed. Sushi is pressed with a hot iron on to sticky vinegar rice. The few desserts are just as ethereal as the savoury food.

Lafayette

NEW *380 Lafayette Street, at Great Jones Street (1-212 533 3000, www.lafayette ny.com). Subway B, D, F, M to Broadway-Lafayette Street; 6 to Bleecker Street.* **Open** 7.30-11.30am, noon-11pm Mon-Wed; 7.30-11.30am, noon-midnight Thur, Fri; 8am-midnight Sat; 8am-11pm Sun. $$. **French**. Map p55 D3 92

Ace culinary crew Andrew Carmellini, Josh Pickard and Luke Ostrom – the winning team behind blockbusters Locanda Verde (see p172) and the Dutch (see p63) – followed up with this souped-up, all-day French bistro, which marks Carmellini's return to his Francophilic roots (exemplified by runs at Café Boulud and Lespinasse). The menu focuses on the country's rustic south. A zinc-hooded rotisserie twirls roasted chicken *pour deux* in the spacious, mahogany-floored eaterie, while an in-house bakery churns out Provençal staples like pain de campagne, and pretty people gab over their niçoise salads. While some dishes fail to excite, it's a solid choice for brunch.

McSorley's Old Ale House

15 E 7th Street, between Second & Third Avenues (1-212 473 9148). Subway F to Lower East Side-Second Avenue. **Open** 11am-1am Mon-Sat; 1pm-1am Sun. No credit cards. **Bar**. Map p55 D3 93

Ladies should probably leave the Manolos at home. In traditional Irish-pub fashion, McSorley's floor has been thoroughly scattered with sawdust to take care of the spills and other messes that often accompany large quantities of cheap beer. Established in 1854, McSorley's became an institution by remaining steadfastly authentic and providing only two choices: McSorley's Dark Ale and McSorley's Light Ale.

Mighty Quinn's

103 Second Avenue, at E 6th Street (1-212 677 3733, www. mightyquinnsbbq.com). Subway 6 to Astor Place. **Open** 11.30am-11pm Mon-Thur, Sun; 11.30am-midnight Fri, Sat. **$$. Barbecue. Map** p55 D3 ❸❹

Drummer-turned-chef Hugh Mangum first hawked his Texalina (Texas spice meets Carolina vinegar) specialities at his immensely popular stand at Smorgasburg (see p32). When the operation went brick-and-mortar, the hungry throngs followed. Lines of customers snake through the steel-tinged East Village joint, watching as black-gloved carvers give glistening meat porn a dash of Maldon salt before slinging it down the assembly line. Paprika-rubbed brisket is slow-cooked for 22 hours, and the Jurassic-sized beef rib is so impossibly tender, one bite will quiet the pickiest barbecue connoisseur.

Momofuku Ssäm Bar

207 Second Avenue, at 13th Street (1-212 254 3500, www.momofuku.com). Subway L to First or Third Avenue; L, N, Q, R, 4, 5, 6 to 14th Street-Union Square. **Open** noon-4.30pm, 5.30-11pm Mon-Thur; noon-4.30pm, 5.30pm-2am Fri; noon-4pm, 5.30pm-2am Sat; noon-4pm, 5.30pm-11pm Sun. **$$. Korean. Map** p55 D2 ❸❺

At celebrated chef David Chang's second modern Korean restaurant, waiters hustle to loud rock music in the 50-seat space, which feels expansive compared with the crowded counter dining of its nearby predecessor, Momofuku Noodle Bar (171 First Avenue, between 10th & 11th Streets, 1-212 777 7773). Try the wonderfully fatty pork-belly

steamed bun with hoisin sauce and cucumbers, or one of the ham platters. But you'll need to come with a crowd to sample the house speciality, *bo ssäm* (a slow-roasted hog butt that is consumed wrapped in lettuce leaves, with a dozen oysters and other accompaniments); it serves six to eight people and must be ordered in advance. David Chang has further expanded his E Vill empire with a bar, Booker and Dax, at this location, and a sweet annexe, Milk Bar (one of several in the city), across the street.

PDT

113 St Marks Place, between First Avenue & Avenue A (1-212 614 0386). Subway L to First Avenue; 6 to Astor Place. **Open** 6pm-2am Mon-Thur, Sun; 6pm-4am Fri, Sat. **Bar. Map** p55 D3 ❾❻

Word has got out about 'Please Don't Tell', the faux speakeasy inside gourmet hot dog joint Crif Dogs (see p79), so it's a good idea to reserve a booth in advance. Once you arrive, you'll notice people lingering outside an old wooden phone booth near the front. Slip inside, pick up the receiver and the host opens a secret panel to the dark, narrow space. The cocktails surpass the gimmicky entry: try the house old-fashioned, made with bacon-infused bourbon, which leaves a smoky aftertaste.

Porchetta

110 E 7th Street, between First Avenue & Avenue A (1-212 777 2151, www. porchettanyc.com). Subway F to Lower East Side-Second Avenue; L to First Avenue; 6 to Astor Place. **Open** 11.30am-10pm Mon-Thur, Sun; 11.30am-11pm Fri, Sat. **Italian/ sandwiches. Map** p55 E3 ❸❼

This small, subway-tiled space has a narrow focus: central Italy's classic boneless roasted pork. The meat – available as a sandwich or a platter – is amazingly moist and tender, having been slowly roasted with rendered pork fat, seasoned with fennel pollen, herbs and spices, and flecked with brittle shards of skin. The other menu items (a mozzarella sandwich, humdrum sides) seem incidental; the pig is the point.

Proletariat

102 St Marks Place, between First Avenue & Avenue A (no phone, www. proletariatny.com). Subway 6 to Astor Place. **Open** 5pm-2am Mon-Thur; 2pm-2am Fri-Sun. **Bar. Map** p55 D3 ❾❽

Proletariat is a welcome look into no-holds-barred beer geekdom, blissfully free of TVs and generic pub grub. With just 12 stools and a space so tight that clunky menus have been replaced with a QR code (scan it with your smartphone), brewhounds get the type of intimacy usually afforded only to the cocktail and wine crowds. The expert servers have a story for every keg they tap, from the newest local brews to obscure New Zealand ales and deep cuts from the Belgian canon.

Terroir

413 E 12th Street, between First Avenue & Avenue A (1-646 602 1300, www. wineisterroir.com). Subway L to First Avenue; L, N, Q, R, 4, 5, 6 to 14th Street-Union Square. **Open** 5pm-2am Mon-Sat; 5pm-midnight Sun. **Wine bar. Map** p55 D2 ❾❾

The surroundings are stripped-back basic at this wine-bar offspring of nearby restaurant Hearth – the focus is squarely on the drinks. Co-owner and oenoevangelist Paul Grieco preaches the powers of *terroir* – grapes that express a sense of place – and the knowledgeable waitstaff deftly help patrons to navigate nearly 50 by-the-glass options. Pair the stellar sips with their restaurant-calibre small plates.

Shopping

Bond Street Chocolate

63 E 4th Street, between Bowery & Second Avenue (1-212 677 5103, www.bondstchocolate.com). Subway

6 to Bleecker Street. **Open** noon-8pm Tue-Sat; 1-6pm Sun. **Map** p55 D3 ❿⓿

Former pastry chef Lynda Stern's East Village spot is a grown-up's candy store, with quirky chocolate confections in shapes ranging from gilded Buddhas (and other religious figures) to skulls, and flavours from elderflower to bourbon and absinthe.

Fabulous Fanny's

335 E 9th Street, between First & Second Avenues (1-212 533 0637, www.fabulous fannys.com). Subway L to First Avenue; 6 to Astor Place. **Open** noon-8pm daily. **Map** p55 D2 ❿①

Formerly a Chelsea flea market booth, this two-room shop is the city's best source of period glasses, stocking more than 30,000 pairs of spectacles, from Jules Verne-esque wire rims to 1970s rhinestone-encrusted Versace shades.

The Future Perfect

55 Great Jones Street, between Bowery & Lafayette Street (1-212 473 2500, www.thefutureperfect.com). Subway 6 to Bleecker Street. **Open** 10am-7pm Mon-Fri; noon-7pm Sat, Sun. **Map** p59 D3 ❿②

Championing avant-garde interior design, this innovative store specialises in artist-made, limited-edition and one-of-a-kind pieces. The Future Perfect is the exclusive US stockist of Dutch designer Piet Hein Eek's elegant woodwork and pottery, but it also showcases local talent. Check out spare gold jewellery and branching metal light fixtures by New Yorker Lindsey Adelman and concrete vessels cast from real fruit and gourds in Chen Chen and Kai Williams's Brooklyn studio.

Kiehl's

109 Third Avenue, between 13th & 14th Streets (1-212 677 3171, www.kiehls. com). Subway L to Third Avenue; L, N, Q, R, 4, 5, 6 to 14th Street-Union Square. **Open** 10am-8pm Mon-Sat; 11am-6pm Sun. **Map** p55 D2 ❿③

Lafayette p80

The apothecary founded on this East Village site in 1851 has morphed into a major skincare brand, but the products, in their minimal packaging, are still good value and effective. Lip balms and the thick-as-custard Creme de Corps have become cult classics.

Obscura Antiques & Oddities

207 Avenue A, between 12th & 13th Streets (1-212 505 9251, www. obscuraantiques.com). Subway L to First Avenue. **Open** noon-8pm Mon-Sat; noon-7pm Sun. **Map** p55 E2 **104**

Housed inside a former funeral home, this eccentric shop, immortalised in a Science Channel reality TV series, specialises in bizarre items like medical and scientific antiques, human skulls and 19th-century taxidermied animals. Owners Evan Michelson and Mike Zohn scour flea markets, auctions and even museums for rare artefacts.

Other Music

15 E 4th Street, between Broadway & Lafayette Street (1-212 477 8150, www.othermusic.com). Subway B, D, F, M to Broadway-Lafayette Street; 6 to Bleecker Street. **Open** 11am-9pm Mon-Fri; noon-8pm Sat; noon-7pm Sun. **Map** p54 C3 **105**

Other Music opened in the shadow of Tower Records in the mid '90s, a pocket of resistance to chain-store tedium. All these years later, the Goliath across the street is gone, but tiny Other Music carries on. Whereas the shop's mishmash of indie rock, experimental music and stray slabs of rock's past once seemed adventurous, the curatorial foundation has proved prescient, amid the emergence of mixed-genre venues in the city.

Patricia Field

306 Bowery, between Bleecker & E Houston Streets (1-212 966 4066, www. patriciafield.com). Subway 6 to Bleecker Street. **Open** 11am-8pm Mon-Thur, Sun; 11am-9pm Fri, Sat. **Map** p55 D3 **106**

The iconic redheaded designer and stylist has moved her boutique two doors down from the original, into a space that's nearly double the size, combining Field's former apartment with a vacated store behind it – her old bedroom is now a full-service hair salon. In addition to funky, flamboyant threads for men and women, stock up on whimsical accessories such as polka-dot shades, taxi cab-shaped wristlets by Betsey Johnson and cube-shaped rings.

Screaming Mimi's

382 Lafayette Street, at 4th Street (1-212 677 6464, www.screamingmimis.com). Subway B, D, F, M to Broadway-Lafayette Street; N, R to Prince Street; 6 to Bleecker Street. **Open** noon-8pm Mon-Sat; 1-7pm Sun. **Map** p55 D3 **107**

This vintage mecca has been peddling men's and women's clothing and accessories since 1978. Owner Laura Wills travels the world, scouting eclectic finds that span the 1950s to the 1990s, and organises clothing racks by decade. Do you need sunglasses from the 1970s? How about a Duran Duran T-shirt from the '80s? Head upstairs to check out higher-end garments by designers such as Hattie Carnegie, Jean Paul Gaultier and Vivienne Westwood.

Strand Book Store

828 Broadway, at 12th Street (1-212 473 1452, www.strandbooks.com). Subway L, N, Q, R, 4, 5, 6 to 14th Street-Union Square. **Open** 9.30am-10.30pm Mon-Sat; 11am-10.30pm Sun. **Map** p54 C2 **108**

Established in 1927, the Strand has a mammoth collection of more than two million discount volumes (both new and used), and the store is made all the more daunting by its chaotic, towering shelves and sometimes crotchety staff. You can find just about anything here, from that out-of-print Victorian book on manners to the kitschiest of sci-fi pulp. Note that the rare book room upstairs closes at 6.20pm.

Nightlife

Duane Park

308 Bowery, between Bleecker & E Houston Streets (1-212 732 5555, www.duaneparknyc.com). Subway F to Lower East Side-Second Avenue; 6 to Astor Place. **Map** p55 D3 ⓵⓪⓽

Formerly the Bowery Poetry Club, the venue now operates as Southern-inflected supper club Duane Park from Tuesday to Saturday, but Bowery Poetry (www.bowerypoetry.com) still holds events on Sundays and Mondays. Get dinner and a show – burlesque, jazz, vaudeville or magic – in decadent surroundings featuring crystal chandeliers and Corinthian-topped columns.

Joe's Pub

Public Theater, 425 Lafayette Street, between Astor Place & E 4th Street (1-212 967 7555, www.joespub.com). Subway N, R to 8th Street-NYU; 6 to Astor Place. **Map** p55 D3 ⓵⓵⓪

One of the city's premier small spots for sit-down audiences, the recently refurbished Joe's Pub brings in impeccable talent of all genres and origins. While some well-established names play here, Joe's also lends its stage to up-and-comers (this is where Amy Winehouse made her debut in the United States), drag acts and cabaret performers (Justin Vivian Bond is a mainstay). The food menu – a mix of snacks, shareable plates and main courses – has been revitalised by hot chef Andrew Carmellini.

Nowhere

322 E 14th Street, between First & Second Avenues (1-212 477 4744, www.nowhere barnyc.com). Subway L to First Avenue. **Open** 3pm-4am daily. **Map** p55 D2 ⓵⓵⓵

Low ceilings and dim lighting help to create a speakeasy vibe at this subterranean LGBT bar. The place attracts everyone from young lesbians to bears, thanks to an entertaining line-up of theme nights. Tuesday nights are especially fun, when DJ Damian Cote's long-running Buddies party takes over. The pool table is another big draw.

UCBEast

153 E Third Street at Avenue A (1-212 366 9231, www.ucbtheatre.com). Subway F to Lower East Side-Second Avenue. **Map** p55 E3 ⓵⓵⓶

When it opened in 2011, the East Village offshoot of longstanding alternative-comedy hub Upright Citizens Brigade Theatre gave the enormous community another space – and a bar. The warm lighting and low, rounded ceiling of the ex-arthouse cinema create immediate intimacy, whether the fare is improv or stand-up, and the venue snapped up some of the fledgling comedy variety shows that were scattered in East Side venues.

Webster Hall

125 E 11th Street, between Third & Fourth Avenues (1-212 353 1600, www.websterhall.com). Subway L to Third Avenue; L, N, Q, R, 4, 5, 6 to 14th Street-Union Square. **Map** p55 D2 ⓵⓵⓷

The grand Webster Hall isn't exactly on clubland's A-list, due to a populist DJ policy and a crowd that favours muscle shirts and gelled hair. But it's been open, on and off, since 1866, so it must be doing something right. Friday night's Girls & Boys bash attracts music makers of the stature of Grandmaster Flash and dubstep duo Nero. Concerts are booked by Bowery Presents, who run Bowery Ballroom and Mercury Lounge. Expect to find high-calibre indie acts (Black Lips, Battles, Tune-Yards), but be sure to arrive early for a decent view. A smaller space downstairs, the Studio, hosts mainly by local bands.

Arts & leisure

Anthology Film Archives

32 Second Avenue, at 2nd Street (1-212 505 5181, www.anthologyfilm archives.org). Subway F to Lower East Side-Second Avenue; 6 to Bleecker Street. No credit cards. **Map** p55 D3 ⓵⓵⓸

This red-brick building feels a bit like a fortress – and, in a sense, it is one, protecting the legacy of NYC's fiercest film experimenters. Dedicated to the preservation, study and exhibition of independent, avant-garde and artist-made work, Anthology houses two screens and a film museum.

Great Jones Spa

29 Great Jones Street, at Lafayette Street (1-212 505 3185, www.gjspa.com). Subway 6 to Astor Place. **Open** 9am-10pm daily. **Map** p55 D3 ⓯
Based on the theory that water brings health, Great Jones has a popular water lounge complete with subterranean pools, saunas, steam rooms and a three-and-a-half-storey waterfall. Access to the 15,000sq ft paradise is free with services over $100 – treat yourself to a scented body scrub, a massage or one of the many indulgent packages. Alternatively, a three-hour pass costs $50.

New York Theatre Workshop

79 E 4th Street, between Bowery & Second Avenue (1-212 460 5475, www.nytw.org). Subway F to Lower East Side-Second Avenue; 6 to Astor Place. **Map** p55 D3 ⓰
Founded in 1979, the New York Theatre Workshop works with emerging directors eager to take on challenging pieces. Besides presenting plays by world-class artists such as Caryl Churchill and Tony Kushner, this company also premièred *Rent*, Jonathan Larson's seminal 1990s musical. The iconoclastic Flemish director Ivo van Hove has made the NYTW his New York pied-à-terre.

Public Theater

425 Lafayette Street, between Astor Place & E 4th Street (1-212 539 8500, tickets 1-212 967 7555, www.publictheater.org). Subway N, R to 8th Street-NYU; 6 to Astor Place. **Map** p55 D3 ⓱
Under the guidance of the civic-minded Oskar Eustis, this local institution – dedicated to producing the work of new American playwrights, but also known for its Shakespeare in the Park productions – has regained its place at the forefront of the Off Broadway world. The ambitious, multicultural programming ranges from new works by major playwrights to the annual Under the Radar festival for emerging artists. The company's home building, an Astor Place landmark, has five stages and was recently extensively renovated.

The Stone

Avenue C, at E 2nd Street (no phone, www.thestonenyc.com). Subway F to Lower East Side-Second Avenue. No credit cards. **Map** p55 E3 ⓲
Don't call sax star John Zorn's not-for-profit venture a 'club'. You'll find no food or drinks here, and no nonsense, either: the Stone is an art space dedicated to 'the experimental and the avant-garde'. If you're down for some rigorously adventurous sounds (intense improvisers like Tim Berne and Okkyung Lee, or moonlighting rock mavericks such as Thurston Moore), Zorn has made it easy: no advance sales, and all ages admitted (under-19s get discounts, under-12s get in free). The bookings are left to a different artist-curator each month.

Greenwich Village

Stretching from Houston Street to 14th Street, between Broadway and Sixth Avenue, the Village has been inspiring bohemians for almost a century. Now that it's one of the most expensive neighbourhoods in the city, you need a lot more than a struggling artist's income to inhabit its leafy streets, but it's still a fine place for idle wandering, candlelit dining and hopping between bars and cabaret venues.

Sights & museums

Washington Square Park

Subway A, B, C, D, E, F, M to W 4th Street. **Map** p54 C3 ⓳

An art hub on the Hudson

The Whitney Museum moves into new downtown digs.

Once the gritty domain of wholesale butchers and gay nightspots with evocative names such as the Mineshaft and the Ramrod, the Meatpacking District became a fashionable hub in the 1990s and early noughties before giving way to more mainstream popularity. What the neighbourhood has lacked, however, is culture – though since 2009, the High Line has provided a direct pedestrian link to Chelsea's galleries (and plenty of temporary public art installations along its length). That's set to change in spring 2015, when the **Whitney Museum of American Art** (1-212 570 3600, www.whitney.org) opens its striking new digs at the southern foot of the park.

Founded by sculptor and art patron Gertrude Vanderbilt Whitney in 1931, the Whitney holds more than 19,000 pieces by around 2,900 artists, including Willem de Kooning, Edward Hopper, Jasper Johns, Georgia O'Keeffe and Claes Oldenburg. Yet, until now, its reputation has rested primarily on its temporary shows – particularly the prestigious and controversial Whitney Biennial. The nine-storey, steel-and-glass building, designed by Renzo Piano, is roughly three times the size of the old Upper East Side premises. For the first time, there will be space for a comprehensive display of the collection.

The dramatic, asymmetrical structure features a series of outdoor terraces that rise like steps above the High Line. The art isn't restricted to the museum's interior. On the fifth, sixth and seventh floors you can take in alfresco sculptures and installations while admiring views of the Hudson River and city landmarks including the Empire State Building and 1 World Trade Center. An 8,500-square-foot public plaza beneath the High Line leads to the cantilevered glass entrance. Inside, you'll find a ground-floor restaurant helmed by dining guru Danny Meyer, a gift shop and a free-admission lobby gallery. Four elevators, commissioned by Richard Artschwager before his death in 2013, have a dual function as passenger lifts and an art installation, entitled *Six in Four*. Using six themes that have featured in the artist's work since the 1970s – door, window, table, basket, mirror and rug – they will transport visitors not only to the upper floors, but also to an alternative reality.

The city's main burial ground until 1825, Washington Square Park has served ever since as the spiritual home, playground and meeting place for Greenwich Village. The Washington Square Arch at the northern end was designed by Stanford White and dedicated in 1895. It marks the southern end of Fifth Avenue. The central fountain, completed in 1872, was recently shifted to align it with the arch, as part of extensive park renovations. In the 1960s, the park was a gathering spot for the Beat poets – with Allen Ginsberg giving several impromptu readings here – and it retains its vitality, thanks to the street performers, NYU students, chess players, political agitators and hustlers who congregate when the weather is fine.

Eating & drinking

Blue Hill

75 Washington Place, between Sixth Avenue & Washington Square West (1-212 539 1776, www.bluehillfarm. com). Subway A, B, C, D, E, F, M to W 4th Street. **Open** 5-11pm Mon-Sat; 5-10pm Sun. **$$$**. **American**. Map p54 C3 **120**
More than a mere crusader for sustainability, Dan Barber is also one of the most talented cooks in town, building his menu around whatever's at its peak on his family farm in Great Barrington, Massachusetts, and the not-for-profit Stone Barns Center for Food and Agriculture in Westchester, NY (home to a sibling restaurant), among other suppliers. The evening may begin with a sophisticated seasonal spin on a pig-liver terrine and move on to a sweet slow-roasted parsnip 'steak' with creamed spinach and beet ketchup.

Caffe Reggio

119 MacDougal Street, at W 3rd Street (1-212 475 9557, www.cafereggio.com). Subway A, B, C, D, E, F, M to W 4th Street. **Open** 8am-3am daily. No credit cards. **$**. **Café**. Map p54 C3 **121**

Legend has it that the original owner of this classic café introduced Americans to the cappuccino in 1927 and, apart from its acquired patina, we bet the interior hasn't changed much since then. It's since traded in the coal-fuelled espresso machine for a sleeker Caffè Sacco model, but you can still admire the old custom chrome-and-bronze contraption on the bar. Tuck into a house-made tiramisu and espresso under the Italian Renaissance paintings.

Carbone

181 Thompson Street, between Bleecker & W Houston Streets (1-212 254 3000, www.carbonenewyork.com). Subway C, E to Spring Street. **Open** noon-2pm, 5.30pm-midnight Mon-Fri; 5.30pm-midnight Sat, Sun. **$$$**. **Italian**. Map p54 C3 **122**
Nostalgia specialists Rich Torrisi and Mario Carbone honour Gotham's legendary red-sauce relics (Rao's, Bamonte's) with their high-profile revamp of historic Rocco's Ristorante. Suave, tuxedo-clad waiters – Bronx accents intact, but their burgundy threads designed by Zac Posen – tote an avalanche of complimentary extras: chunks of chianti-infused Parm, olive-oil-soaked 'Grandma Bread' and slivers of smoky prosciutto. Follow updated renditions of classic pasta like a spicy, über-rich rigatoni alla vodka with mains such as sticky cherry-pepper ribs and lavish takes on tiramisu for dessert.

Corkbuzz Wine Studio

13 E 13th Street, between Fifth Avenue & University Place (1-646 873 6071, www.corkbuzz.com). Subway L, N, Q, R, 4, 5, 6 to 14th Street-Union Square. **Open** 4.30pm-midnight Mon-Wed; 4.30pm-1am Thur, Fri; 11am-3pm, 4.30pm-1am Sat; 11am-3pm, 4.30pm-midnight Sun (hours vary seasonally). **Wine bar**. Map p54 C2 **123**
This intriguing and elegant hybrid, owned by the world's youngest

master sommelier, Laura Maniec, comprises a restaurant, a wine bar and an educational centre. Before you drink anything, chat with one of the staffers, who preach the Maniec gospel to patrons as they navigate 35 by-the-glass options and around 250 bottles.

Kin Shop

469 Sixth Avenue, between 11th & 12th Streets (1-212 675 4295, www. kinshopnyc.com). Subway F, M to 14th Street; L to Sixth Avenue. **Open** 11.30am-3pm, 5.30-10pm Mon-Wed; 11.30am-3pm, 5.30-11pm Thur-Sat; 11.30am-3pm, 5-10pm Sun. **$$**. **Thai**. **Map** p54 B2 **124**

Top Chef champ Harold Dieterle channels his South-east Asian travels into the menu at this eaterie, which serves classic Thai street food alongside more upmarket Thai-inspired dishes. The traditional fare seems extraneous, but Dieterle's auteur creations are often inspired. A salad of crispy oysters, slivered celery and fried pork belly is bright and refreshing, while a sophisticated riff on massaman curry features long-braised goat with a silky sauce infused with toasted coconut, fried shallots and purple yams.

Minetta Tavern

113 MacDougal Street, between Bleecker & W 3rd Streets (1-212 475 3850, www. minettatavernny.com). Subway A, B, C, D, E, F, M to W 4th Street. **Open** 5.30pm-1am Mon, Tue; noon-2.30pm, 5.30pm-1am Wed-Fri; 11am-3pm, 5.30pm-1am Sat, Sun. **$$**. **Eclectic**. **Map** p54 C3 **125**

Thanks to restaurateur extraordinaire Keith McNally's spot-on restoration, the Minetta is as buzzy now as it must have been when it was frequented by Hemingway and Fitzgerald in its heyday. The big-flavoured bistro fare includes classics such as roasted bone marrow, trout meunière topped with crabmeat, and an airy Grand Marnier soufflé. But the most illustrious thing on the menu is the Black Label burger. You might find the $28 price tag a little

hard to swallow, but the superbly tender sandwich – essentially chopped steak in a bun smothered in caramelised onions – is worth every penny.

Num Pang Sandwich Shop

21 E 12th Street, between Fifth Avenue & University Place (1-212 255 3271, www.numpangnyc.com). Subway L, N, Q, R, 4, 5, 6 to 14th Street-Union Square. **Open** 11am-10pm Mon-Sat; noon-9pm Sun. **$**. **Cambodian**. **Map** p54 C2 **126**

At this small shop, the rotating varieties of *num pang* (Cambodia's answer to the Vietnamese *banh mi*) include pulled duroc pork with spiced honey, peppercorn catfish, and hoisin veal meatballs, each stuffed into a crusty baguette. There's counter seating upstairs, or get it to go and eat in nearby Washington Square Park.

Stumptown Coffee Roasters

NEW *30 W 8th Street, at MacDougal Street (1-347 414 7802, www.stumptown coffee.com). Subway A, B, C, D, E, F, M to W 4th Street.* **Open** 7am-8pm daily. **$**. **Café**. **Map** p54 C3 **127**

The lauded Portland, Oregon, outfit has expanded its New York holdings – which include a branch inside the Ace Hotel – with this stand-alone café. Coffee purists can find single-origin espresso from a La Marzocco GS3 machine and slow brews prepared via java-geek speciality drips like Chemex pour-overs, ceramic filter-cone Bee House drippers or a siphon vacuum brewer. It also offers the chain's full line of 20 seasonal coffees, plus pastries from Momofuku Milk Bar, Ovenly and Doughnut Plant.

Sweetwater Social

NEW *643 Broadway, at Bleecker Street (1-212 253 7467, www.sweetwater socialny.com). Subway B, D, F, M to Broadway-Lafayette Street; 6 to Bleecker Street.* **Open** 5pm-2am Tue-Sat. **Bar**. **Map** p54 C3 **128**

Washington Square Park p86

Channelling an '80s basement rec room, cocktail-world vets Tim Cooper and Justin Noel concoct a lively playground of game-hall amusements and well-executed quaffs at this throwback bar. The witty drinks menu is laid out on a New York subway map, with each cocktail reminiscent of a particular stop: the Ivan Drago, for example, a nod to Russian-heavy Brighton Beach and the Soviet opponent in *Rocky IV*, updates a classic Moscow mule with aromatic cardamom, clove and cinnamon. Leather-jacketed gents huddle over foosball tables – unearthed from Cooper's own childhood basement – while off-duty suits loosen their ties during high-octane Galaga game play.

ZZ's Clam Bar

NEW *169 Thompson Street, between Bleecker & W Houston Streets (1-212 254 3000, www.zzsclambar.com). Subway B, D, F, M to Broadway-Lafayette Street; 6 to Bleecker Street.* **Open** 6pm-11pm Tue-Sat. **$$$. Seafood. Map** p54 C3 ❷❾

A powerhouse trio – Rich Torrisi, Mario Carbone and Jeff 'ZZ' Zalaznick – continues its neo-Italian-American hot streak with a 12-seat raw bar highlighting first-rate cocktails and *crudo*. At the marble bar, acclaimed barman Thomas Waugh (Death & Company) concocts the likes of rum, house-made coconut cream, acacia honey and lime juice served in a frozen coconut. In bar-friendly small plates, the chefs explore raw fish in all forms, with East Coast oysters on the half-shell and the titular clams. Composed *crudos* might feature *shimaaji* (striped horse mackerel) tartare topped with whipped ricotta and Petrossian caviar.

Shopping

CO Bigelow Chemists

414 Sixth Avenue, between 8th & 9th Streets (1-212 473 7324, www.bigelowchemists.com). Subway A, B, C, D, F, M to W 4th Street; 1 to Christopher Street. **Open** 7.30am-9pm

Mon-Fri; 9.30am-7pm Sat; 9.30am-5.30pm Sun. **Map** p54 C3 ❶❸⓿

Established in 1838, Bigelow is the oldest apothecary in America. Its simply packaged and appealingly old-school line of toiletries include such tried-and-trusted favourites as Mentha Lip Shine, Barber Cologne Elixirs and Lemon Body Cream. The spacious, chandelier-lit store is packed with natural and homeopathic remedies, organic skincare products and drugstore essentials – and the place still fills prescriptions.

Nightlife

Blue Note

131 W 3rd Street, between MacDougal Street & Sixth Avenue (1-212 475 8592, www.bluenote.net). Subway A, B, C, D, E, F, M to W 4th Street. **Map** p54 C3 ❶❸❶

The Blue Note prides itself on being 'the jazz capital of the world'. Bona fide musical titans (Jimmy Heath, Lee Konitz) rub against contemporary heavyweights (The Bad Plus), while the close-set tables in the club get patrons rubbing up against each other. The Sunday brunch is the best bargain bet.

Comedy Cellar

117 MacDougal Street, between Minetta Lane & W 3rd Street (1-212 254 3480, www.comedycellar.com). Subway A, B, C, D, E, F, M to W 4th Street. **Map** p54 C3 ❶❸❷

Despite being named one of NYC's best stand-up clubs year after year, the Cellar maintains a hip, underground feel. It gets packed, but no-nonsense comics such as Dave Chapelle, Jim Norton and Marina Franklin will distract you from your bachelorette-party neighbours. **Other location** Comedy Cellar at the Village Underground, 130 W 3rd Street, between Sixth Avenue & MacDougal Street (1-212 254 3480).

Le Poisson Rouge

158 Bleecker Street, at Thompson Street (1-212 505 3474, www.lepoissonrouge. com). Subway A, B, C, D, E, F, M to W 4th Street. **Map** p54 C3 ❶❸❸

Tucked into the basement of the long-gone Village Gate – a legendary performance space that hosted everyone from Miles Davis to Jimi Hendrix – Le Poisson Rouge was opened in 2008 by a group of young music enthusiasts with ties to both the classical and indie rock worlds. The booking policy reflects both camps, often on a single bill. No other joint in town offers such a wide range of great music, whether from a feverish Malian band (Toumani Diabaté's Symmetric Orchestra), rising indie talent (Zola Jesus) or young classical stars (pianist Simone Dinnerstein).

Arts & leisure

IFC Center

323 Sixth Avenue, at W 3rd Street (1-212 924 7771, www.ifccenter.com). Subway A, B, C, D, E, F, M to W 4th Street. **Map** p54 B3 ⓵⓷⓸

The long-darkened 1930s Waverly was once again illuminated back in 2005 when it was reborn as a modern five-screen arthouse cinema, showing the latest indie hits, along with choice midnight cult items and occasional foreign classics. You may come face to face with the directors or the actors on the screen, as many introduce their work on opening night.

West Village & Meatpacking District

The area west of Sixth Avenue to the Hudson River, from 14th Street to Houston Street, has held on to much of its picturesque charm. Bistros abound along Seventh Avenue and Hudson Street and high-rent shops proliferate on this stretch of Bleecker Street, including no fewer than three Marc Jacobs boutiques. The West Village is also a long-standing gay mecca, although the scene has largely moved north to Chelsea and Hell's Kitchen. The north-west corner of the neighbourhood is known as the

Meatpacking District, dating from its origins as a wholesale meat market in the 1930s. In recent years designer stores, trendy eateries and nightclubs have moved in, and the area is the starting point for the High Line and the new location of the Whitney Museum of American Art (see p87).

Sights & museums

High Line

1-212 500 6035, www.thehighline.org. **Open** usually 7am-10pm daily (hours vary seasonally; see website for updates). **Map** p54 A2 ⓵⓷⓹

Running from Gansevoort Street in the Meatpacking District through Chelsea's gallery district to 30th Street, this slender, sinuous green strip – formerly an elevated freight train track – has been designed by landscape architects James Corner Field Operations and architects Diller Scofidio + Renfro. In autumn 2012, construction began on the final section, which will open in three phases, starting in late 2014. Stretching from 30th to 34th Streets, it skirts the West Side Rail Yards, which are being developed into a long-planned residential and commercial complex, Hudson Yards.

Eating & drinking

Blind Tiger Ale House

281 Bleecker Street, at Jones Street (1-212 462 4682, www. blindtigeralehouse.com). Subway A, B, C, D, E, F, M to W 4th Street; 1 to Christopher Street-Sheridan Square. **Open** 11.30am-4am daily. **Bar.** **Map** p54 B3 ⓵⓷⓺

Brew geeks descend upon this hops heaven for boutique ales and more than two dozen daily rotating, hard-to-find drafts (like Southern Tier Krampus and Singlecut Half-Stack). The clubby room features windows that open on to the street. Late afternoons and early evenings are ideal for serious sippers enjoying plates of Murray's

Cheese, while the after-dark set veers dangerously close to Phi Kappa territory.

Buvette

42 Grove Street, between Bedford & Bleecker Streets (1-212 255 3590, www.ilovebuvette.com). Subway 1 to Christopher Street-Sheridan Square. **Open** 8am-2am Mon-Fri; 10am-2am Sat, Sun. **$$. French. Map** p54 B3 **137**
Chef Jody Williams has filled every nook of tiny, Gallic-themed Buvette with old picnic baskets, teapots and silver trays, among other vintage ephemera. The food is just as thoughtfully curated – Williams's immaculate renditions of coq au vin, goose-fat rillettes or intense, lacquered wedges of tarte Tatin arrive on tiny plates, in petite jars or in miniature casseroles, her time-warp flavours recalling an era when there were classic bistros on every corner.

Corner Bistro

331 W 4th Street, at Jane Street (1-212 242 9502, www.cornerbistrony. com). Subway A, C, E to 14th Street; L to Eighth Avenue. **Open** 11.30am-4am Mon-Sat; noon-4am Sun. No credit cards. **Bar. Map** p54 B2 **138**
There's one compelling reason to come to this legendary pub: it serves what some New Yorkers say are the city's best burgers – plus the beer is just $3 for a mug of McSorley's. The patties are no-frills and served on a flimsy paper plate. To get one, you may have to queue for a good hour, especially on weekend nights; if the wait is too long for a table, try to slip into a space at the bar.

Employees Only

510 Hudson Street, between Christopher & W 10th Streets (1-212 242 3021, www.employeesonlynyc.com). Subway 1 to Christopher Street-Sheridan Square. **Open** 6pm-4am daily. **Bar. Map** p54 B3 **139**
This Prohibition-themed bar cultivates an exclusive vibe, but there's no cover and no trouble at the door. Pass by the palm reader in the window (it's a front) and you'll find an amber-lit art deco interior where formality continues to flourish: servers wear custom-designed frocks and bartenders are in waitstaff whites. The real stars are cocktails such as the West Side, a lethal mix of lemon vodka, lemon juice, mint and club soda.

Fedora

239 W 4th Street, between Charles & W 10th Streets (1-646 449 9336, www.fedoranyc.com). Subway A, B, C, D, E, F, M to W 4th Street; 1 to Christopher Street-Sheridan Square. **Open** 5.30pm-midnight Mon, Sun; 5.30pm-2am Tue-Sat. **$$. Canadian.** **Map** p54 B3 **140**
This French-Canadian knockout is part of restaurateur Gabriel Stulman's West Village mini-empire (his other local eateries are Joseph Leonard, Jeffrey's Grocery, Italian spot Perla and Bar Sardine). Mehdi Brunet-Benkritly produces some of the most exciting toe-to-tongue cooking in town, plying epicurean hipsters with Quebecois party food that's eccentric, excessive and fun – crisp pig's head with enoki, for example, or maple-smoked salmon with almonds and curry cream.

Kesté Pizza & Vino

271 Bleecker Street, between Cornelia & Jones Streets (1-212 243 1500, www.kestepizzeria.com). Subway 1 to Christopher Street-Sheridan Square. **Open** noon-11pm Mon-Sat; noon-10.30pm Sun. **$. Pizza. Map** p54 B3 **141**
If anyone can claim to be an expert on Neapolitan pizza, it's Kesté's Roberto Caporuscio: as president of the US branch of the Associazione Pizzaiuoli Napoletani, he's top dog for the training and certification of *pizzaioli*. At his intimate, 46-seat space, it's all about the crust – blistered, salty and elastic, it could easily be eaten plain. Add fantastic toppings such as sweet-tart San Marzano tomato sauce, milky mozzarella and fresh basil, and you have one of New York's finest pies.

Pearl Oyster Bar

18 Cornelia Street, between Bleecker & W 4th Streets (1-212 691 8211, www.pearloysterbar.com). Subway A, B, C, D, E, F, M to W 4th Street. **Open** noon-2.30pm, 6-11pm Mon-Fri; 6-11pm Sat. **$$**. **Seafood.** Map p54 B3 **142**

There's a good reason this convivial, no-reservations, New England-style fish joint always has a queue – the food is outstanding. Signature dishes include the lobster roll – sweet lemon-scented meat laced with mayonnaise on a butter-enriched bun – and a contemporary take on bouillabaisse: a briny lobster broth packed with mussels, cod, scallops and clams, topped with an aïoli-smothered croûton.

RedFarm

529 Hudson Street, between Charles & W 10th Streets (1-212 792 9700, www.redfarmnyc.com). Subway 1 to Christopher Street-Sheridan Square. **Open** 5-11.45pm Mon-Fri; 11am-2.30pm, 5-11.45pm Sat; 11am-2.30pm, 5-11pm Sun. **$$**. **Chinese.** Map p54 B3 **143**

High-end ingredients and whimsical plating at Ed Schoenfeld's interpretive Chinese restaurant have helped to pack the dining room since opening night. Chef Joe Ng is known for his dim sum artistry: scallop and squid *shu mai* come skewered over shot glasses of warm carrot and ginger bisque – designed to be eaten and gulped in rapid succession; other nouveau creations include Katz's pastrami-stuffed egg rolls and shrimp dumplings decorated with 'eyes' and pursued on the plate by a sweet-potato Pac-Man.

Rosemary's

NEW *18 Greenwich Avenue, at W 10th Street (1-212 647 1818, www.rosemarysnyc.com). Subway A, B, C, D, E, F, M to W 4th Street.* **Open** 8am-4.30pm, 5pm-midnight Mon-Fri; 10am-4pm, 5pm-midnight Sat, Sun. **$$**. **Italian.** Map p54 B2 **144**

While gastronomy isn't the primary focus in most of the pheromone factories clustered on this stretch of Seventh Avenue, this rustic, farmhouse-vibe celebrity magnet ought to be packed with food fanatics. Chef Wade Moises, who worked for Mario Batali at Babbo and Lupa, is a talent to watch. Pair pasta with one of the showstopping large-format feasts – big platters for two that in fact serve three or four. House-made cavatelli with braised beef, heirloom tomato sauce and fresh cherry tomatoes is a mellow foil for the chef's carne misti, a mountain of espresso-glazed pork ribs, smoky lamb shoulder and super-succulent whey-brined chicken.

The Spotted Pig

314 W 11th Street, at Greenwich Street (1-212 620 0393, www.thespottedpig.com). Subway A, C, E to 14th Street; L to Eighth Avenue; 1 to Christopher Street-Sheridan Square. **Open** noon-2am Mon-Fri; 11am-2am Sat, Sun. **$$**. **Eclectic.** Map p54 B3 **145**

With a creaky interior that recalls an ancient pub, this Anglo-Italian hybrid from Ken Friedman and chef April Bloomfield is still hopping more than a decade after opening. The gastropub doesn't take reservations and a wait can always be expected. The burger is a must-order: a secret blend covered with gobs of pungent roquefort, served with a tower of crispy shoestring fries tossed with rosemary. Indulgent desserts, like the flourless chocolate cake, are worth loosening your belt for.

White Horse Tavern

567 Hudson Street, at 11th Street (1-212 989 3956). Subway 1 to Christopher Street-Sheridan Square. **Open** 11am-2am Mon-Thur, Sun; 11am-4am Fri, Sat. No credit cards. **Bar.** Map p54 B3 **146**

Popular lore tells us that in 1953, Dylan Thomas pounded 18 straight whiskeys here before expiring in his Chelsea Hotel residence – a portrait of him hangs in the middle room, above his favourite table in the corner. Now the old-school bar and its adjacent outdoor patio play host to a yuppie crowd and clutches of tourists, drawn by the outdoor seating, a fine selection of beers – and the legend.

Shopping

Aedes de Venustas

9 Christopher Street, between Greenwich Avenue & Waverly Place (1-212 206 8674, www.aedes.com). Subway A, B, C, D, F, M to W 4th Street; 1 to Christopher Street-Sheridan Square. **Open** noon-8pm Mon-Sat; 1-7pm Sun. **Map** p54 B3 **147**

Decked out like a 19th-century boudoir, this perfume collector's palace devotes itself to ultra-sophisticated fragrances and high-end skincare lines, such as Diptyque, Santa Maria Novella and its own glamorously packaged range of fragrances, candles and room sprays. Hard-to-find scents, such as Serge Lutens perfumes, line the walls.

Doyle & Doyle

NEW *412 W 13th Street, between Ninth Avenue & Washington Street (1-212 677 9991, www.doyledoyle.com). Subway A, C, E to 14th Street; L to Eighth Avenue.* **Open** noon-7pm Mon-Wed, Fri-Sun; noon-8pm Thur. **Map** p54 A2 **148**

Whether your taste is art deco or nouveau, Victorian or Edwardian, gemologist sisters Elizabeth and Pamela Doyle, who specialise in vintage and antique jewellery, will have that one-of-a-kind item you're looking for, including engagement and eternity rings. In 2013, they packed up their curated archive and moved from the Lower East Side to larger premises in the Meatpacking District. The sisters have also launched their own collection of new heirlooms.

Jeffrey New York

449 W 14th Street, between Ninth & Tenth Avenues (1-212 206 1272, www.jeffreynewyork.com). Subway A, C, E to 14th Street; L to Eighth Avenue. **Open** 10am-8pm Mon-Wed,

Fri; 10am-9pm Thur; 10am-7pm Sat; 12.30-6pm Sun. **Map** p54 A2 **149**

Jeffrey Kalinsky, a former Barneys shoe buyer, was a Meatpacking District pioneer when he opened his store in 1999. Designer clothing abounds here – by Yves Saint Laurent, Céline and Christopher Kane, among others. But the centrepiece is the shoe salon, featuring Manolo Blahnik, Prada and Christian Louboutin, as well as newer names to watch.

Murray's Cheese

254 Bleecker Street, between Sixth & Seventh Avenues (1-212 243 3289, www.murrayscheese.com). Subway A, B, C, D, E, F, M to W 4th Street. **Open** 8am-8pm Mon-Sat; 10am-7pm Sun. **Map** p54 B3 **150**

For the last word in curd, New Yorkers have been flocking to Murray's since 1940 to sniff out the best international and domestic cheeses. The helpful staff will guide you through hundreds of stinky, runny, washed-rind and aged comestibles. Murray's also has a Cheese Bar at 264 Bleecker Street serving cheese-focused dishes.

Owen

809 Washington Street, between Gansevoort & Horatio Streets (1-212 524 9770, www.owennyc.com). Subway A, C, E to 14th Street; L to Eighth Avenue. **Open** 11am-7pm Mon-Thur; 10am-8pm Fri-Sat; noon-7pm Sun. **Map** p54 A2 **151**

FIT grad Phillip Salem founded this upscale boutique featuring more than 30 emerging and already-established brands. Anchoring the stock is Phillip Lim's cool, urban menswear and edgy dresses by Alexander Wang. The modern threads for both genders are displayed atop quartz slab tables and hung on blackened steel bars.

Rag & Bone General Store

425 W 13th Street, at Washington Street (1-212 249 3331, www.rag-bone. com). Subway A, C, E to 14th Street.

Open 11am-8pm Mon-Sat; noon-7pm Sun. **Map** p54 A2 ⓲

The Meatpacking District location of this enduringly hip brand, which began as a denim line in 2002, retains much of the former factory's industrial vibe with unfinished concrete floors, brick walls and an original Dave's Quality Veal sign. Sip a latte from the in-store Jack's Stir Brew Coffee before or after browsing the impeccably cut jeans, luxurious knitwear and well-tailored jackets for men and women.

Nightlife

Cielo

18 Little West 12th Street, between Ninth Avenue & Washington Street (1-212 645 5700, www.cielodub.com). Subway A, C, E to 14th Street; L to Eighth Avenue. **Open** 10pm-4am Mon, Wed-Sat. **Map** p54 A2 ⓳

You'd never guess from all the Kardashian wannabes hanging out in the neighbourhood that the attitude inside this exclusive club is close to zero – at least once you get past the bouncers. On the sunken dancefloor, hip-to-hip crowds gyrate to deep beats from top DJs, including NYC old-schoolers François K, Tedd Patterson and Louie Vega. Cielo, which features a crystal-clear sound system, has won a bevy of 'best club' awards – and it deserves them all.

Henrietta Hudson

438 Hudson Street, at Morton Street (1-212 924 3347, www.henriettahudson. com). Subway 1 to Christopher Street-Sheridan Square. **Open** 5pm-2am Mon, Tue; 5pm-4am Wed-Sun. Map p54 B3 ⓴

A much-loved lesbian hangout, this glam lounge attracts women from all over the New York area. Every night is different, with hip hop, pop, rock and live shows among the musical offerings.

Smalls

183 W 10th Street, at W 4th Street (no phone, www.smallsjazzdub.com).

Subway A, B, C, D, E, F, M to W 4th Street; 1 to Christopher Street-Sheridan Square. **Open** 4pm-4am daily. No credit cards. **Map** p54 B3 ⓯

For those looking for an authentic jazz club experience – rather than the cheesy dinner-club vibe that prevails at too many other spots around town – Smalls is a must. The cosy basement space feels like a speakeasy, or more specifically, one of those hole-in-the-wall NYC jazz haunts of yore over which fans obsess. Best of all, the booking skews towards retro, yet not stubbornly so. You'll hear classic hardbop as well as more adventurous, contemporary approaches.

Stonewall Inn

53 Christopher Street, between Seventh Avenue South & Waverly Place (1-212 488 2705, www.thestonewallinnnyc. com). Subway 1 to Christopher Street-Sheridan Square. **Open** 2pm-4am daily. **Map** p54 B3 ⓰

This gay landmark is the site of the famous 1969 rebellion against police harassment (though back then it also included the building next door). Though it's not exactly hip, it's one of the few LGBT bars that cater equally to males and females. Special nights range from dance soirées and drag shows to bingo gatherings.

Village Vanguard

178 Seventh Avenue South, at Perry Street (1-212 255 4037, www.village vanguard.com). Subway A, C, E, 1, 2, 3 to 14th Street; L to Eighth Avenue. **Map** p54 B2 ⓱

Still going strong after more than three-quarters of a century, the Village Vanguard is one of New York's legendary jazz centres. History surrounds you: John Coltrane, Miles Davis and Bill Evans have all grooved in this hallowed hall. Big names both old and new still fill the schedule, and the Grammy Award-winning Vanguard Jazz Orchestra has been the Monday-night regular for almost 50 years.

Times Square p117

Midtown

Soaring office towers, crowded pavements and taxi-choked streets – that's the image most people have of midtown, the area roughly between 14th Street and 59th Street, from river to river. This part of town draws visitors to some of the city's best-known landmarks, including the Empire State Building, the Chrysler Building, Rockefeller Center and the electronic spectacle that is Times Square. But there's more to the busy midsection of Manhattan than iconic architecture and commerce. It contains the city's most concentrated contemporary gallery district (Chelsea), its hottest gay enclave (Hell's Kitchen), some of its swankiest shops (Fifth Avenue) and most of its big theatres.

Chelsea

The corridor between 14th and 29th Streets west of Sixth Avenue emerged as the nexus of New York's queer life in the 1990s, though it's since been eclipsed by Hell's Kitchen to the north as a gay hotspot. Chelsea's cityscape shifts from leafy side streets lined with pristine 19th-century brownstones to an eclectic array of striking industrial and contemporary architecture on the far west side. In recent years, the local buzz has shifted to the previously neglected Hudson-hugging strip that has evolved into the city's main gallery district.

Sights & museums

Museum at FIT

Building E, Seventh Avenue, at 27th Street (1-212 217 4558, www.fitnyc. edu/museum). Subway 1 to 28th Street. **Open** noon-8pm Tue-Fri; 10am-5pm Sat. **Admission** free. **Map** p98 C3 **①**
The Fashion Institute of Technology owns one of the largest and most impressive collections of clothing, textiles and accessories in the world,

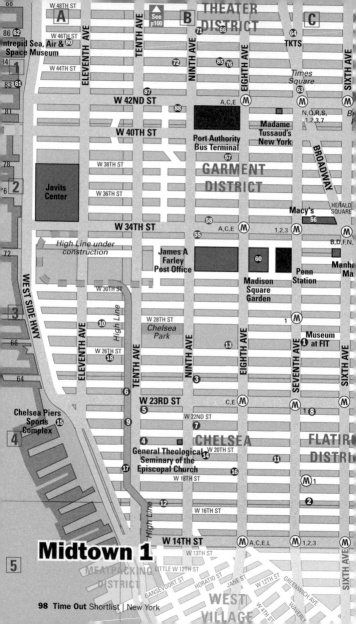

Midtown 1

D | **E** | **F**

E 48TH ST

See p101

Japan Society

1

E 46TH ST

Grand Central
Terminal

E 44TH ST

105
107

106

United Nations
Headquarters

Chrysler
Building
104

Ⓜ 7 | Ⓜ S,4,5,6,7

E 42ND ST

NY Public
Library

QUEENS-MIDTOWN TUNNEL

TUDOR CITY PL

E 40TH ST

Scandinavia House:
The Nordic Center
in America ■

46 | 49

E 38TH ST

East River

2

Morgan
Library

42

E 36TH ST

Empire State
Building

E 34TH ST

6 Ⓜ

Ⓜ MADISON AVE

48

E 32ND ST

35

50

PARK AVE SOUTH

E 30TH ST

7

44

LEXINGTON AVE

E 28TH ST

SECOND AVE

E 28TH ST

3

Museum
22 of Sex

6 Ⓜ

E 26TH ST

MT CARMEL PL

FIRST AVE

21 Museum of
Mathematics
(MoMath)
20

THIRD AVE

E 24TH ST

0 _____ 300 m

0 _____ 300 yds

© Copyright Time Out Group 2014

*Madison
Square*

25

51

ASSER LEVY PL

Manhattan
Marina

FRANKLIN D ROOSEVELT DR

tiron
lding

33

Ⓜ
19

28

6 Ⓜ

E 23RD ST

70

**GRAMERCY
PARK**

Peter Cooper
Village

4

69

E 22ND ST

37

Theodore
Roosevelt
Birthplace

47

*Gramercy
Park*

E 20TH ST

32

30

43

National
Arts Club

PARK AVE SOUTH

IRVING PL

E 18TH ST

BROADWAY

RUTHERFORD PL

NATHAN D
PERLMAN PL

Stuyvesant
Town

45

FIFTH AVE

36

39

E 16TH ST

41 52

*Stuyvesant
Square*

Ⓜ Sights & museums

Ⓜ Eating & drinking

Ⓜ Shopping

Ⓜ Nightlife

Ⓜ Arts & leisure

*Union
Square*

L,N,Q,R,
4,5,6

Ⓜ

Ⓜ L

Ⓜ L

**DOWNTOWN
(pp50-96)**

E 12TH ST

5

St Mark's Church
✚ in-the-Bowery

E 11TH ST

E 10TH ST

*Grace
Church* ✚

E 9TH ST

Time Out Shortlist | New York **99**

Midtown 2

Strawber Fields

Sheep Meadow

W 72ND ST

W 70TH ST

W 68TH ST

W 66TH ST

W 64TH ST

Lincoln Center

W 62ND ST

W 60TH ST

Heckscher Playground

Columbus Circle

Time Warner Center

Hearst Tower

Museum of Arts & Design

Carnegie Hall

W 58TH ST

W 57TH ST

W 56TH ST

W 54TH ST

De Witt Clinton Park

W 52ND ST

HELL'S KITCHEN

W 50TH ST

W 48TH ST

Intrepid Sea, Air & Space Museum

THEATER DISTRICT

W 46TH ST

W 44TH ST

Times Square

TKTS

W 42ND ST

Port Authority Bus Terminal

Madame Tussaud's New York

LINCOLN TUNNEL

W 40TH ST

W 38TH ST

GARMENT DISTRICT

Javits Center

W 36TH ST

See p98

W 34TH ST

Macy's

UPTOWN
(pp130-153)

MIDTOWN EAST

Asia Society and Museum

The Frick Collection

China Institute

Tisch Children's Zoo

Delacorte Musical Clock

Zoo

Trump Wollman Rink

Scholars' Gate

Grand Army Plaza

Rockefeller University

ED KOCH QUEENSBORO (59TH ST) BRIDGE

Trump Tower

Museum of Modern Art

Paley Center for Media

Radio City Music Hall

St Patrick's Cathedral

NBC

efeller nter

Christie's

Japan Society

United Nations Headquarters

Grand Central Terminal

Chrysler Building

Bryant Park

NY Public Library

Scandinavia House: The Nordic Center in America

Morgan Library

Empire State Building

1 Sights & museums
1 Eating & drinking
1 Shopping
1 Nightlife
1 Arts & leisure

E 72ND ST
E 70TH ST
E 68TH ST
E 66TH ST
E 64TH ST
E 62ND ST
E 60TH ST
E 58TH ST
E 57TH ST
E 56TH ST
E 54TH ST
E 52ND ST
E 50TH ST
E 48TH ST
E 46TH ST
E 44TH ST
E 42ND ST
E 40TH ST
E 38TH ST
E 36TH ST
E 34TH ST

FRANKLIN D ROOSEVELT DR

FIFTH AVE
MADISON AVE
PARK AVE
LEXINGTON AVE
THIRD AVE
SECOND AVE
FIRST AVE
YORK AVE
SUTTON PL SOUTH
SUTTON
BEEKMAN PL
MITCHELL PL
TUDOR CITY PL
PARK AVE SOUTH

TRAMWAY

QUEENS-MIDTOWN TUNNEL

300 m
300 yds

© Copyright Time Out Group 2014

including some 50,000 costumes and fabrics dating from the fifth century to the present. Under the directorship of fashion historian Valerie Steele, the museum showcases a selection from the permanent collection, as well as a programme of temporary exhibitions on individual designers or spotlighting fashion from cultural angles.

Rubin Museum of Art

150 W 17th Street, at Seventh Avenue (1-212 620 5000, www.rmanyc.org). Subway A, C, E to 14th Street; L to Eighth Avenue; 1 to 18th Street. **Open** 11am-5pm Mon, Thur; 11am-9pm Wed; 11am-10pm Fri; 11am-6pm Sat, Sun. **Admission** $15; free-$10 reductions; free 6-10pm Fri. **Map** p98 C4 ❷

Dedicated to Himalayan art, the Rubin is a very stylish museum – a fact that falls into place when you learn that the six-storey space was once occupied by famed fashion store Barneys. Rich-toned walls are classy foils for the serene statuary and intricate, multicoloured painted textiles. The second level is dedicated to 'Gateway to Himalayan Art', an annually rotating display of selections from the permanent collection of more than 2,000 pieces dating from the second century to the present day. The upper floors are devoted to changing exhibitions.

Eating & drinking

Co

230 Ninth Avenue, at 24th Street (1-212 243 1105, www.co-pane.com). Subway C, E to 23rd Street. **Open** 5-11pm Mon; 11.30am-11pm Tue- Fri; 11am-11pm Sat; 11am-10pm Sun. **$$. Pizza. Map** p98 B4 ❸

This unassuming pizzeria was the restaurant debut of Jim Lahey, whose Sullivan Street Bakery supplies bread to many top restaurants. Lahey's crust is so good, in fact, it doesn't need any toppings (try the Pizza Bianca, sprinkled with sea salt and olive oil). The most compelling individual-sized pies come from non-traditional sources, such as the ham and cheese, essentially a croque-monsieur in pizza form.

Cookshop

156 Tenth Avenue, at 20th Street (1-212 924 4440, www.cookshopny. com). Subway C, E to 23rd Street. **Open** 8-11am, 11.30am-4pm, 5.30-11.30pm Mon-Fri; 10.30am-4pm, 5.30-11.30pm Sat; 10.30am-4pm, 5.30-10pm Sun. **$$. American. Map** p98 B4 ❹

Chef Marc Meyer and his wife/co-owner Vicki Freeman want Cookshop to be a platform for sustainable ingredients from independent farmers. True to the restaurant's mission, the ingredients are consistently top-notch, and the menu changes daily. While organic ingredients alone don't guarantee a great meal, Meyer knows how to let the natural flavours speak for themselves, and Cookshop scores points for getting the house-made ice-cream to taste as good as Ben & Jerry's.

Empire Diner

NEW *210 Tenth Avenue, at 22nd Street (1-212 596 7523, www.empire-diner. com). Subway C, E to 23rd Street.* **Open** 11am-11pm Mon-Sat; 11am-10pm Sun. **$$. American. Map** p98 B4 ❺

Despite attaining celebrity-chef status through appearances on *Chopped* and *Iron Chef*, Amanda Freitag (formerly of the Harrison) had one space left to fill on her résumé – running her own restaurant. In 2013, the Chelsea resident took over this shuttered local fixture. Freitag preserved the classic looks of the 1940s Fodero dining car – immortalised by Woody Allen in the 1979 movie *Manhattan* – but gave the menu a contemporary, locavore revamp. Fare includes smoked whitefish wrapped up with radishes in crêpes and Greek salad studded with charred octopus, and the ice-cream for the banana splits is churned in house.

Half King

505 W 23rd Street, between Tenth & Eleventh Avenues (1-212 462 4300, www.thehalfking.com). Subway C, E to 23rd Street. **Open** 11am-4am Mon-Fri; 9am-4am Sat, Sun. **Bar**. **Map** p98 B4 **❻**

Don't let their blasé appearance fool you – the creative types gathered at the Half King's yellow pine bar are probably as excited as you are to catch a glimpse of the part-owner, author Sebastian Junger. While you're waiting, order one of the 16 draught beers – including several local brews – or a seasonal cocktail.

Shopping

Billy's Bakery

184 Ninth Avenue, between 21st & 22nd Streets (1-212 647 9956, www.billys bakerynyc.com). Subway C, E to 23rd Street. **Open** 8.30am-11pm Mon-Thur; 8.30am-midnight Fri; 9am-midnight Sat; 9am-9pm Sun. **Map** p98 B4 **❼**

If you crave a large serving of nostalgia, come here for such super-sweet delights as classic cupcakes, Key Lime or coconut cream pie, Hello Dollies (indulgent graham cracker treats), Red Velvet Cake and the Famous Chocolate Icebox Cake, all dispensed in a retro setting.

Mantiques Modern

146 W 22nd Street, between Sixth & Seventh Avenues (1-212 206 1494, www.mantiquesmodern.com). Subway 1 to 23rd Street. **Open** 10.30am-6.30pm Mon-Fri; 11am-7pm Sat, Sun. **Map** p98 C4 **❽**

Specialising in industrial and modernist furnishings and art from the 1880s to the 1980s, Mantiques Modern is a fantastic repository of beautiful and bizarre items, from kinetic sculptures and early-20th-century wooden artists' mannequins to a Soviet World War II telescope. Pieces by famous designers such as Hermès sit side by side with natural curiosities, and skulls (in metal or Lucite), crabs, animal horns and robots are all recurring themes.

Printed Matter

195 Tenth Avenue, between 21st & 22nd Streets (1-212 925 0325, www.printed matter.org). Subway C, E to 23rd Street. **Open** 11am-7pm Mon-Wed, Sat; 11am-8pm Thur, Fri. **Map** p98 B4 **❾**

This non-profit organisation is devoted to artists' books – ranging from David Shrigley's deceptively naïve illustrations to provocative photographic self-portraits by Matthias Herrmann – and operates a public reading room as well as a shop. Works by unknown and emerging artists share shelf space with those by veterans such as Yoko Ono and Edward Ruscha.

Nightlife

The Eagle

554 W 28th Street, between Tenth & Eleventh Avenues (1-646 473 1866, www.eaglenyc.com). Subway C, E to 23rd Street. **Open** 9pm-4am Mon; 10pm-4am Tue-Sat; 4pm-4am Sun. No credit cards. **Map** p98 A3 **❿**

You don't have to be a kinky leather daddy to enjoy this manly outpost, but it definitely doesn't hurt. The gay fetish bar is home to an array of beer blasts, foot-worship fêtes and leather soirées, plus simple pool playing and cruising nights. In summer, the rooftop is a surprising oasis.

G Lounge

225 W 19th Street, between Seventh & Eighth Avenues (1-212 929 1085, www.glounge.com). Subway 1 to 18th Street. **Open** 4pm-4am daily. No credit cards. **Map** p98 C4 **⓫**

The neighbourhood's original slick boy lounge – a moodily lit cave with a cool brick-and-glass arched entrance – wouldn't look out of place in an upscale boutique hotel. An excellent roster of DJs stays on top of the mood at this popular gay after-work cocktail spot.

Highline Ballroom

431 W 16th Street, between Ninth & Tenth Avenues (1-212 414 5994,

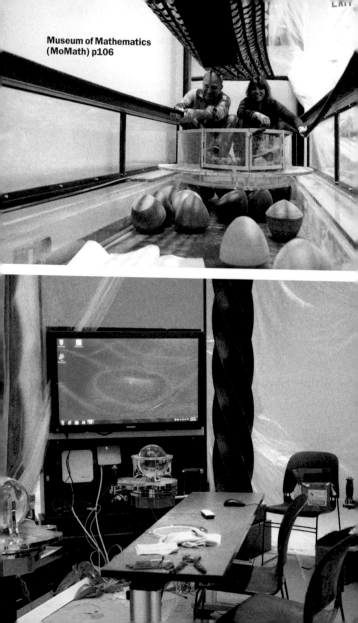

Museum of Mathematics
(MoMath) p106

www.highlineballroom.com). Subway
A, C, E to 14th Street; L to Eighth
Avenue. Map p98 B5 **12**
This West Side club has a slick, LA feel,
but it has a lot to recommend it. The
acoustics are first class, the sightlines
are pretty good and the bookings are
impressive, ranging from hip hop
heatseekers such as Yelawolf and
Wiz Khalifa, to singer-songwriter pop,
world music and burlesque.

Upright Citizens Brigade Theatre

307 W 26th Street, between Eighth &
Ninth Avenues (1-212 366 9176, www.
ucbtheatre.com). Subway C, E to 23rd
Street; 1 to 28th Street. No credit cards.
Map p98 B3 **13**
The Upright Citizens Brigade, which
migrated from Chicago in the 1990s,
has been the most visible catalyst in
New York's current alternative comedy
boom. The improv troupes and sketch
groups here are some of the best in the
city. Stars of Saturday Night Live and
writers for late-night talk shows gather
on Sunday nights to wow crowds in
the long-running ASSSSCAT 3000.
Other premier teams include the
Stepfathers (Fridays) and Death by
Roo Roo (Saturdays). Arrive early so
you can choose a good seat – the venue
has challenging sightlines.

Arts & leisure

Atlantic Theater Company

336 W 20th Street, between Eighth
& Ninth Avenues (1-212 691 5919,
www.atlantictheater.org). Map p98 B4 **14**
Created in 1985 as an offshoot of
acting workshops led by playwright
David Mamet and actor William H
Macy, the dynamic Atlantic Theater
Company has presented dozens of
new plays, including Steven Sater and
Duncan Sheik's rock musical Spring
Awakening, and Conor McPherson's
The Night Alive. New musicals are
a strong feature of the company's

programme, and it also has a smaller
second stage deep underground at 330
W 16th Street.

Chelsea Piers

Piers 59-62, W 17th to 23rd Streets,
at Eleventh Avenue (1-212 336 6666,
www.chelseapiers.com). Subway C, E
to 23rd Street. **Open** times vary;
phone or check website for details.
Map p98 A4 **15**
Chelsea Piers is still the most
impressive all-in-one athletic facility in
New York. Between the ice rink (Pier 61,
1-212 336 6100), the bowling alley
(Pier 60, 1-212 835 2695), the driving
range (Pier 59, 1-212 336 6400) and
scads of other choices, there's definitely
something for everyone. The Field
House (between Piers 61 & 62, 1-212
336 6500) has a gymnastics centre, a
climbing wall, basketball courts and
batting cages. At the Sports Center
Health Club (Pier 60, 1-212 336 6000),
you'll find classes covering everything
from boxing to triathlon training in
the pool, as well as a gym complete
with comprehensive weight deck and
cardiovascular machines.

Joyce Theater

175 Eighth Avenue, at 19th Street (1-
212 242 0800, www.joyce.org). Subway
A, C, E to 14th Street; 1 to 18th Street;
L to Eighth Avenue. Map p98 B4 **16**
This intimate space houses one of the
finest theatres – we're talking about
sightlines – in town. Companies and
choreographers that present work
here, among them Ballet Hispanico,
Pilobolus Dance Theater and
Doug Varone, tend to be somewhat
traditional. The Joyce hosts dance
throughout much of the year –
Pilobolus is a summer staple.

The Kitchen

512 W 19th Street, between Tenth &
Eleventh Avenues (1-212 255 5793,
www.thekitchen.org). Subway A, C, E
to 14th Street; L to Eighth Avenue.
Map p98 B4 **17**

The Kitchen offers some of the best experimental dance around – inventive, provocative and rigorous. Some of New York's finest artists have performed here: Sarah Michelson (who has also served as a guest curator for specific programmes), Dean Moss, Ann Liv Young and Jodi Melnick.

Sleep No More

McKittrick Hotel, 530 W 27th Street, between Tenth & Eleventh Avenues (Ovationtix 1-866 811 4111, www. sleepnomorenyc.com). Subway 1 to 28th Street; C, E to 23rd Street. **Map** p98 A3 ⓭

A multitude of searing sights awaits at this dazzling and uncanny installation by British company Punchdrunk. Your sense of space is blurred as you wend your way through more than 90 discrete spaces, from a cloistral chapel to a ballroom floor. A Shakespearean can check off *Macbeth* allusions; others can just revel in the haunted-house vibe.

Flatiron District & Union Square

Taking its name from the distinctive wedge-shaped Flatiron Building, this district spans 14th to 29th Streets, between Sixth and Lexington Avenues. But, as with many neighbourhoods in NYC, the borders are disputed and evolving – NoMad is slowly catching on as the new name for the blocks north of Madison Square Park. Once predominantly commercial, the area became more residential in the 1980s, with buyers drawn to its 19th-century brownstones and early 20th-century industrial architecture; restaurants and shops followed.

Sights & museums

Flatiron Building

175 Fifth Avenue, between 22nd & 23rd Streets. Subway N, R, 6 to 23rd Street. **Map** p99 D4 ⓲

One of New York's most celebrated structures, the Flatiron Building was the world's first steel-frame skyscraper when it was completed in 1902. The 22-storey Beaux Arts edifice is clad in white limestone and terracotta, but it's its unique triangular shape as well as its singular position at the crossing of Fifth Avenue and Broadway that draws admiration from sightseers and natives alike.

Madison Square Park

23rd to 26th Streets, between Fifth & Madison Avenues (www.madison squarepark.org). Subway N, R, 6 to 23rd Street. **Map** p99 D3/D4 ⓴

This elegant green space opened in 1847 and is now surrounded by illustrious buildings. The world's tallest skyscraper from 1909 to 1913, the Metropolitan Life Tower at 1 Madison Avenue was designed to resemble the Campanile in Venice's Piazza San Marco, whose reconstruction (after a collapse in 1902) Met Life had funded. The Appellate Division Courthouse at 27 Madison Avenue is one of the finest Beaux Arts buildings in New York. The park hosts summer concerts, literary readings, childrens' events and Mad Sq Art, a year-round 'gallery without walls', featuring changing installations by big-name artists such as Antony Gormley and Jaume Plensa.

Museum of Mathematics (MoMath)

11 E 26th Street, between Fifth & Madison Avenues (1-212 542 0566, www.momath.org). Subway N, R, 6 to 23rd Street. **Open** 10am-5pm daily (10am-2.30pm 1st Wed of each mth). **Admission** $16; free-$10 reductions. **Map** p99 D3 ㉑

Think a ride on a square-wheeled trike could never be smooth? Find out just how bump-free it can be when you take said tricycle over a sunflower-shaped track, where the petals create strategically placed catenaries – curves used in geometry and physics – that make a level ride possible. The country's first Museum of Mathematics, designed for visitors of all ages, replaces lectures and textbooks with more than 30 eclectic exhibits covering topics such as algebra and geometry.

Museum of Sex

233 Fifth Avenue, at 27th Street (1-212 689 6337, www.museumofsex. com). Subway N, R, 6 to 28th Street. **Open** 10am-8pm Mon-Thur, Sun; 10am-9pm Fri, Sat. **Admission** $17.50; $15.25 reductions. Under-18s not admitted. **Map** p99 D3 ②

Situated in the former Tenderloin district, which was bumping and grinding with dance halls and brothels in the 19th century, MoSex explores its subject within a cultural context. Highlights of the museum's permanent collection of more than 15,000 objects range from the tastefully erotic to the outlandish: an 1890s anti-onanism device looks as uncomfortable as the BDSM gear donated by a local dominatrix, and there is kinky art courtesy of Picasso and Keith Haring. Rotating exhibitions in the three-level space include the likes of 'The Sex Lives of Animals'. The gift shop stocks books and arty sex toys, while the museum's bar dispenses aphrodisiac cocktails, stimulating soft drinks and light bites.

Eating & drinking

230 Fifth

230 Fifth Avenue, between 26th & 27th Streets (1-212 725 4300, www.230-fifth. com). Subway N, R to 28th Street. **Open** 4pm-4am Mon-Fri; 10am-4am Sat, Sun. **Bar**. **Map** p99 D3 ㉓

The 14,000sq ft roof garden dazzles with truly spectacular views, including a close-up of the Empire State Building, but the glitzy indoor lounge – with its floor-to-ceiling windows, wraparound sofas and bold lighting – shouldn't be overlooked. While the sprawling outdoor space gets mobbed on sultry nights, it's less crowded in the cooler

months when heaters, fleece robes and hot ciders make it a winter hotspot.

Breslin Bar & Dining Room

Ace Hotel New York, 16 W 29th Street, at Broadway (1-212 679 1939, www.thebreslin.com). Subway N, R to 28th Street. **Open** 7am-4pm, 5.30pm-midnight daily. $$$. **Eclectic**. **Map** p99 D3 ㉔

The third project from restaurant savant Ken Friedman and Anglo chef April Bloomfield, the Breslin broke gluttonous new ground. Expect a wait at this no-reservations hotspot – you can quell your appetite at the bar with an order of scrumpets (fried strips of lamb belly). The overall ethos could best be described as late-period Henry VIII: groaning boards of house-made terrines feature thick slices of guinea hen, rabbit and pork. The pig's foot for two – half a leg, really – could feed the whole Tudor court. Desserts include amped-up childhood treats like ice-cream sundaes.

Eleven Madison Park

11 Madison Avenue, at E 24th Street (1-212 889 0905, www.elevenmadison park.com). Subway N, R, 6 to 23rd Street. **Open** 5.30-10pm Mon-Wed, Sun; noon-1pm, 5.30-10pm Thur-Sat. $$$$. **American**. **Map** p99 D4 ㉕

Chef Daniel Humm and impresario partner Will Guidara – who bought Eleven Madison Park from their old boss, legendary restaurateur Danny Meyer – are masters of reinvention. And once again, they've hit on a winning formula, this time for a 16-course meal themed around Gotham – marked by stagecraft and tricks – that departs imaginatively from the city's upper echelons of Old World-dominated fine dining. During a recent meal, a glass cloche rose over a puff of smoke, unveiling smoked sturgeon above smouldering embers. Rib eye, aged an astonishing 140 days, was served

with a side of oxtail jam with melted
foie gras and whipped potato icing
that's as rich as it sounds, and a waiter
performed a card trick with a chocolate
payoff – a nod to the city's old street-
corner shysters.

Hanjan

*36 W 26th Street, between Broadway
& Sixth Avenue (1-212 206 7226,
www.hanjan26.com). Subway N, R to
28th Street.* **Open** *5.30-11pm Mon-Wed,
Sun; 5.30pm-midnight Thur-Sat.* **$$**.
Korean. Map p98 C3 **26**
Hanjan is a shining example of a
joomak, the Korean equivalent of the
English gastropub. Expect a barrage
of deeply satisfying dishes: glutinous
rice cakes licked with spicy pork fat;
crispy scallion pancakes studded
with squid; and juicy skewers of fresh
chicken thighs that you can swab with
funky *ssamjang*. Each plate packs
its own surprises, but the whole feast
is tied together by a soulful bass note
melding spice, sweetness, and just the
right amount of fishy funk.

John Dory Oyster Bar

*Ace Hotel New York, 1196 Broadway,
at W 29th Street (1-212 792 9000,
www.thejohndory.com). Subway N,
R to 28th Street.* **Open** *noon-midnight
daily.* **$$**. **American**. Map p99 D3 **27**
April Bloomfield and Ken Friedman's
original John Dory, in the Meatpacking
District, was an ambitious, pricey
endeavour, but its reincarnation in the
Ace Hotel is an understated knockout.
Tall stools face a raw bar stocked
with East and West Coast oysters,
all expertly handled and impeccably
sourced. True to form, the rest of
Bloomfield's tapas-style seafood dishes
are intensely flavoured – cold poached
lobster with tomalley vinaigrette, for
example, or chorizo-stuffed squid with
smoked tomato.

Milk and Honey

*30 E 23rd Street, between Madison
Avenue & Park Avenue South (no phone,*
*www.mlkhny.com). Subway N, R, 6 to
23rd Street.* **Open** *6pm-4am daily.* **Bar**.
Map p99 D4 **28**
See box p112.

The NoMad

*1170 Broadway, at 28th Street (1-347
472 5660, www.thenomadhotel.com).
N, R to 28th Street.* **Open** *7-10am, noon-
2am Mon-Sat; 7-10am, noon-2pm, 5.30-
10pm Sun.* **$$$**. **American**. Map p99
D3 **29**
The NoMad is another restaurant from
chef Daniel Humm and front-of-house
partner Will Guidara, also behind
Eleven Madison Park (see p107).
Featuring plush armchairs around
well-spaced tables, it offers a stylish
return to three-course dining. The
food, like the space, exudes decadence:
a slow-cooked egg stars in one over-
the-top starter, with mushrooms,
black garlic and kale for crunch. And
while New York offers diners plenty
of rich-man roast chickens for two,
the amber-hued bird here – with a foie
gras, brioche and black truffle stuffing
– is surely the new gold standard, well
worth its $79 price tag.

Old Town Bar & Grill

*45 E 18th Street, between Broadway &
Park Avenue South (1-212 529 6732,
www.oldtownbar.com). Subway L, N, Q,
R, 4, 5, 6 to 14th Street-Union Square.*
Open *11.30am-11.30pm Mon-Fri; 10am-
11.30pm Sat; 11am-10pm Sun.* **Bar**.
Map p99 D4 **30**
Amid the swank food and drink
sanctums sprouting up around Park
Avenue South, this classic and elegant
old-school tavern remains a shrine
to unchanging values. Grab a sweet
wooden booth or belly up to the long
bar and drain a few pints alongside the
regulars who gather on stools 'south
of the pumps' (their lingo for taps).
If you work up an appetite, skip the
much-praised burger in favour of the
chilli dog: a grilled and scored all-beef
Sabrett with spicy home-made beef-
and-red-kidney-bean chilli.

Rave on

Fuerza Bruta returns in part three of the De La Guarda trilogy.

When the sensory-wraparound rave known as *De La Guarda* swung into town 16 years ago, it was the only show of its kind. Even in 2007, when environmental-kinesthetic mastermind Diqui James unveiled a sequel, *Fuerza Bruta*, there was no *Sleep No More, Then She Fell* or *Queen of the Night*. So has James tried to reinvent the wheel and beat the competition – say, by introducing narrative or literary allusions? Not a chance. *Fuerza Bruta: Wayra* (see p111) is of a piece with its predecessors, still offering unique thrills for a remarkably young and diverse audience that, we're guessing, doesn't get to Playwrights Horizons very much. And there's nothing wrong with that. Immersive theatre may be more common now, but no one blasts through boundaries like these guys.

The crowd enters the cavernous Daryl Roth Theatre to be raked with coloured lights and encouraged to shake its booty to ambient music. The show then begins with a white-suited man (familiar if you saw *Fuerza Bruta*) running on an accelerating treadmill, dodging furniture and other performers, until he's shot in the chest. Is what follows his dying dream?

The next 70 minutes include the customary flying stunts and, best of all, a return of the clear-bottomed pool that descends to within touching distance, allowing us to gaze at women swimming in shallow water, belly flopping on the clear plastic to create percussive slaps. Eventually, a huge grid-covered balloon is stretched over the audience, with performers peering down through holes.

What it all means is anyone's guess. Images of humans tethered to the grid far above suggest our status as cosmic marionettes. Are the women swimming in the pool mermaids? Watery angels? That visual trope of performers dropping out of the sky, grabbing a spectator and hoisting them up to the heavens – a manifestation of flying, or a visitation from death? Perhaps best to switch off the analytic apparatus and just enjoy the thrills – of which there are plenty.

NEW YORK BY AREA

Rye House

11 W 17th Street, between Fifth & Sixth Avenues (1-212 255 7260, www. ryehousenyc.com). Subway F, M to 14th Street; L to Sixth Avenue. **Open** noon-11pm Mon, Sun; noon-2am Thur-Sat. **Bar. Map** p99 D4 ⓛ

As the name suggests, American spirits are the emphasis at this dark, sultry bar. As well as bourbons and ryes, there are gins, vodkas and rums, most distilled in the States. Check out the jalapeño-infused Wake-up Call, one of the venue's most popular bourbon cocktails. While the focus is clearly on drinking, there's excellent upscale pub grub, such as truffle grilled cheese or potato pierogies.

Shopping

ABC Carpet & Home

888 Broadway, at 19th Street (1-212 473 3000, www.abchome.com). Subway L, N, Q, R, 4, 5, 6 to 14th Street-Union Square. **Open** 10am-7pm Mon-Wed, Fri, Sat; 10am-8pm Thur; 11am-6pm Sun. **Map** p99 D4 ⓛ

Most of ABC's 35,000-strong carpet range is housed in the store across the street at no.881 – except the rarest rugs, which reside on the sixth floor of the main emporium. Browse everything from organic soap to hand-beaded lampshades on the ground floor. Furniture, on the upper floors, spans every style, from antique Asian to mid-century modern. Jean-Georges Vongerichten's artfully decorated on-site seasonal restaurant, ABC Kitchen, makes an excellent lunch (or dinner) stop.

Eataly

200 Fifth Avenue, between 23rd & 24th Streets (1-212 229 2560, www.eataly. com). Subway F, M, N, R to 23rd Street. **Open** 10am-11pm daily. **Map** p99 D4 ⓛ

This massive foodie destination, from Mario Batali and Joe and Lidia Bastianich, sprawls across 50,000sq

ft. A spin-off of an operation by the same name just outside of Turin, the complex encompasses six restaurants and a rooftop beer garden. Adjacent retail areas offer gourmet provisions, including artisanal breads baked on the premises, fresh mozzarella, salumi and a vast array of olive oils.

Idlewild Books

12 W 19th Street, between Fifth & Sixth Avenues (1-212 414 8888, www.idle wildbooks.com). Subway F, M to 14th Street; L to Sixth Avenue. **Open** noon-7.30pm Mon-Thur; noon-6pm Fri, Sat; noon-5pm Sun. **Map** p99 D4 ⓛ

Opened by a former United Nations press officer, Idlewild stocks travel guides to more than 100 countries and all 50 states, which are grouped with related works of fiction and non-fiction. It also has a large selection of works in French, Spanish and Italian. Fun fact: Idlewild was the original name for JFK Airport.

JJ Hat Center

310 Fifth Avenue, at W 32nd Street (1-212 239 4368, www.jjhatcenter.com). Subway B, D, F, M, N, Q, R to 34th Street-Herald Square. **Open** 9am-6pm Mon-Fri; 9.30am-5.30pm Sat. **Map** p99 D3 ⓛ

Traditional hats may currently be back in fashion, but this venerable shop, in business since 1911, is oblivious to passing trends. Dapper gents sporting the shop's wares will help you choose from more than 4,000 fedoras, pork pies, caps and other styles on display in the splendid, chandelier-illuminated, wood-panelled showroom. Prices start at around $35 for a wool-blend cap.

Kiosk

Room 925, 41 Union Square West, at 17th Street (1-212 226 8601, www. kioskkiosk.com). Subway N, Q, R, 4, 5, 6 to 14th Street-Union Square. **Open** noon-7pm Thur, Fri. **Map** p99 D4 ⓛ

Alisa Grifo has collected an array of inexpensive items – mostly simple and functional but with a strong design aesthetic – from around the world. At her gem of a shop, you can pick up anything from cool Japanese can openers to colourful net bags from Germany and Shaker onion baskets handmade in New Hampshire. Hours may be extended, so call before visiting.

LA Burdick

5 E 20th Street, between Fifth Avenue & Broadway (1-800 229 2419, www.burdickchocolate.com). Subway N, R to 23rd Street. **Open** 8.30am-9pm Mon-Sat; 10am-7pm Sun. **Map** p99 D4 37

Best known for its cute little chocolate penguins and mice, the family-owned, New Hampshire-based chocolatier now has a shop and café in NYC. Pastries share display space with marzipan, dipped caramels and an array of truffles. Ponder the choices over a cup of dark, white or milk hot chocolate, or plump for dealer's choice with a wide selection of assorted boxes, including a tempting range of gift baskets and boxes – including those signature mice and penguins.

Showplace Antique & Design Center

40 W 25th Street, between Fifth & Sixth Avenues (1-212 633 6063, www.nyshowplace.com). Subway F, M to 23rd Street. **Open** 10am-6pm Mon-Fri; 8.30am-5.30pm Sat, Sun. **Map** p98 C3 38

Set over four expansive floors, this indoor market houses more than 200 high-quality dealers selling everything from vintage furniture to Greek and Roman antiquities. Among the highlights are Joe Sundlie's spot-on-trend vintage pieces from Lanvin and Alaïa, and Mood Indigo – arguably the best source in the city for collectible bar accessories and dinnerware. The array of Bakelite jewellery and table accessories and Fiestaware is dazzling.

Union Square Greenmarket

From 16th to 17th Streets, between Union Square East & Union Square West (1-212 788 7476, www.grownyc.org/greenmarket). Subway L, N, Q, R, 4, 5, 6 to 14th Street-Union Square. **Open** 8am-6pm Mon, Wed, Fri, Sat. **Map** p99 D4 39

Shop elbow-to-elbow with top chefs for locally grown produce, handmade breads and baked goods, preserves and cheeses at the city's flagship farmers' market on the periphery of Union Square Park. Between Thanksgiving and Christmas, a holiday market sets up shop here too.

Nightlife

Metropolitan Room

34 W 22nd Street, between Fifth & Sixth Avenues (1-212 206 0440, www.metropolitanroom.com). Subway F, M, N, R to 23rd Street. **Map** p98 C4 40

The Met Room occupies a comfortable middle zone on the city's cabaret spectrum, less expensive than the fancier supper clubs and more polished than the cheaper spots. Regular performers range from rising jazz artists to established cabaret acts such as Baby Jane Dexter and Gabrielle Stravelli, plus legends like Annie Ross.

Arts & leisure

Fuerza Bruta: Wayra

Daryl Roth theatre, 101 E 15th Street, at Union Square East (Telecharge 1-212 239 6200, www.fuerzabrutanyc.com). Subway L, N, Q, R, 4, 5, 6 to 14th Street-Union Square. **Map** p99 D5 41

See box p109.

Gramercy Park & Murray Hill

A key to Gramercy Park, the gated square at the southern end of Lexington Avenue (between 20th & 21st Streets), is the preserve of residents of the surrounding homes (and members of a couple of venerable private clubs). Murray Hill spans 30th to 40th Streets,

Frat-town gets fashionable

An influx of upscale spots is transforming postgrad territory.

Dover Street Market

NEW YORK BY AREA

For years dominated by the hard-partying post-frat set, Murray Hill hasn't exactly been known for style. But food-and-drink scene movers and shakers have started migrating east of the bar-and-restaurant-saturated Flatiron District and NoMad (North of Madison Square). In 2012, visionary barman Sasha Petraske, who paved the way for the modern cocktail bar with Milk and Honey in 2000, planted a flag here for artisanal tipples with **Middle Branch** (see p114), a bi-level drinkery with open french windows welcoming an after-work crowd to its crimson banquettes. A year later, Petraske relocated his original cocktail den nearby to the Flatiron District. The new **Milk and Honey** (see p108) may be more accessible than the reservations-only original – walk-ins are welcome – but cocktail menus are still absent. Ask for one of the bar's contemporary classics like the ginger-and-Scotch Penicillin.

The decor of **Salvation Taco** (see p114) – coloured Christmas lights, fake fruit – may evoke that Cancun vacation, but the fiesta fare doled out at this Murray Hill cantina has an upscale bent, thanks to ace restaurant duo April Bloomfield and Ken Friedman (of the Spotted Pig and the Ace Hotel's Breslin). Exotic fillings include Moroccan-spiced lamb and Korean-barbecue-style beef. It's easy to find a cheap ramen joint in this postgrad mecca, but house-made soba crowned with shaved black truffles? That's only at **Kajitsu** (see p113). The minimalist, Michelin-starred den displays a devotion to produce, influenced by the monk-approved shojin-ryori (vegetarian) tradition. The sublime fare has made it a cult favourite among top-notch toques like Momofuku's David Chang.

Now the area even has destination retail – the third **Dover Street Market** (see p114) opened in the former home of the New York School of Applied Design, bringing Comme des Garçons designer Rei Kawakubo's quirky, upscale interpretation of a London fashion market to NYC, complete with a with an outpost of the cult Paris eaterie, Rose Bakery.

between Third and Fifth Avenues. Townhouses of the rich and powerful were once clustered around Madison and Park Avenues, but these days, only a few streets retain their former elegance. For years largely populated by upwardly mobiles fresh out of university, the area is becoming more fashionable.

Sights & museums

Morgan Library & Museum
225 Madison Avenue, at E 36th Street (1-212 685 0008, www.themorgan.org). Subway 6 to 33rd Street. **Open** 10.30am-5pm Tue-Thur; 10.30am-9pm Fri; 10am-6pm Sat; 11am-6pm Sun. **Admission** $18; free-$12 reductions; free 7-9pm Fri. **Map** p99 D2/p101 D5 ❷

This Madison Avenue institution began as the private library of financier Pierpont Morgan. It houses first-rate works on paper, including drawings by Michelangelo, Rembrandt and Picasso; a copy of *Frankenstein* annotated by Mary Shelley; manuscripts by Steinbeck, Twain and Wilde; and sheet music handwritten by Beethoven and Mozart. Each Yuletide, it displays an original edition of Dickens's *A Christmas Carol*.

Eating & drinking

71 Irving Place Coffee & Tea Bar
71 Irving Place, between 18th & 19th Streets (1-212 995 5252, www.irvingfarm.com). Subway L, N, Q, R, 4, 5, 6 to 14th Street-Union Square. **Open** 7am-10pm Mon-Sat; 8am-10pm Sun. **$. Café. Map** p99 D4 ❸

Irving Farm's beans are roasted in a 100-year-old carriage house in the Hudson Valley; fittingly, its Gramercy Park café, located on the ground floor of a stately brownstone, also has a rustic edge. Breakfast (the likes of granola, oatmeal, waffles and bagels), sandwiches and salads accompany the excellent java.

The Cannibal
116 E 29th Street, between Park & Lexington Avenues (1-212 686 5480, www.thecannibalnyc.com). Subway 6 to 28th Street. **Open** 11am-11.30pm Mon-Sat; 11am-10.30pm Sun. **$-$$. Steakhouse. Map** p99 D3 ❹

The Cannibal, run by restaurateur Christian Pappanicholas (and connected to his Belgian-American eaterie Resto), is an unusual retail-restaurant hybrid – a beer store and a butcher's shop but also a laid-back place to eat and drink. The meat counter supplies whole beasts for Resto's large-format feasts, but the carnivore's paradise is otherwise autonomous, with its own chef, Preston Clark (formerly of Jean-Georges), and beer master, Julian Kurland. The food is best ordered in rounds, pairing beer and bites – wispy shavings of Kentucky ham, pâtés, sausages and tartares – as you sample some of the 450 selections on the drinks list.

Casa Mono
52 Irving Place, at E 17th Street (1-212 253 2773, www.casamononyc.com). Subway L to Third Avenue; L, N, Q, R, 4, 5, 6 to 14th Street-Union Square. **Open** noon-midnight daily. **$-$$. Spanish.** Map p99 E4 ❺

In 2003 offal-loving chef-partners Mario Batali and Andy Nusser broke new ground in NYC with their adventurous Spanish fare, and they're still going strong, with dishes including crispy pigs' ears, fried sweetbreads with fennel, foie gras with *cinco cebollas* (five types of onion), and fried duck egg with black truffles. For a slightly cheaper option, the attached Bar Jamón (125 E 17th Street; open 5pm-2am Mon-Fri; noon-2am Sat, Sun) offers tapas, Ibérico hams and Spanish cheeses.

Kajitsu
125 E 39th Street, between Park & Lexington Avenues (1-212 228 4873, www.kajitsunyc.com). Subway S, 4, 5, 6, 7 to 42nd Street-Grand Central.

Open 11.45am-1.45pm, 5.30-10pm Tue-Sat; 5.30-10pm Sun (and 1st day of each month). **$$$**. **Japanese/vegetarian**. Map p99 D2 **46**
See box p112.

Maialino

Gramercy Park Hotel, 2 Lexington Avenue, at E 21st Street (1-212 777 2410, www.maialinonyc.com). Subway 6 to 23rd Street. **Open** 7.30-10am, noon-2pm, 5.30-10.30pm Mon-Thur; 7.30-10am, noon-2pm, 5.30-11pm Fri; 10am-2.30pm, 5.30-11pm Sat; 10am-2.30pm, 5.30-10.30pm Sun. **$$**. **Italian**. Map p99 D4 **47**
Danny Meyer's first full-fledged foray into Italian cuisine is a homage to the neighbourhood trattorias that kept him well fed as a 20-year-old tour guide in Rome. Salumi and bakery stations between the front bar and the wood-beamed dining room – hog jowls and sausages dangling near shelves stacked with crusty bread – mimic a market off the Appian Way. Executive chef Nick Anderer's menu offers exceptional facsimiles of dishes specific to Rome, such as carbonara and suckling pig.

Middle Branch

154 E 33rd Street, between Lexington & Third Avenues (1-212 213 1350). Subway 6 to 33rd Street. **Open** 5pm-2am daily. **Bar**. Map p99 E2 **48**
See box p112.

Salvation Taco

145 E 39th Street, between Lexington & Third Avenues (1-212 865 5800, www.salvationtaco.com). Subway S, 4, 5, 6, 7 to 42nd Street-Grand Central. **Open** 7am-midnight daily. **$**. **Mexican**. Map p99 E2 **49**
See box p112.

Shopping

Dover Street Market New York

NEW *160 Lexington Avenue, at 30th Street (1-646 837 7750, www.dover streetmarket.com). Subway 6 to 28th or*

33rd Street. **Open** 11am-7pm Mon-Sat; noon-6pm Sun. Map p99 D3 **50**
Like the original, named for its London location, DSMNY is a multilevel store that blurs the line between art and commerce. A transparent elevator whisks shoppers through the seven-floor consumer playground. Three pillars running through six of the levels have been transformed into art installations: a stripey patchwork knitted sheath by Magda Sayeg, London Fieldworks' wooden metropolis, and 3D collages by 'junk sculptor' Leo Sewell. All of the Comme lines – more than 15 of them – are here, alongside mini boutiques for luxury labels like Louis Vuitton and Prada, streetwear brands such as Nike and Supreme, a showroom spotlighting emerging talent, and a raft of cool names and exclusive items.

Nightlife

Gramercy Theatre

127 E 23rd Street, between Park & Lexington Avenues (1-212 614 6932, www.thegramercytheatre.com). Subway N, R, 6 to 23rd Street. Map p99 D4 **51**
The Gramercy Theatre looks exactly like what it actually is, a run-down former movie theatre; yet it has a decent sound system and good sightlines. Concert-goers can lounge in raised seats on the top level or get closer to the stage lower down. Bookings have included such Baby Boom underdogs as Todd Rundgren and Loudon Wainwright III, and the occasional comedy show, but tilt towards niche metal and emo bands.

Irving Plaza

17 Irving Place, at E 15th Street (1-212 777 6800, www.irvingplaza. com). Subway L, N, Q, R, 4, 5, 6 to 14th Street-Union Square. Map p99 D5 **52**
Lying just east of Union Square, this mid-size rock venue has served as a Democratic Party lecture hall (in the 19th century), a Yiddish theatre and a burlesque house (Gypsy

Rose Lee made an appearance). Most importantly, it's a great place to see big stars keeping a low profile (Jeff Beck, Jane's Addiction and Lenny Kravitz), along with medium heavies on their way up.

Herald Square & Garment District

Seventh Avenue is the main drag of the Garment District (roughly from 34th to 40th Streets, between Broadway & Eighth Avenue), where designers feed America's multibillion-dollar clothing industry. The world's largest store, Macy's, looms over Herald Square (at the junction of Broadway and Sixth Avenue). To the east, the spas, restaurants and karaoke bars of Koreatown line 32nd Street, between Fifth and Sixth Avenues.

Eating & drinking

Keens Steakhouse

72 W 36th Street, between Fifth & Sixth Avenues (1-212 947 3636, www. keens.com). Subway B, D, F, M, N, Q, R to 34th Street-Herald Square. **Open** 5.30-10.30pm Mon-Fri; 5-10.30pm Sat; 5-9.30pm Sun. **$$. Steakhouse**. Map p98 C2 ❺❸

The ceiling and walls are hung with pipes, some from such long-ago Keens regulars as Babe Ruth, JP Morgan and Teddy Roosevelt. Even in these nonsmoking days, you can catch a whiff of the restaurant's 120-plus years of history. Bevelled-glass doors, two working fireplaces and a forest's worth of dark wood suggest a time when 'Diamond Jim' Brady piled his table with bushels of oysters, slabs of seared beef and troughs of ale. The menu still lists a three-inch-thick mutton chop (imagine a saddle of lamb but with more punch), and the porterhouse (for two or three) holds its own against any steak in the city.

Mandoo Bar

2 W 32nd Street, between Fifth Avenue & Broadway (1-212 279 3075, www. mandoobarnyc.com). Subway B, D, F, M, N, Q, R to 34th Street-Herald Square. **Open** 11.30am-10pm daily. **$. Korean**. Map p99 D3 ❺❹

If the staff members painstakingly filling and crimping little dough squares in the front window don't give things away, we will – this wood-wrapped industrial-style eaterie elevates *mandoo* (Korean dumplings) above mere appetiser status. Six varieties of the tasty morsels are filled with such delights as subtly piquant kimchi, juicy pork, succulent shrimp and vegetables. Try them miniaturised, as in the 'baby mandoo', swimming in a soothing beef broth or atop springy, soupy ramen noodles.

Shopping

B&H

420 Ninth Avenue, at W 34th Street (1-212 444 5040, www.bhphotovideo. com). Subway A, C, E to 34th Street-Penn Station. **Open** 9am-7pm Mon-Thur; 9am-1pm Fri; 10am-6pm Sun. Map p98 B2 ❺❺

B&H is the ultimate one-stop shop for all your photographic, video and audio needs. In this huge, busy store, goods are transported from the stock room via an overhead conveyor belt. Note that, due to the largely Hasidic Jewish staff, the store is closed on Saturdays and other Jewish holidays.

Macy's

151 W 34th Street, between Broadway & Seventh Avenue (1-212 695 4400, www.macys.com). Subway B, D, F, M, N, Q, R to 34th Street-Herald Square; 1, 2, 3 to 34th Street-Penn Station. **Open** 9am-9.30pm Mon-Fri; 10am-9.30pm Sat. Map p98 C2/p100 C5 ❺❻

It may not be as glamorous as New York's other famous stores but for sheer breadth of stock, the 34th Street behemoth is hard to beat. Mid-price fashion for all ages, big beauty names and housewares have traditionally been the store's bread and butter, but a $400 million redesign, which should be wrapping up in late 2015, has introduced new luxury boutiques including Gucci and Burberry. The cosmetics department has been luxed up with high-end brands such as Jo Malone London and Laura Mercier, plus a Blow hair-styling bar. Pick up a Macy's visitors guide at the entrance for a list of departments and designers available on each floor, and if you need any tourist guidance or information, stop by the store's Official NYC Information Center. Food and drink options have also been improved, and include a trattoria with prosecco bar.

Nepenthes New York

307 W 38th Street, between Eighth & Ninth Avenues (1-212 643 9540, www.nepenthesny.com). Subway A, C, E, 1, 2, 3 to 34th Street-Penn Station. **Open** noon-7pm Mon-Sat; noon-5pm Sun. **Map** p98 B2 ⑤⑦

Well-dressed dudes with an eye on the Japanese style scene will already be familiar with this Tokyo fashion retailer. The narrow, ground-floor Garment District shop – its first US location – showcases expertly crafted urban-rustic menswear from house label Engineered Garments, such as plaid flannel shirts and workwear-inspired jackets. There is also a small selection of its women's line, FWK.

Sam Ash Music

NEW *333 W 34th Street, between Eighth & Ninth Avenues (1-212 719 2299, www.samashmusic.com). Subway A, C, E to 34th Street-Penn Station.* **Open** 10am-8pm Mon-Sat; 11am-7pm Sun. **Map** p98 B2 ⑤⑧

Established in Brooklyn in 1924, this musical instrument emporium moved from Times Square's now-silent 'music row' in 2013. The 30,000sq ft store offers new, vintage and custom guitars of all varieties, along with amps, DJ equipment, drums, keyboards, recording equipment, turntables and an array of sheet music.

Arts & leisure

Juvenex

5th Floor, 25 W 32nd Street, between Fifth Avenue & Broadway (1-646 733 1330, www.juvenexspa.com). Subway B, D, F, M, N, Q, R to 34th Street-Herald Square. **Open** 24hrs daily. **Map** p99 D3 ⑤⑨

This bustling Koreatown relaxation hub may be slightly rough around the edges (frayed towels, dingy sandals), but we embrace it for its bathhouse-meets-Epcot feel (igloo saunas, tiled 'soaking ponds' and a slatted bridge), and 24-hour availability (and it's women only between 8am and 5pm). A basic Purification Program – including soak and sauna, face, body and hair cleansing and a salt scrub – is great value at $115.

Madison Square Garden

Seventh Avenue, between 31st & 33rd Streets (1-212 465 6741, www.thegarden. com). Subway A, C, E, 1, 2, 3 to 34th Street-Penn Station. **Map** p98 C3 ⑥⓪

Some of music's biggest acts – Jay-Z, Lady Gaga, Rush – come out to play at the world's most famous basketball arena, home to the Knicks and also hockey's Rangers. Whether you'll be able to see them depends on your seat number or the quality of your binoculars. While it is undoubtedly a part of the fabric of New York, the storied venue is too vast for a rich concert experience, but it has been improved by a major renovation. The three-year revamp brought new seating and food from top New York City chefs, among other improvements, while respecting the Garden's history. The striking circular ceiling has been restored, while the north and south corridors on the entry level have been returned to their original appearance, including ads and posters from 1968.

Theater District & Hell's Kitchen

Times Square is the gateway to the Theater District, the zone located roughly between 41st Street and 53rd Street, from Sixth Avenue to Ninth Avenue. Thirty-eight of the opulent show houses here – those with more than 500 seats – are designated as being part of Broadway (plus the Vivian Beaumont Theater, uptown at Lincoln Center; p150). Just west of Times Square is Hell's Kitchen, which maintained a crime-ridden, tough veneer well into the 1970s. Today, it's emerging as the city's new queer mecca. Pricey Restaurant Row (46th Street, between Eighth & Ninth Avenues) caters to theatregoers, but Ninth Avenue itself, with its cornucopia of cheap ethnic eateries, is a better bet.

Sights & museums

Circle Line Cruises

Pier 83, W 42nd Street, at the Hudson River (1-212 563 3200, www.circle line42.com). Subway A, C, E to 42nd Street-Port Authority. **Tickets** $28-$39; $21-$34 reductions. **Map** p98 A1/p100 A4 ⑥①

Circle Line's famed three-hour guided circumnavigation of Manhattan Island is a fantastic way to get your bearings and see many of the city's sights as you pass under its iconic bridges. If you don't have time for the full round trip, try the semi-circle cruise of lower and midtown Manhattan, or the two-hour 'Liberty' tour that takes you around Downtown to the Brooklyn Bridge and back.

Intrepid Sea, Air & Space Museum

USS Intrepid, Pier 86, Twelfth Avenue & 46th Street (1-877 957 7447, www. intrepidmuseum.org). Subway A, C, E to 42nd Street-Port Authority, then M42

bus to Twelfth Avenue or 15min walk. **Open** *Apr-Oct* 10am-5pm Mon-Fri; 10am-6pm Sat, Sun. *Nov-Mar* 10am-5pm daily. **Admission** $24-$31; free-$27 reductions. **Map** p98 A1/p100 A4 ⑥②

Commissioned in 1943, this 27,000-ton, 898ft aircraft carrier survived torpedoes and kamikaze attacks in World War II, served during the Vietnam War and the Cuban Missile Crisis, and recovered two space capsules for NASA. It was decommissioned in 1974, then resurrected as an educational institution. On its flight deck and portside aircraft elevator are top-notch examples of American military might, including the US Navy F-14 Tomcat (as featured in *Top Gun*), an A-12 Blackbird spy plane and a fully restored Army AH-1G Cobra gunship helicopter. In summer 2011, the museum became home to the *Enterprise* (OV-101), the first Space Shuttle Orbiter (entry to the Space Shuttle Pavilion costs extra).

Times Square

From 42nd to 47th Streets, between Broadway & Seventh Avenue. Subway N, Q, R, S, 1, 2, 3, 7 to 42nd Street-Times Square; N, Q, R to 49th Street. **Map** p98 C1/p100 C4 ⑥③

Times Square's evolution from a traffic-choked fleshpot to a tourist-friendly theme park has accelerated in the past few years. Not only has the 'crossroads of the world' gained an elevated viewing platform atop the rebuilt TKTS discount booth, but pedestrian plazas have also been developed in the 'Bowtie' from 42nd to 47th Streets.

Originally called Longacre Square, Times Square was renamed after the *New York Times* moved here in the early 1900s. The first electrified billboard graced the district in 1904. The same year, the inaugural New Year's Eve party in Times Square doubled as the *Times*' housewarming party in its new HQ. Today, around a million people gather here to watch a mirrorball descend every 31 December. The paper

NEW YORK BY AREA

left the building only a decade after it arrived. However, it retained ownership of its old headquarters until the 1960s, and erected the world's first scrolling electric news 'zipper' in 1928. The read-out, now sponsored by Dow Jones, still trumpets the latest breaking stories.

TKTS

Father Duffy Square, Broadway & 47th Street (1-212 912 9770, www.tdf. org). Subway N, Q, R to 49th Street; N, Q, R, S, 1, 2, 3, 7 to 42nd Street-Times Square. **Open** *Evening tickets* 3-8pm Mon, Wed-Sun; 2-8pm Tue. *Same-day matinée tickets* 10am-2pm Wed, Sat; 11am-3pm Sun. **Map** p98 C1/p100 C4 **64**

At the architecturally striking TKTS base, you can get theatre and event tickets on the day of the performance for as much as 50% off face value. Although there's often a queue when it opens for business, this has usually dispersed one to two hours later, so it's worth trying your luck an hour or two before the show. While you're there, ascend the red structural glass steps behind the ticket windows for a great view of the surrounding light show.

Eating & drinking

Ardesia

510 W 52nd Street, between Tenth & Eleventh Avenues (1-212 247 9191, www.ardesia-ny.com). Subway C, E to 50th Street. **Open** 4pm-midnight Mon-Wed; 4pm-2am Thur, Fri; 2pm-2am Sat; 2pm-midnight Sun. **$. Wine bar.** **Map** p100 B3 **65**

Le Bernardin vet Mandy Oser's iron-and-marble gem, tucked away on a peaceful Hell's Kitchen street, offers a winning range of superior wines in a laid-back, relaxed setting. The 75-strong collection of international bottles is a smart balance of Old and New World options that pair beautifully with the varied selection of small plates. A grüner veltliner – a dry, oaky white from Austria – had

enough backbone to stand up to a duck *banh mi* layered with spicy duck pâté and Sriracha aioli. One for the serious oenophile.

Café Edison

Hotel Edison, 228 W 47th Street, between Broadway & Eighth Avenues (1-212 354 0368). Subway N, Q, R to 49th Street; 1 to 50th Street. **Open** 6am-9.30pm Mon-Sat; 6am-7.30pm Sun. No credit cards. **$. American.** **Map** p100 C4 **66**

This old-school, no-frills eaterie draws tourists, theatregoers, actors and just about everyone else in search of deli staples such as cheese blintzes and giant open-faced Reubens. The matzo ball soup is so restorative, you can almost feel it bolstering your immune system.

Don Antonio by Starita

309 W 50th Street, between Eighth & Ninth Avenues (1-646 719 1043, www.donantoniopizza.com). Subway C, E to 50th Street. **Open** 11.30am-3.30pm, 4.30-11pm Mon-Thur; 11.30am-3.30pm, 4.30pm-1am Fri, Sat; 11.30am-10.30pm Sun. **$$. Pizza.** **Map** p100 C3 **67**

Pizza aficionados have been busy colonising this collaboration between Kesté's (see p94) talented Roberto Caporuscio and his Naples mentor, Antonio Starita. Start with tasty bites like the *frittatine* (a deep-fried spaghetti cake oozing *prosciutto cotto* and béchamel sauce). The main event should be the habit-forming Montanara Starita, which gets a quick dip in the deep fryer before hitting the oven to develop its puffy, golden crust. Topped with tomato sauce, basil and intensely smoky buffalo mozzarella, it's a worthy addition to the pantheon of classic New York pies.

Gotham West Market

NEW *600 Eleventh Avenue, between 44th & 45th Streets (1-212 582 7940, www.gothamwestmarket.com). Subway A, C, E to 42nd Street-Port Authority.*

Open 7am-11pm Mon-Fri; 8am-11pm Sat, Sun. $-$$. **Eclectic/bar**. Map p100 B4 ⑬

In 2013, Hell's Kitchen welcomed this hip take on a food court, perfect for lunch or a quick pre-theatre bite. The 15,000sq ft retail-dining mecca is divided into eight culinary stalls – such as Blue Bottle Coffee and an outpost of gourmet grocer/cooking-supply store Brooklyn Kitchen – as well as a full-service NYC Velo bike shop. Dine-in or take-out options include Ivan Ramen Slurp Shop, where Tokyo noodle guru Ivan Orkin offers his famed shio, shoyu and chilli-sesame varieties (see p72); Little Chef, the salad-and-soup-focused offshoot of Caroline Fidanza's Saltie sandwich shop; El Colmado tapas bar from Seamus Mullen of Tertulia; and a cocktail-and-charcuterie outpost of the Cannibal (see p113). Seating is at chef's counters or communal tables.

Kashkaval Garden

852 Ninth Avenue, between 55th & 56th Streets (1-212 245 1758, www. kashkavalgarden.com). Subway C, E to 50th Street. **Open** 4pm-2am daily. **$$**. **Wine bar**. Map p100 B3 ⑭

This charming tapas and wine bar evokes fondue's peasant origins, with deep cast-iron pots and generous baskets of crusty bread. Steer clear of the bland and rubbery kashkaval (a Balkan sheep's-milk cheese) and order the gooey gruyère and truffle. Or choose from the selection of tangy Mediterranean spreads – roasted artichoke dip with breadcrumbs or beet houmous – and the impressive roster of skewers. End the meal with the crowd-pleasing chocolate torte.

Rum House

228 W 47th Street, between Seventh & Eighth Avenues (1-646 490 6924, www. edisonrumhouse.com). Subway N, Q, R to 49th Street. **Open** noon-4am daily. **Bar**. Map p100 C4 ⑰

In 2009, this rakish, 1970s-vintage piano bar in the Edison Hotel seemed destined to go the way of the Times Square peep show. But the team behind Tribeca mixology den Ward III has ushered in a second act, introducing some key upgrades (including serious cocktails) while maintaining the charmingly offbeat flavour of the place. Sip dark spirit-heavy tipples, such as a funky old-fashioned riff that showcases the rich, tropical complexity of Banks 5 Island Rum, while listening to a pianist or jazz trio most nights of the week.

Shopping

Amy's Bread

672 Ninth Avenue, between 46th & 47th Streets (1-212 977 2670, www. amysbread.com). Subway C, E to 50th Street; N, Q, R to 49th Street. **Open** 7.30am-10pm Mon, Tue; 7.30am-11pm Wed-Fri; 8am-11pm Sat; 8am-10pm Sun. Map p98 B1/p100 B4 ⑰

Whether you want sweet (double chocolate pecan Chubbie cookies) or savoury (hefty French sourdough boules), Amy's never disappoints. Breakfast and snacks such as the grilled cheese sandwich (made with New York State cheddar) are served in the on-site café.

Domus

413 W 44th Street, between Ninth & Tenth Avenues (1-212 581 8099, www.domusnewyork.com). Subway A, C, E to 42nd Street-Port Authority. **Open** noon-8pm Tue-Sat; noon-6pm Sun. Map p100 B4 ⑫

Scouring the globe for unusual design products is nothing new, but owners Luisa Cerutti and Nicki Lindheimer take the concept a step further; each year they visit a far-flung part of the world to forge links with and support co-operatives and individual craftspeople. The beautiful results, such as vivid baskets woven from telephone wire by South African Zulu tribespeople, reflect a fine attention to detail and a sense of place. It's a great spot to find reasonably priced home goods and gifts, from Tunisian bath towels to Italian throws.

Fine and Dandy

445 W 49th Street, between Ninth & Tenth Avenues (1-212 247 4847, www. fineanddandyshop.com). Subway C, E to 50th Street. **Open** noon-8pm Mon-Sat; 1-8pm Sun. **Map** p100 B4 ⓭

Following the success of several pop-ups around the city, owner Matt Fox opened his first permanent location. The accessories-only shop – decked out in flourishes such as collegiate trophies and ironing boards repurposed as tables – is a prime location for the modern gent to score of-the-moment retro accoutrements like bow ties, suspenders (braces) and spats. House-label printed ties are hung in propped-open vintage trunks, while patterned socks are displayed in old briefcases.

Nightlife

54 Below

254 W 54th Street, between Broadway & Eighth Avenues (1-646 476 3551, www.54below.com). Subway B, D, E to Seventh Avenue; C, E, 1 to 50th Street; R to 57th Street. **Map** p100 C3 ⓮

A team of Broadway producers is behind this swank supper club in the bowels of the legendary Studio 54 space. The schedule is dominated by big Broadway talent – such as Patti LuPone, Ben Vereen and Sherie Rene Scott – but there's also room for edgier talents like Justin Vivian Bond and Jackie Hoffman.

Atlas Social Club

NEW *753 Ninth Avenue, between 50th & 51st Streets (1-212 262 8527, www. atlassocialclub.com). Subway C, E to 50th Street.* **Open** 4pm-4am daily. **Map** p100 B3 ⓯

This straight-friendly gay drinkery, designed to look like a cross between an old-school athletic club and a speakeasy, is one of the more relaxed options on the HK strip – at least when it's not packed to the gills, which it can be at weekends. Be sure to check out the bathrooms, which are brightly papered with images from vintage beefcake and sports magazines.

Birdland

315 W 44th Street, between Eighth & Ninth Avenues (1-212 581 3080, www. birdlandjazz.com). Subway A, C, E to 42nd Street-Port Authority. **Map** p98 B1/ p100 C4 ⓰

The flagship venue for Midtown's jazz resurgence, Birdland takes its place among the neon lights of Times Square seriously. That means it's a haven for great jazz musicians (Joe Lovano, Kurt Elling) as well as performers like John Pizzarelli and Aaron Neville. The club is also notable for its roster of bands-in-residence. Sundays belong to the Arturo O'Farrill Afro-Cuban Jazz Orchestra.

Carolines on Broadway

1626 Broadway, between 49th & 50th Streets (1-212 757 4100, www.carolines. com). Subway N, Q, R to 49th Street; 1 to 50th Street. **Map** p100 C3 ⓱

This New York City institution's long-term relationships with national comedy headliners, sitcom stars and cable-special pros ensure that its stage always features marquee names – including Emmy-nominated actor Rob Schneider and *Curb Your Enthusiasm* regular Richard Lewis. The majority of the bookings lean towards mainstream appetites, but the club also makes time for darker fare such as Louis CK.

Fairytail Lounge

500 W 48th Street, between Tenth & Eleventh Avenues (1-646 684 3897, www.facebook.com/fairytaillounge). Subway C, E to 50th Street. **Open** 5pm-2am Mon, Tue; 5pm-3am Thur-Sun. **Map** p100 B4 ⓲

An easy-to-miss entrance-way belies the pseudo-Victorian, psychedelic enchanted forest interior to this gay

Gotham West Market p118

watering hole. Whether you find a mellow happy-hour crowd or a hyper dance party, the vibe is more arty than you'd expect in pretty-boy central.

Flaming Saddles

793 Ninth Avenue, at W 53rd Street (1-212 713 0481, www.flamingsaddles. com). Subway C, E to 50th Street. **Open** 3pm-4am Mon-Fri; noon-4am Sat, Sun. No credit cards. **Map** p100 B3 ⑦

City guys can party honky-tonk-style at this country and western gay bar. The place is outfitted to look like a Wild West bordello, complete with red velvet drapes, antler sconces and rococo wallpaper. Dancing bartenders in cowboy boots add to the raucous vibe.

Pacha

618 W 46th Street, between Eleventh & Twelfth Avenues (1-212 209 7500, www.pachanyc.com). Subway C, E to 50th Street. **Open** 10pm-6am Fri; 10pm-8am Sat. **Map** p98 A1/p100 A4 ⑳

The worldwide glam-club chain Pacha hit the US market in 2005 with this swanky joint helmed by superstar spinner Erick Morillo. The spot attracts heavyweights ranging from local hero Danny Tenaglia to international crowd-pleasers such as Fedde Le Grande and Benny Benassi. As with most big clubs, it pays to check the line-up in advance if you're into underground beats.

Arts & leisure

Avenue Q

New World Stages, 340 W 50th Street, between Eighth & Ninth Avenues (Telecharge 1-212 239 6200, www. avenueq.com). Subway C, E, 1 to 50th Street. **Map** p100 C3 ㉛

After many years, which have included a Broadway run followed by a return to its Off Broadway roots, the sassy and clever puppet musical doesn't show its age. Robert Lopez and Jeff Marx's deft *Sesame Street*-esque novelty tunes about porn and racism

still earn their laughs, and *Avenue Q* remains a sly and winning piece of metamusical tomfoolery.

The Book of Mormon

Eugene O'Neill Theatre, 230 W 49th Street, between Broadway & Eighth Avenue (Telecharge 1-212 239 6200, www.bookofmormonbroadway.com). Subway C, E to 50th Street; N, Q, R, S, 1, 2, 3, 7 to 42nd Street-Times Square; N, R to 49th Street. **Map** p100 C4 ㉜

This gleefully obscene and subversive satire is one of the funniest shows to grace the Great White Way since *The Producers* and *Urinetown*. Writers Trey Parker and Matt Stone of *South Park*, along with composer Robert Lopez (*Avenue Q*), find the perfect blend of sweet and nasty for this tale of mismatched Mormon proselytisers in Uganda.

Carnegie Hall

154 W 57th Street, at Seventh Avenue (1-212 247 7800, www.carnegiehall.org). Subway N, Q, R to 57th Street. **Map** p100 C3 ㉝

Artistic director Clive Gillinson continues to put his stamp on Carnegie Hall. The stars – both soloists and orchestras – still shine brightly inside this renowned concert hall in the Isaac Stern Auditorium. But it's the spunky upstart Zankel Hall that has generated the most buzz, offering an eclectic mix of classical, contemporary, jazz, pop and world music. Next door, the Weill Recital Hall hosts intimate concerts and chamber music programmes.

Jersey Boys

August Wilson Theatre, 245 W 52nd Street, between Broadway & Eighth Avenue (Telecharge 1-212 239 6200, www.jerseyboysinfo.com/broadway). Subway C, E, 1 to 50th Street. **Map** p100 C3 ㉞

The Broadway musical finally does right by the jukebox with this nostalgic behind-the-music tale, presenting the Four Seasons' infectiously energetic

1960s tunes (including 'Walk Like a Man' and 'Big Girls Don't Cry') as they were intended to be performed. Sleek direction by Des McAnuff ensures that Marshall Brickman and Rick Elice's script feels canny instead of canned.

Kinky Boots

Al Hirschfeld Theatre, 302 W 45th Street, between Eighth & Ninth Avenues (Telecharge 1-212 239 6200, www. kinkybootsthemusical.com). Subway A, C, E to 42nd Street-Port Authority; N, Q, R, S, 1, 2, 3, 7 to 42nd Street-Times Square. **Map** p100 C4 ⑧⑤

Harvey Fierstein and Cyndi Lauper's fizzy crowd-pleaser, in which a sassy-dignified drag queen kicks an English shoe factory into gear, feels familiar at every step. But it has been manufactured with solid craftsmanship and care (Lauper is a musical-theatre natural), and is boosted by a heart-strong cast. The overall effect of Kinky Boots is nigh irresistible.

New York City Center

131 W 55th Street, between Sixth & Seventh Avenues (1-212 581 7907, www.nycitycenter.org). Subway B, D, E to Seventh Avenue; F, N, Q, R to 57th Street. **Map** p100 C3 ⑧⑥

Before Lincoln Center changed the city's cultural geography, this was the home of American Ballet Theatre, the Joffrey Ballet and the New York City Ballet. City Center's lavish decor is golden – as are the companies that pass through here. Regular events include Alvin Ailey American Dance Theater in December and the popular Fall for Dance Festival, in autumn, which features mixed bills for just $15.

Pershing Square Signature Center

480 W 42nd Street, at Tenth Avenue (1-212 244 7529, www.signaturetheatre. org). Subway A, C, E to 42nd Street-Port Authority. **Map** p100 B4 ⑧⑦

Founded in 1991 by James Houghton, the award-winning Signature Theatre Company focuses on exploring and celebrating playwrights in depth, with whole seasons devoted to works by individual living writers. Over the past years, the company has delved into the oeuvres of August Wilson, John Guare, Horton Foote and many more. Special programmes are designed to keep prices low. In 2012 the troupe expanded hugely into a new home – a theatre complex designed by Frank Gehry, with three major spaces and ambitious long-term commission programmes, cementing it as one of the city's key cultural institutions.

Playwrights Horizons

416 W 42nd Street, between Ninth & Tenth Avenues (1-212 564 1235, Ticket Central 1-212 279 4200, www. playwrightshorizons.org). Subway A, C, E to 42nd Street-Port Authority. **Map** p100 B4 ⑧⑧

More than 300 important contemporary plays have had their première here, including dramas (*Driving Miss Daisy*, *The Heidi Chronicles*) and musicals (Stephen Sondheim's *Assassins* and *Sunday in the Park with George*). More recent seasons have included new works by Edward Albee and Craig Lucas, as well as Bruce Norris's Pulitzer Prize-winning *Clybourne Park*.

Ziegfeld Theater

141 W 54th Street, between Sixth & Seventh Avenues (1-212 307 1862, www. bowtiecinemas.com). Subway B, D, E to Seventh Avenue; F, N, Q, R to 57th Street; 1 to 50th Street. **Map** p100 C3 ⑧⑨

Despite its Jazz Age moniker, this movie palace actually opened in 1969; since then, its red carpets and gilded staircases have served as a last stand against stadium-seated sameness. Temporarily endangered but saved by Bow Tie Cinemas, the city's largest single-screen theatre seats 1,162 citizens under chandeliers, harking back to when going to motion pictures was an aspirational experience.

NEW YORK BY AREA

Fifth Avenue & around

The stretch of Fifth Avenue between Rockefeller Center and Central Park South showcases retail palaces bearing names that were famous long before the concept of branding was developed. Bracketed by Saks Fifth Avenue (49th to 50th Streets) and Bergdorf Goodman (57th to 58th Streets), tenants include Gucci, Prada and Tiffany & Co – and the parade of A-list brand names continues east along 57th Street. A number of landmarks and first-rate museums are on, or in the vicinity of, the strip.

Sights & museums

Empire State Building

350 Fifth Avenue, between 33rd & 34th Streets (1-212 736 3100, www. esbnyc.com). Subway B, D, F, M, N, Q, R to 34th Street-Herald Square. **Open** 8am-2am daily (last elevator 1.15am). **Admission** *86th floor* $29; free-$26 reductions. *102nd floor* $17 extra (see website for express ticket options). **Map** p99 D2 ⑩

Financed by General Motors executive John J Raskob at the height of New York's skyscraper race, the Empire State sprang up in a mere 14 months, weeks ahead of schedule and $5 million under budget. Since its opening in 1931, it's been immortalised in countless photos and films, from the original *King Kong* to *Sleepless in Seattle*. Following the destruction of the World Trade Center in 2001, the 1,250ft tower resumed its title as New York's tallest building but has since been overtaken by 1 World Trade Center. The nocturnal colour scheme of the tower lights – recently upgraded to flashy LEDs – often honours holidays, charities or special events. The enclosed observatory on the 102nd floor is the city's highest lookout point, but the panoramic deck on the 86th floor, 1,050ft above the street, is roomier. From here,

you can enjoy views of all five boroughs and five neighbouring states too (when the skies are clear).

International Center of Photography

1133 Sixth Avenue, at 43rd Street (1-212 857 0000, www.icp.org). Subway B, D, F, M to 42nd Street-Bryant Park; N, Q, R, S, 1, 2, 3 to 42nd Street-Times Square; 7 to Fifth Avenue. **Open** 10am-6pm Tue-Thur, Sat, Sun; 10am-8pm Fri. **Admission** $14; free-$10 reductions. Pay what you wish 5-8pm Fri. **Map** p101 D4 ㉛

Since 1974, the ICP has served as a pre-eminent library, school and museum devoted to the photographic image. Photojournalism remains a vital facet of the centre's programming, which also includes contemporary photos and video. Recent shows in the two-floor exhibition space have focused on the work of Elliott Erwitt, Richard Avedon and Lewis Hine.

Museum of Modern Art (MoMA)

11 W 53rd Street, between Fifth & Sixth Avenues (1-212 708 9400, www.moma. org). Subway E, M to Fifth Avenue-53rd Street. **Open** 10.30am-5.30pm Mon-Thur, Sat, Sun; 10.30am-8pm Fri; 10.30am-8pm 1st Thur of the month & every Thur in July, Aug. **Admission** (incl admission to film programmes) $25; free-$18 reductions; free 4-8pm Fri. **Map** p101 D3 ㉜

Following a two-year redesign by Japanese architect Yoshio Taniguchi, MoMA reopened in 2004 with almost double the space to display some of the world's most impressive artworks from the 19th to the 21st centuries. The museum's permanent collection is divided into seven curatorial departments: Architecture and Design; Drawings; Film; Media and Performance Art; Painting and Sculpture; Photography; and Prints and Illustrated Books. Among the collection's highlights are Picasso's

Les Demoiselles d'Avignon, Dalí's *The Persistence of Memory* and Van Gogh's *The Starry Night* as well as masterpieces by Giacometti, Hopper, Matisse, Monet, O'Keefe, Pollock, Rothko, Warhol and others. Outside the building, the Philip Johnson-designed Abby Aldrich Rockefeller Sculpture Garden contains works by Calder, Rodin and Moore. There's also a destination restaurant: the Modern, which overlooks the garden.

New York Public Library

Fifth Avenue, at 42nd Street (1-917 275 6975, www.nypl.org). Subway B, D, F, M to 42nd Street-Bryant Park; 7 to Fifth Avenue. **Open** *Sept-June* 10am-6pm Mon, Thur-Sat; 10am-8pm Tue, Wed; 1-5pm Sun. *July, Aug* 10am-6pm Mon, Thur-Sat; 10am-8pm Tue, Wed (see website for gallery hours). **Admission** free. **Map** p99 D1/p101 D5 ❸❸

Guarded by the marble lions Patience and Fortitude, this austere Beaux Arts edifice, designed by Carrère and Hastings, was completed in 1911. The building was renamed in honour of philanthropist Stephen A Schwarzman in 2008, but Gothamites still know it as the New York Public Library, although the citywide library system consists of 92 locations. Free hour-long tours (11am, 2pm Mon-Sat; 2pm Sun, except July & Aug) take in the Rose Main Reading Room on the third floor, which at 297ft long and 78ft wide is almost the size of a football field. Specialist departments include the Map Division, containing some 431,000 maps and 16,000 atlases, and the Rare Books Division boasting Walt Whitman's personal copies of the first (1855) and third (1860) editions of *Leaves of Grass*. The library also stages major exhibitions and high-profile events.

Rockefeller Center

From 48th to 51st Streets, between Fifth & Sixth Avenues (tours & Top of the Rock 1-212 698 2000, NBC Studio Tours 1-212 664 3700, www.rockefellercenter.
com). Subway B, D, F, M to 47th-50th Streets-Rockefeller Center. **Open** *Observation deck* 8am-midnight daily (last elevator 11pm). **Admission** *Rockefeller Center tours* $17 (under-6s not admitted). *Observation deck* $29; free-$27 reductions. *NBC Studio tours* $24; $21 reductions (under-6s not admitted). **Map** p101 D3/D4 ❾❹

Constructed under the aegis of industrialist John D Rockefeller in the 1930s, this art deco city-within-a-city is inhabited by NBC, Simon & Schuster, McGraw-Hill and other media giants, as well as Radio City Music Hall, Christie's auction house, and an underground shopping arcade. Guided tours of the entire complex are available daily, and there's a separate NBC Studio tour too.

The buildings and grounds are embellished with works by several well-known artists; look out for Isamu Noguchi's stainless-steel relief, *News*, above the entrance to 50 Rockefeller Plaza, and José Maria Sert's mural *American Progress* in the lobby of 30 Rockefeller Plaza. The most breathtaking sights are those seen from the 70th-floor Top of the Rock observation deck. In winter, the Plaza's courtyard transforms into an ice-skating rink.

St Patrick's Cathedral

Fifth Avenue, between 50th & 51st Streets (1-212 753 2261, www.saint patrickscathedral.org). Subway B, D, F, M to 47th-50th Streets-Rockefeller Center; E, M to Fifth Avenue-53rd Street. **Open** 6.30am-8.45pm daily. **Admission** free. **Map** p101 D3 ❾❺

The largest Catholic church in the US, St Patrick's was built 1858-79. The Gothic-style façade features intricate white-marble spires, but just as impressive is the interior, including the Louis Tiffany-designed altar, the solid bronze baldachin, and rose window by stained-glass master Charles Connick. Note that due to crucial restoration work, part of the exterior may be under scaffolding.

Rockefeller Center p125

Eating & drinking

Bar Room at the Modern

9 W 53rd Street, between Fifth & Sixth Avenues (1-212 333 1220, www.themodernnyc.com). Subway E, M to Fifth Avenue-53rd Street. **Open** 11.30am-3pm, 5-10.30pm Mon-Sat; 11.30am-3pm, 5-9.30pm Sun. **$$**. **American creative**. Map p101 D3 **96**

Those who can't afford to drop a pay cheque at award-winning chef Gabriel Kreuther's formal MoMA dining room, the Modern, can still dine in the equally stunning and less pricey bar at the front. The Alsatian-inspired menu is constructed of around 30 small and medium-sized plates that can be mixed and shared. Desserts come courtesy of pastry chef Marc Aumont, and the wine list is extensive to say the least.

Benoit

60 W 55th Street, between Fifth & Sixth Avenues (1-646 943 7373, www. benoitny.com). Subway E, M to Fifth Avenue-53rd Street; F to 57th Street. **Open** 11.45am-3pm, 5.30-11pm Mon-Sat; 11.30am-3.30pm, 5.30-11pm Sun. **$$$**. **French**. Map p101 D3 **97**

Alain Ducasse's classic brasserie attempts to reclaim 55th Street's former Francophile row. Come for successful, seasonality-snubbing relics like a cassoulet packed with hearty meat (pork loin, garlic sausage, duck confit) under a canopy of white beans. At the Sunday-only brunch, the dessert bar (per item $6, all-you-can-eat $18) offers a dozen seasonal pastries and tarts.

Betony

NEW *41 W 57th Street, between Fifth & Sixth Avenues (1-212 465 2400, www.betony-nyc.com). Subway F, N, Q, R to 57th Street.* **Open** noon-2pm, 5.30-10.45pm Mon-Fri; 5.30-10.45pm Sat, Sun. **$$$**. **American creative**. Map p101 D3 **98**

Eleven Madison Park alumni Bryce Shuman and Eamon Rockey have created a rare treat: a serious New American restaurant that doesn't take itself too seriously. Hyper-professional service is softened with a heaped dose of humanity, and the fun-loving à la carte menu includes stellar riffs on crunchy fried pickles and toasty tuna melts. Dishes such as seared foie gras plugged with smoked ham hock and draped with crisp, vinegar-twanged kale combine upmarket cachet with down-home comforts.

Shopping

Bergdorf Goodman

754 Fifth Avenue, between 57th & 58th Streets (1-212 753 7300, www. bergdorfgoodman.com). Subway E, M to Fifth Avenue-53rd Street; N, Q, R to Fifth Avenue-59th Street. **Open** 10am-8pm Mon-Fri; 10am-7pm Sat; 11am-6pm Sun. Map p101 D3 **99**

Synonymous with understated luxury, Bergdorf's is known for its designer clothes (the fifth floor is dedicated to younger, trend-driven labels) and accessories. For something more unusual, seek out Kentshire's wonderful cache of vintage jewellery on the seventh floor. Descend to the basement for the wide-ranging beauty department. The men's store is across the street at 745 Fifth Avenue.

FAO Schwarz

767 Fifth Avenue, at 58th Street (1-212 644 9400, www.fao.com). Subway N, Q, R to Fifth Avenue-59th Street; 4, 5, 6 to Lexington Avenue-59th Street. **Open** 10am-8pm Mon-Thur, Sun; 10am-9pm Fri, Sat. Map p101 D2 **100**

Although it's now owned by the ubiquitous Toys 'R' Us company, this three-storey emporium is still the ultimate NYC toy box. Most people head straight to the 22ft-long floor piano that Tom Hanks famously tinkled in Penny Marshall's endearing *Big*. Children will marvel at the giant stuffed animals, the detailed and imaginative Lego figures and the revolving Barbie fashion catwalk.

NEW YORK BY AREA

Henri Bendel

712 Fifth Avenue, at 56th Street (1-212 247 1100, www.henribendel.com). Subway E, M to Fifth Avenue-53rd Street; N, Q, R to Fifth Avenue-59th Street. **Open** 10am-8pm Mon-Sat; noon-7pm Sun. **Map** p101 D3 ⑩

While Bendel's merchandise (a mix of jewellery, accessories, cosmetics and fragrances) is comparable to that of other upscale stores, it somehow seems more desirable when viewed in its opulent premises, a conglomeration of three 19th-century townhouses – and those darling brown-and-white striped shopping bags don't hurt, either. If you find you haven't a thing to wear while you're in NYC, but don't want to add to your luggage, you can select designer duds and accessories in the on-site showroom of popular e-tailer Rent the Runway. Bendel's is also the home of celebrity hairdresser Frédéric Fekkai's flagship salon.

Nightlife

Radio City Music Hall

1260 Sixth Avenue, at 50th Street (1-212 247 4777, www.radiocity.com). Subway B, D, F, M to 47th-50th Streets Rockefeller Center. **Map** p101 D3 ⑩

Few rooms scream 'New York City!' more than this gilded hall, which in recent years has drawn Leonard Cohen, Drake and Bon Iver as headliners. The greatest challenge for any performer is to not be upstaged by the awe-inspiring art deco surroundings, although those same surroundings lend historic heft to even the flimsiest showing. Bookings are all over the map – expect everything from seasonal staples like resident dance troupe the Rockettes to lectures with the Dalai Lama.

Arts & leisure

Caudalie Vinothérapie Spa

4th Floor, 1 W 58th Street, at Fifth Avenue (1-212 265 3182, www.caudalie-usa.com). Subway N, Q, R to Fifth
Avenue-59th Street. **Open** 10am-7pm Tue-Sat; 10am-5pm Sun. **Map** p101 D2 ⑩

The first Vinothérapie outpost in the US, this original spa harnesses the antioxidant power of grapes and vine leaves. The 8,000sq ft facility in the Plaza offers such treatments as a Red Vine bath ($75) in one of its cherrywood 'barrel' tubs.

Midtown East

Shopping, dining and entertainment options wane east of Fifth Avenue in the 40s and 50s. However, this area is home to a number of landmarks. What the area lacks in street-level attractions it makes up for with an array of world-class architecture.

Sights & museums

Chrysler Building

405 Lexington Avenue, between 42nd & 43rd Streets. Subway S, 4, 5, 6, 7 to 42nd Street-Grand Central. **Map** p99 E1/p101 E4 ⑩

Completed in 1930 by architect William Van Alen, the gleaming 77-storey Chrysler Building is a pinnacle of art deco architecture, paying homage to the automobile industry with vast radiator-cap eagles in lieu of traditional gargoyles and a brickwork relief sculpture of racing cars complete with chrome hubcaps. During the famed three-way race for New York's tallest building, a needle-sharp stainless-steel spire was added to the blueprint to make it taller than 40 Wall Street, under construction at the same time – but less than a year after its completion the 1,046ft Chrysler Building was outdone by the Empire State Building.

Grand Central Terminal

From 42nd to 44th Streets, between Lexington & Vanderbilt Avenues (audio tours 1-917 566 0008, www.grandcentralterminal.com). Subway

S, 4, 5, 6, 7 to 42nd Street-Grand Central.
Map p99 D1/p101 D4 **106**
Each day, the world's largest rail terminal sees more than 750,000 people shuffle through its Beaux Arts threshold. Designed by Warren & Wetmore and Reed & Stern, the gorgeous transportation hub opened in 1913 with lashings of Botticino marble and staircases modelled after those of the Paris opera house. After midcentury decline, the terminal underwent extensive restoration between 1996 and 1998 and is now a destination in itself, with shopping and dining options, including the Campbell Apartment (1-212 953 0409), the Grand Central Oyster Bar & Restaurant (see right), and a sprawling Apple Store (1-212 284 1800) on the East Balcony. Check the website for information about self-guided audio tours ($8; $6-$7 reductions).

United Nations Headquarters

Temporary visitors' entrance: First Avenue, at 47th Street (tours 1-212 963 8687, http://visit.un.org). Subway S, 4, 5, 6, 7 to 42nd Street-Grand Central.
Tours (must be booked in advance online) 10.15am-4.15pm Mon-Fri.
Admission $18; $9-$11 reductions (under-5s not admitted). **Map** p99 F1/p101 F4 **106**
The United Nations is undergoing extensive renovations that have left the Secretariat building, designed by Le Corbusier, gleaming – though that structure is off-limits to the public. The hour-long public tours discuss the history and role of the UN, and visit the Security Council Chamber (when not in session) in the newly renovated Conference Building. The General Assembly Hall is currently closed for building work until autumn 2014 or later. Although some artworks and objects given by member nations are not on public display during this period, it's now possible to see other pieces for the first time in years; among

them Norman Rockwell's mosaic *The Golden Rule*, on the third floor of the Conference Building.

Eating & drinking

Grand Central Oyster Bar & Restaurant

Grand Central Terminal, Lower Concourse, 42nd Street, at Park Avenue (1-212 490 6650, www.oysterbarny. com). Subway S, 4, 5, 6, 7 to 42nd Street-Grand Central. **Open** 11.30am-9.30pm Mon-Sat. **$$. Seafood. Map** p99 D1/p101 D4 **107**
The legendary Grand Central Oyster Bar has been a fixture of the gorgeous hub that shares its name since 1913. The surly countermen at the mile-long bar (the best seats in the house) are part of the charm. Avoid the more complicated fish concoctions and play it safe with a reliably awe-inspiring platter of iced, just-shucked oysters (there can be a whopping 30 varieties to choose from, including many from nearby Long Island).

Monkey Bar

60 E 54th Street, between Madison & Park Avenues (1-212 288 1010, www. monkeybarnewyork.com). Subway E, M to Lexington Avenue-53rd Street; 6 to 51st Street. **Open** 11.30am-2.30pm, 5.30-10pm Mon-Fri; 5.30-10pm Sat. **$$$. American. Map** p101 D3 **108**
After the repeal of Prohibition in 1933, this one-time piano bar in the swank Hotel Elysée (see p180) became a boozy clubhouse for the glitzy artistic figures of the age, among them Dorothy Parker and Tennessee Williams. The Monkey Bar is now owned by publishing titan Graydon Carter, who has brought new buzz to the historic space. Perched at the bar with a pitch-perfect glass of Gonet-Medeville champagne or ensconced in a booth with a plate of fettuccine carbonara with bacon lardons, you'll find yourself seduced by that rare alchemy of old New York luxury and new-school flair.

NEW YORK BY AREA

Central Park

Uptown

In the 19th century, the area above 59th Street was a bucolic getaway for locals living at the southern tip of the island. Today, much of this locale maintains an air of serenity, thanks largely to Central Park and the presence of a number of New York's premier cultural institutions.

Central Park

In 1858, the newly formed Central Park Commission chose landscape designer Frederick Law Olmsted and architect Calvert Vaux to turn a vast tract of rocky swampland into a rambling oasis of lush greenery. When their vision of an urban 'greensward' was realised in 1873, Central Park became the first man-made public park in the US.

As well as a wide variety of landscapes, from open meadows to woodland, the park offers numerous family-friendly attractions and activities, from the **Central Park**

Zoo (830 Fifth Avenue, between 63rd & 66th Streets, 1-212 439 6500, www.centralparkzoo.org; $12, free-$9 reductions) to marionette shows in the quaint **Swedish Cottage** (west side, at 81st Street). Stop by the visitor centre in the 1870 Gothic Revival **Dairy** (midpark at 65th Street, 1-212 794 6564, www.centralparknyc.org) for information on activities and events. In winter, ice-skaters lace up at the picturesque **Trump Wollman Rink** (midpark at 62nd Street, 1-212 439 6900, www.wollmanskatingrink. com). A short stroll to about 64th Street brings you to the **carousel** (open Apr-Oct), a bargain at $3 a ride.

Come summer, sunbathers, picnickers and Frisbee players fill the **Sheep Meadow**, the designated quiet zone that begins at 66th Street (sheep did indeed graze here until 1934). To the east, between 66th and 72nd Streets, is the **Mall**, an elm-lined promenade that attracts street performers and in-line skaters. One of the most popular meeting places in the park is north of the Mall: the grand **Bethesda Fountain & Terrace**, near the midpoint of the 72nd Street Transverse Road. *Angel of the Waters*, the sculpture in the centre of the fountain, was created by Emma Stebbins, the first woman to be granted a major public art commission in New York.

To the west of the fountain, near the W 72nd Street entrance, sits **Strawberry Fields**, a section of the park that memorialises John Lennon, who lived in the nearby Dakota Building. It features a mosaic of the word 'imagine' and more than 160 species of flowers and plants from all over the world. Just north of the Bethesda Fountain is the **Loeb Boathouse** (midpark, between 74th & 75th Streets, 1-212 517 2233, www.thecentralparkboathouse.com). From here, you can take a rowing boat or a gondola out on the lake, which is crossed by the elegant Bow Bridge. The Loeb houses a restaurant and bar (closed dinner Nov-mid Apr), and lake views make it a lovely place for brunch or drinks.

Further north, the picturesque **Belvedere Castle**, a restored Victorian folly, sits atop the park's second-highest peak. Besides offering excellent views, it also houses the Henry Luce Nature Observatory. The nearby **Delacorte Theater** hosts Shakespeare in the Park (see p35). And further north still sits the **Great Lawn** (midpark, between 79th & 85th Streets), a sprawling stretch of grass that serves as sports fields, a rallying point for political protests, and a summer concert spot. East of the Great Lawn, behind the **Metropolitan Museum of Art** (see p137), is the **Obelisk**, a 69-foot hieroglyphics-covered granite monument dating from around 1500 BC, which was given to the US by the Khedive of Egypt in 1881.

In the mid 1990s, the **Jacqueline Kennedy Onassis Reservoir** (midpark, between 85th & 96th Streets) was renamed in honour of the late first lady, who used to jog around it. From the path, admire the classic apartment buildings and skyscrapers surrounding the park.

In the northern section of the park, the exquisite **Conservatory Garden** (entrance on Fifth Avenue, at 105th Street) comprises formal gardens inspired by English, French and Italian styles.

Upper East Side

Although Manhattan's super-rich now live all over town, the air of old money is most pronounced on the Upper East Side. Along Fifth, Madison and Park Avenues, stately mansions and townhouses rub shoulders with deluxe apartment buildings guarded by uniformed doormen. Fifth Avenue from 82nd to 105th Streets is known as Museum Mile because it's lined with more than half a dozen celebrated institutions.

Sights & museums

Cooper Hewitt, Smithsonian Design Museum

2 E 91st Street, at Fifth Avenue (1-212 849 8400, www.cooperhewitt.org). Subway 4, 5, 6 to 86th Street. **Open** (reopening December 2014) 10am-6pm Mon-Fri, Sun; 10am-9pm Sat. **Admission** $18; free-$12 reductions; pay what you wish 6-9pm Sat. **Map** p133 D2 ❶

The museum began as a collection created for students of the Cooper Union for the Advancement of Science and Art by the Hewitt sisters – grand-daughters of the institution's founder, Peter Cooper – and opened to the public in 1897. Part of the Smithsonian since the 1960s, it is the only museum in the US solely dedicated to historic and contemporary design. In 1976, it took up residence

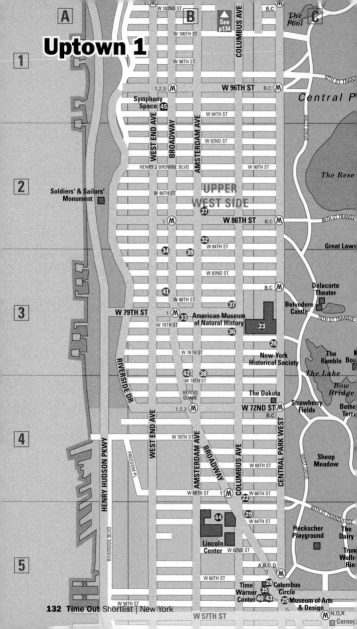

Uptown 1

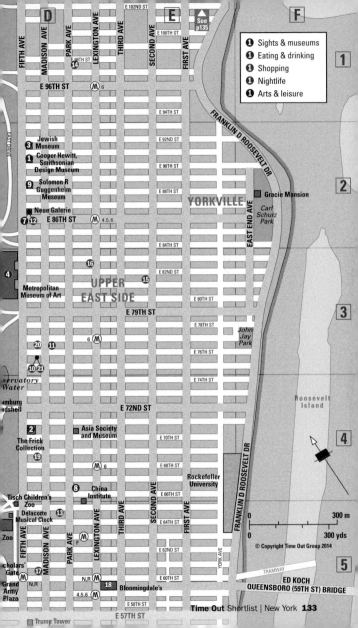

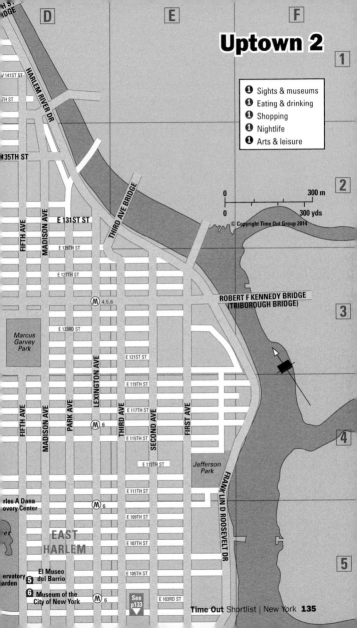

Uptown 2

- **1** Sights & museums
- **1** Eating & drinking
- **1** Shopping
- **1** Nightlife
- **1** Arts & leisure

© Copyright Time Out Group 2014

D **E** **F**

W 141ST ST

TH ST

135TH ST

HARLEM RIVER DR

FIFTH AVE
MADISON AVE

E 131ST ST

E 129TH ST

E 127TH ST

THIRD AVE BRIDGE

ROBERT F KENNEDY BRIDGE
(TRIBOROUGH BRIDGE)

Ⓜ 4,5,6

E 123RD ST

Marcus
Garvey
Park

E 121ST ST

E 119TH ST

LEXINGTON AVE

E 117TH ST

FIFTH AVE
MADISON AVE
PARK AVE
THIRD AVE
SECOND AVE
FIRST AVE

Ⓜ 6

E 115TH ST

E 113TH ST

Jefferson
Park

E 111TH ST

rles A Dana
overy Center

Ⓜ 6

E 109TH ST

FRANKLIN D ROOSEVELT DR

er

E 107TH ST

**EAST
HARLEM**

E 105TH ST

ervatory
arden

5 El Museo
del Barrio

6 Museum of the
City of New York

Ⓜ 6

E 103RD ST

See
p133 ▼

Grand designs

NYC's premier design institution debuts a dramatic restoration.

Home to 217,000 objects, the **Cooper Hewitt, Smithsonian Design Museum** (see p131) occupies the Carnegie mansion – itself an example of ground-breaking design. The 64-room Georgian-style pile was among the first private homes to have an elevator, central heating and even a precursor of air-conditioning. Historic spaces such as the Teak Room, with its intricate wall panelling and cabinets, have been painstakingly restored, and the addition of a 6,000-square-foot gallery on the third floor – formerly occupied by the National Design Library, now housed in an adjacent building – provides more room for rotating exhibitions.

Architects Diller Scofidio + Renfro have created contemporary, interactive displays that respect the period surroundings. Each visitor receives a high-tech pen, allowing them to 'collect' objects and partake in the design process. The entire second floor now showcases objects from the permanent collection, with wall coverings, textiles, product design, decorative arts, drawings, prints and graphic design, organised by theme. The varied holdings include oil sketches by Hudson River School painter Frederic Church, which reflect the museum's origins as a 'visual library' for Cooper Union students that included preparatory drawings as well as completed works. 'The real strength of our collection is 19th century,' says curatorial director Cara McCarty, 'although in recent years we've been making a concerted effort to add to the contemporary collection.'

You'll also see a 1996 concept design for the Air Jordan XIII sneaker, by the shoe's original designer, Tinker Hatfield, which emphasises the Cooper Hewitt's commitment to collecting drawings and prototypes that illuminate the design process. The reimagined museum includes a Models & Prototypes Gallery, a hands-on Process Lab and a digital Immersion Room that lets you fully experience the institution's impressive collection of wallcoverings – the largest in the US.

in the former home of steel magnate Andrew Carnegie. December 2014 sees the completion of a three-year renovation and expansion project, which has increased the exhibition space by 60%. See box p136.

Frick Collection

1 E 70th Street, between Fifth & Madison Avenues (1-212 288 0700, www.frick.org).
Subway 6 to 68th Street-Hunter College.
Open 10am-6pm Tue-Sat; 11am-5pm Sun. **Admission** $20; $10-$15 reductions; under-10s not admitted. Pay what you wish 11am-1pm Sun. **Map** p133 D4 **❷**
Industrialist, robber baron and collector Henry Clay Frick commissioned this opulent mansion with a view to leaving his legacy to the public. Designed by Thomas Hastings of Carrère & Hastings (the firm behind the New York Public Library), the 1914 building was inspired by 18th-century British and French architecture. In an effort to preserve the feel of a private residence, labelling is minimal, but a free audio guide and a $2 booklet are available. Works spanning the 14th to the 19th centuries include masterpieces by Rembrandt, Vermeer, Bellini, Whistler and Monet, exquisite period furniture and objects. A gallery in the enclosed garden portico is devoted to decorative arts and sculpture.

Jewish Museum

1109 Fifth Avenue, at 92nd Street (1-212 423 3200, www.thejewishmuseum.org).
Subway 4, 5, 6 to 86th Street; 6 to 96th Street. **Open** 11am-5.45pm Mon, Tue, Sat, Sun; 11am-8pm Thur; 11am-5.45pm Fri (11am-4pm Nov-Mar). Closed on Jewish holidays. **Admission** $15; free-$12 reductions; free Sat. Pay what you wish 5-8pm Thur. **Map** p133 D2 **❸**
The Jewish Museum is housed in a magnificent 1908 French Gothic-style mansion – the former home of the financier, collector and Jewish leader Felix Warburg. Inside, 'Culture and Continuity: The Jewish Journey' traces the evolution of Judaism from

antiquity to the present day. The two-floor permanent exhibition comprises thematic displays of 800 of the museum's cache of 25,000 works of art, artefacts and media installations. The excellent temporary shows appeal to a broad audience.

Metropolitan Museum of Art

1000 Fifth Avenue, at 82nd Street (1-212 535 7710, www.metmuseum.org).
Subway 4, 5, 6 to 86th Street. **Open** 10am-5.30pm Mon-Thur, Sun; 10am-9pm Fri, Sat. **Admission** suggested donation (incl same-week admission to the Cloisters) $25; free-$17 reductions. **Map** p133 D3 **❹**
Now occupying 13 acres of Central Park, the Metropolitan Museum of Art opened in 1880. The original Gothic Revival building was designed by Calvert Vaux and Jacob Wrey Mould, but is now almost completely hidden by subsequent additions. A redesign of the museum's four-block-long plaza is expected to be completed around the publication of this guide, bringing new fountains and tree-shaded seating.

The first floor's north wing contains the collection of ancient Egyptian art and the glass-walled atrium housing the Temple of Dendur, which was moved from its Nile-side setting and overlooks a reflective pool. In the north-west corner is the American Wing, which underwent a multi-phase renovation that culminated in 2012 with the reopening of its Galleries for Paintings, Sculpture and Decorative Arts; the centrepiece is Emanuel Gottlieb Leutze's iconic 1851 painting *Washington Crossing the Delaware*. The wing's grand Engelhard Court is flanked by the façade of Wall Street's Branch Bank of the United States (saved when the building was torn down in 1915) and a stunning loggia designed by Louis Comfort Tiffany for his Long Island estate.

In the southern wing are the halls housing Greek and Roman art. Turning west brings you to the Arts of Africa, Oceania and the Americas collection; it was donated by Nelson Rockefeller as a memorial to his son Michael, who disappeared in New Guinea in 1961.

A wider-ranging bequest, the two-storey Robert Lehman Wing, is at the western end of the floor. This eclectic collection is housed in a re-creation of the Lehman family townhouse and features works by Botticelli, Bellini, Ingres and Rembrandt, among others. At ground level, the renovated and rechristened Anna Wintour Costume Center is the site of the Met's blockbuster fashion exhibitions.

Upstairs, the central western section is dominated by the recently expanded and rehung European Paintings galleries, which hold an amazing reserve of old masters – the museum's five Vermeers are now shown together for the first time. To the south, the 19th-century European galleries contain some of the Met's most popular works – in particular the two-room Monet holdings and a colony of Van Goghs that includes his oft-reproduced *Irises*.

Walk eastward and you'll reach the galleries of the Art of the Arab Lands, Turkey, Iran, Central Asia and Later South Asia. In the north-east wing of the floor, you'll find the sprawling collection of Asian art; be sure to check out the ceiling of the Jain Meeting Hall in the South-east Asian gallery. If you're still on your feet, give them a deserved rest in the Astor Court, a tranquil re-creation of a Ming Dynasty garden, or head up to the Iris & B Gerald Cantor Roof Garden (usually May-late Oct). For the Cloisters, which houses the Met's medieval art collection, see p150.

El Museo del Barrio

1230 Fifth Avenue, at 104th Street (1-212 831 7272, www.elmuseo.org). Subway 6 to 103rd Street. **Open** 11am-6pm Wed-Sat. **Admission** suggested donation $9; free-$5 reductions. *Sept-Dec, Feb-May* free 3rd Sat of each month. **Map** p135 D5 **5**

Founded in 1969 by the artist (and former MoMA curator) Rafael Montañez Ortiz, El Museo del Barrio takes its name from its East Harlem locale (though this stretch of Fifth Avenue is an extension of the Upper East Side's Museum Mile). Dedicated to the art and culture of Puerto Ricans and Latin Americans all over the US, El Museo reopened in 2009 following a $35-million renovation. The redesigned spaces within the museum's 1921 Beaux Arts building provide a polished, contemporary showcase for the diversity and vibrancy of Hispanic art. The new galleries allow more space for rotating exhibitions from the museum's 6,500-piece holdings – from pre-Columbian artefacts to contemporary installations – as well as temporary shows.

Museum of the City of New York

1220 Fifth Avenue, between 103rd & 104th Streets (1-212 534 1672, www. mcny.org). Subway 6 to 103rd Street. **Open** 10am-6pm daily. **Admission** suggested donation $10; free-$6 reductions. **Map** p135 D5 **6**

A great introduction to New York, this institution contains a wealth of city history. *Timescapes*, a 22-minute multimedia presentation that illuminates the history of NYC, is shown free with admission every half hour. The museum's holdings include prints, drawings and photos of the city, decorative arts and furnishings, and a large collection of toys. The undoubted jewel is the amazing Stettheimer Dollhouse: it was created in the 1920s by Carrie Stettheimer, whose artist friends reinterpreted their masterpieces in miniature to hang on the walls. Look closely and you'll even spy a tiny version of Marcel Duchamp's famous *Nude Descending a Staircase*.

A rolling renovation has brought new galleries for temporary exhibitions, which spotlight the city from different angles. Renovations to the museum's North Wing, due to be completed in 2015, will provide space for a core exhibition about the city.

Neue Galerie

1048 Fifth Avenue, at 86th Street
(1-212 628 6200, www.neuegalerie.org).
Subway 4, 5, 6 to 86th Street. **Open**
11am-6pm Mon, Thur-Sun; 11am-8pm
1st Fri of mth. **Admission** $20; $10
reductions (under-12s not admitted).
Map p133 D2 **7**

This elegant gallery is devoted to late
19th- and early 20th-century German
and Austrian fine and decorative arts.
The creation of the late art dealer Serge
Sabarsky and cosmetics mogul Ronald
S Lauder, it has the largest concentra-
tion of works by Gustav Klimt and
Egon Schiele outside Vienna.

Park Avenue Armory

643 Park Avenue, between 66th & 67th
Streets (1-212 616 3930, www.armory
onpark.org). Subway 6 to 68th Street-
Hunter College. **Open** during events;
see website for details. *Tours* $10; free-
$5 reductions. **Map** p133 D4 **8**

Once home to the Seventh Regiment
of the National Guard, this impressive
1881 structure contains a series of
period rooms from the late 19th century, designed by such luminaries as
Louis Comfort Tiffany and the Herter
Brothers. The vast Wade Thompson
Drill Hall has become one of the city's
premier alternative spaces for art, concerts and theatre.

Solomon R Guggenheim Museum

1071 Fifth Avenue, at 89th Street (1-212
423 3500, www.guggenheim.org).
Subway 4, 5, 6 to 86th Street. **Open**
10am-5.45pm Mon-Wed, Fri, Sun;
10am-7.45pm Sat. **Admission** $22; free-
$18 reductions; pay what you wish 5.45-
7.45pm Sat. **Map** p133 D2 **9**

The Guggenheim is as famous for
its landmark building as it is for its
impressive collection and daring temporary shows. Frank Lloyd Wright's
dramatic structure, with its winding,
cantilevered curves, caused quite a stir
when it debuted in 1959. In 1992, the
addition of a ten-storey tower provided

space for a sculpture terrace, a café and
an auditorium; the museum also has a
more upscale restaurant. Solomon R
Guggenheim's original founding collection, amassed in the 1930s, includes
150 works by Kandinsky, in addition to
pieces by Chagall, Picasso, Franz Marc
and others; the Solomon R Guggenheim
Foundation's holdings have since been
enriched by subsequent bequests,
including the Thannhauser Collection
– which includes paintings by
Impressionist and post-Impression-
ist masters such as Manet, Cézanne
and Gaugin – and the Panza di Biumo
Collection of American minimalist and
conceptual art from the 1960s and '70s.

Eating & drinking

Bar Pleiades

The Surrey, 20 E 76th Street, between
Fifth & Madison Avenues (1-212 772
2600, www.danielnyc.com). Subway 6 to
77th Street. **Open** noon-midnight daily.
Bar. **Map** p133 D3 **10**

Designed as a nod to Coco Chanel, Daniel
Boulud's bar is framed in black lacquered
panelling. The luxe setting and moneyed
crowd might seem a little stiff, but the
drinks are so exquisitely executed, you
won't mind sharing your banquette with
a suit. Light eats are provided by Café
Boulud next door.

Bemelmans Bar

The Carlyle, 35 E 76th Street, at
Madison Avenue (1-212 744 1600,
www.thecarlyle.com). Subway 6 to 77th
Street. **Open** 11am-midnight Mon, Sun;
11am-12.30am Tue-Thur; 11am-1am
Fri, Sat. **Bar.** **Map** p133 D3 **11**

The Plaza may have *Eloise*, but the
Carlyle has its own children's book con-
nection – the wonderful 1947 murals
of Central Park by *Madeline* creator
Ludwig Bemelmans in this, the quintessential classy New York bar. A jazz
trio adds to the atmosphere every night
(9.30pm Mon-Sat; 9pm Sun); a cover
charge of $15-$30 applies when the
musicians take up residence.

Café Sabarsky

Neue Galerie, 1048 Fifth Avenue, at 86th Street (1-212 288 0665, www. cafesabarsky.com). Subway 4, 5, 6 to 86th Street. **Open** 9am-6pm Mon, Wed; 9am-9pm Thur-Sun. **$$. Café. Map** p133 D2 ⓬

Purveyor of indulgent pastries to Neue Galerie patrons by day, this sophisticated, high-ceilinged restaurant, inspired by a classic Viennese *kaffeehaus*, is helmed by chef Kurt Gutenbrunner of modern Austrian restaurant Wallsé. Appetisers are most adventurous – the creaminess of the *spätzle* is a perfect base for sweetcorn, tarragon and wild mushrooms – while main course specials, such as *wiener schnitzel*, are capable yet feel like the calm before the *Sturm und Drang* of dessert. Try the *klimttorte*, which masterfully alternates layers of hazelnut cake with chocolate.

Daniel

60 E 65th Street, between Madison & Park Avenues (1-212 288 0033, www. danielnyc.com). Subway F to Lexington Avenue-63rd Street; 6 to 68th Street-Hunter College. **Open** 5.30-11pm Mon-Sat. **$$$$. French. Map** p133 D5 ⓭

The cuisine at Daniel Boulud's elegant fine-dining flagship, designed by Adam Tihany, is rooted in French technique with contemporary flourishes like fusion elements and an emphasis on local produce. Although the menu changes seasonally, it always includes a few signature dishes, such as the chef's oven-baked black sea bass with Syrah sauce, or the duo of beef – a sumptuous pairing of Black Angus short ribs and seared Wagyu tenderloin.

Earl's Beer & Cheese

1259 Park Avenue, between 97th & 98th Streets (1-212 289 1581, www.earlsny. com). Subway 6 to 96th Street. **Open** 4pm-midnight Mon, Tue; 11am-midnight Wed, Thur, Sun; 11am-2am Fri, Sat. **Bar. Map** p133 D1 ⓮

Tucked into the no-man's land between the Upper East Side and East Harlem, this craft-beer cubby hole has the sort of community-hub vibe that makes you want to settle in. The well-priced rotating selection of American craft brews and slapdash set-up appeal to a neighbourhood crowd, but it's Momofuku Ssäm Bar alum Corey Cova's madcap bar menu that makes it destination-worthy. Try the NY State Cheddar – a grilled cheese with braised pork belly, fried egg and house-made kimchi. (Note that the kitchen closes at 11pm.) The crew has since opened a cocktail bar, the Guthrie Inn, next door (1-212 423 9900).

The Gilroy

NEW *1561 Second Avenue, at 81st Street (1-212 734 8800, www.thegilroynyc.com). Subway 4, 5, 6 to 86th Street.* **Open** 5pm-4am daily. **Bar. Map** p133 E3 ⓯

Decorated with art deco chandeliers and red brocade wallpaper, this dimly lit drinkery brings high-wire cocktail culture to the Upper East Side with six variations on the Negroni, a piña colada-margarita hybrid with a coco-nutty cloud of tech-geek 'salt air' and chocolate-banana juleps vacuum-sealed into individual packets, among other creations. Cocktails aren't the whole story, though. Behind the copper-topped bar lies the custom Hoppinator, the latest in a growing line of NYC draft-line gadgetry. Hooked up to the taps, the suds system can adjust a beer's hops to amp up its flavour and intensity.

Lexington Candy Shop

1226 Lexington Avenue, at 83rd Street (1-212 288 0057, www.lexingtoncandy shop.net). Subway 4, 5, 6 to 86th Street. **Open** 7am-7pm Mon-Sat; 8am-5pm Sun. **$. American. Map** p133 D3 ⓰

You won't see much candy for sale here. Instead, you'll find a wonderfully preserved retro diner (it was founded in 1925), its long counter lined with chatty locals on their lunch hours, tucking into burgers and chocolate malts. If you come for breakfast, order the doorstop slabs of french toast.

The Gilroy

Shopping

Madison Avenue, between 57th and 86th Streets, is packed with international designer names: Alexander McQueen, Chloé, Derek Lam, Gucci, Prada, Lanvin, Ralph Lauren, Valentino and more.

Barneys New York

660 Madison Avenue, at 61st Street (1-212 826 8900, www.barneys.com). Subway N, R to Fifth Avenue-59th Street; 4, 5, 6 to 59th Street. **Open** 10am-8pm Mon-Fri; 10am-7pm Sat; 11am-6pm Sun. **Map** p133 D5 ⑰

Barneys has a reputation for spotlighting more independent designer labels than other upmarket department stores, and has its own quirky-classic collection. The ground floor showcases luxe accessories, and cult beauty brands are in the basement. Head to the seventh and eighth floors for contemporary designer and denim lines.

Bloomingdale's

1000 Third Avenue, at 59th Street (1-212 705 2000, www.bloomingdales. com). Subway N, Q, R to Lexington Avenue-59th Street; 4, 5, 6 to 59th Street. **Open** 10am-8.30pm Mon-Sat; 11am-7pm Sun. **Map** p133 D5/E5 ⑱

Ranking among the city's top tourist attractions, Bloomie's is a gigantic, glitzy department store stocked with everything from handbags to home furnishings. The glam beauty section includes an outpost of globe-spanning apothecary Space NK, and you can get a mid-shopping sugar fix at the on-site Magnolia Bakery.

Fivestory

18 E 69th Street, between Fifth & Madison Avenues (1-212 288 1338, www.fivestoryny.com). Subway 6 to 68th Street-Hunter College. **Open** 10am-6pm Mon-Wed, Fri; 10am-7pm Thur; noon-6pm Sat, Sun. **Map** p133 D4 ⑲

At just 26 years old, Claire Distenfeld opened this glamorous, grown-up boutique just off Madison Avenue's swanky designer row. Sprawling over two and a half floors of – you guessed it – a five-storey townhouse, the space is stocked with clothing, shoes and accessories for men, women and children, plus home items. The emphasis is on less ubiquitous American and European labels, including Alexander Wang, Giambattista Valli and Acne, as well as Gianvito Rossi's seductively sleek footwear.

Lisa Perry

988 Madison Avenue, at 77th Street (1-212 431 7464, www.lisaperrystyle. com). Subway 6 to 77th Street. **Open** 10am-6pm Mon-Sat; noon-5pm Sun. **Map** p133 D3 ⑳

Upon graduation from FIT in 1981, designer Lisa Perry launched her line of retro women's threads inspired by her massive personal collection of 1960s and '70s clothing. Ultrabright pieces, such as her signature colour-blocked minidresses, pop against the stark white walls of her Madison Avenue flagship. You'll also find the designer's cheerful accessories and mod home collection.

Arts & leisure

Cornelia Spa at the Surrey

2nd Floor, 20 E 76th Street, between Fifth & Madison Avenues (1-646 358 3600, www.corneliaspaathesurrey.com). Subway 6 to 77th Street. **Open** 10am-8pm Mon-Fri; 9am-7pm Sat; 10am-7pm Sun. **Map** p133 D3 ㉑

Husband and wife Rick Aidekman and Ellen Sackoff reopened their popular boutique spa, which closed in 2009, in a smaller space in upscale hotel the Surrey. The intimate yet luxurious oasis is designed to make you feel like you're lounging in your own living space, complete with savoury and sweet treats. Splurge on the Reparative Caviar and Oxygen Quench facial ($325), or a signature massage ($175 for an hour), which combines deep-tissue, Swedish and shiatsu techniques.

Upper West Side

The gateway to the Upper West Side is Columbus Circle, where Broadway meets 59th Street, Eighth Avenue, Central Park South and Central Park West – a rare rotary in a city that is largely made up of right angles. The cosmopolitan neighbourhood's seat of culture is **Lincoln Center**, a complex of theatres and concert halls that's home to the New York Philharmonic, the New York City Ballet, the Metropolitan Opera and other notable arts organisations.

Further uptown, **Morningside Heights**, between 110th and 125th Streets, from Morningside Park to the Hudson, is dominated by Columbia University. **Riverside Park**, a sinuous stretch of riverbank along the Hudson from 59th Street to 155th Street, was originally designed by Central Park's Frederick Law Olmsted, and subsequently extended.

Sights & museums

American Folk Art Museum

2 Lincoln Square, Columbus Avenue, at 66th Street (1-212 595 9533, www. folkartmuseum.org). Subway 1 to 66th Street-Lincoln Center. **Open** noon-7.30pm Tue-Sat; noon-6pm Sun. **Admission** free. **Map** p132 B4 ㉒
Despite a budget crisis that forced the American Folk Art Museum to give up its midtown premises, the institution is still going strong in the small original space it had retained as a second location. Its unparalleled holdings of folk art include more than 5,000 works from the late 18th century to the present. Exhibitions explore the work of self-taught and outsider artists, as well as showing traditional folk art such as quilts and needlework, and other decorative objects. You can purchase original handmade pieces in the large gift shop.

American Museum of Natural History/Rose Center for Earth & Space

Central Park West, at 79th Street (1-212 769 5100, www.amnh.org). Subway B, C to 81st Street-Museum of Natural History. **Open** 10am-5.45pm daily. **Admission** suggested donation $22; $12.50-$17 reductions. **Map** p132 C3 ㉓
The American Museum of Natural History's fourth-floor dino halls are home to the largest and arguably most fabulous collection of dinosaur fossils in the world. Roughly 80% of the bones on display were dug out of the ground by Indiana Jones types, but during the museum's mid 1990s renovation, several specimens were remodelled to incorporate more recent discoveries. The Tyrannosaurus Rex, for instance, was once believed to have walked upright, *Godzilla*-style; it now stalks prey with its head lowered and tail raised parallel to the ground.

The Hall of North American Mammals, part of a two-storey memorial to Theodore Roosevelt, reopened in autumn 2012 after extensive restoration to its 1940s dioramas. The Hall of Human Origins houses a fine display of our old cousins, the Neanderthals, and the Hall of Biodiversity examines world ecosystems and environmental preservation. A life-size model of a blue whale hangs from the cavernous ceiling of the Hall of Ocean Life, while in the Hall of Meteorites, the focal point is Ahnighito, the largest iron meteor on display in the world, weighing in at 34 tons.

The spectacular Rose Center for Earth & Space offers insight into recent cosmic discoveries via shows in the Hayden Planetarium and a simulation of the origins of the Universe in the Big Bang Theater.

Cathedral Church of St John the Divine

1047 Amsterdam Avenue, at 112th Street (1-212 316 7540, www.stjohndivine.org). Subway B, C, 1 to 110th Street-Cathedral Parkway.

THE AMERICAN MVSEVM OF NATVRAL HISTORY
FOVNDED 1869

American Museum of
Natural History p143

Open 7.30am-6pm daily. **Admission** suggested donation $10. *Tours* $6-$15; $5-$12 reductions. **Map** p134 B4 ㉔

Construction of this massive house of worship, affectionately nicknamed 'St John the Unfinished', began in 1892 in Romanesque style, was put on hold for a Gothic Revival redesign in 1911, then ground to a halt in 1941, when the US entered World War II. It resumed in earnest in 1979, but a fire in 2001 further delayed completion. It's still missing a tower and a north transept, among other things, but the nave has been restored and the entire interior reopened and rededicated. No further work is planned… for now.

In addition to Sunday services, the cathedral hosts concerts and tours (the Vertical Tour, which takes you to the top of the building, is a revelation). It bills itself as a place for all people – and it certainly means it. Annual events include winter and summer solstice celebrations, and even a Blessing of the Bicycles every spring.

Museum of Arts & Design

2 Columbus Cirde, at Broadway (1-212 299 7777, www.madmuseum.org). Subway A, B, C, D, 1 to 59th Street-Columbus Cirde. **Open** 10am-6pm Tue, Wed, Sat, Sun; 10am-9pm Thur, Fri. **Admission** $16; free-$14 reductions. Pay what you wish 6-9pm Thur, Fri. **Map** p132 C5 ㉕

Occupying a revamped 1964 building designed by Radio City Music Hall architect Edward Durell Stone, this institution explores the importance of the creative practice. MAD's permanent collection comprises 3,000 pieces from 1950 to the present in a wide range of media (including clay, glass, wood, metal and cloth). Among the holdings are porcelain ware by Cindy Sherman, stained glass by Judith Schaechter and ceramics by James Turrell. In addition to checking out the roster of imaginative temporary shows, you can watch resident artists create works in studios on the sixth floor. The ninth-floor bistro has views over the park and the gift shop sells a wide selection of hand-crafted jewellery, among other items.

New-York Historical Society

170 Central Park West, between 76th & 77th Streets (1-212 873 3400, www. nyhistory.org). Subway B, C to 81st Street-Museum of Natural History. **Open** 10am-6pm Tue-Thur, Sat; 10am-8pm Fri; 11am-5pm Sun. **Admission** $19; free-$15 reductions. Pay what you wish 6-8pm Fri. **Map** p132 C3 ㉖

Founded in 1804 by a group of prominent New Yorkers that included Mayor Dewitt Clinton, the New-York Historical Society is the city's oldest museum, originally based at City Hall. In autumn 2011, the society's 1908 building reopened after a three-year, $70-million renovation that opened up the interior spaces to make the collection more accessible to a 21st-century audience. The Robert H and Clarice Smith New York Gallery of American History provides an overview of the collection and a broad sweep of New York's place in American history – Revolutionary-era maps are juxtaposed with a piece of the ceiling mural from Keith Haring's Pop Shop (the artist's Soho store, which closed after his death in 1990). Touch-screen monitors offer insight into artwork and documents, and large HD screens display a continuous slide show of highlights of the museum's holdings, such as original watercolours from Audubon's *Birds of America* and some of its 132 Tiffany lamps. The auditorium screens an 18-minute film tracing the city's development, while downstairs the DiMenna Children's History Museum engages the next generation. The upper floors are devoted to changing shows and the Henry Luce III Center for the Study of American Culture, a visible-storage display that spans everything from spectacles and toys to Washington's Valley Forge camp bed.

NEW YORK BY AREA

Eating & drinking

Barney Greengrass

541 Amsterdam Avenue, between 86th & 87th Streets (1-212 724 4707, www. barneygreengrass.com). Subway B, C, 1 to 86th Street. **Open** 8.30am-4pm Tue-Thur; 8.30am-5pm Fri-Sun. No credit cards. **$$. American. Map** p132 B2 **㉗**

This legendary deli is a madhouse at breakfast and brunch. Egg platters come with the usual choice of smoked fish (such as sturgeon or Nova Scotia salmon). Prices are on the high side, but portions are large, and that goes for the sandwiches too. Soup – matzo-ball or cold pink borscht – is a less costly option.

Bouchon Bakery

3rd Floor, Time Warner Center, 10 Columbus Circle, at Broadway (1-212 823 9366, www.bouchonbakery.com). Subway A, B, C, D, 1 to 59th Street-Columbus Circle. **Open** 11.30am-7pm Mon-Wed, Sun; 11.30am-8pm Thur-Sat. **$. Café. Map** p132 C5 **㉘**

Chef Thomas Keller's café, in the same mall as his lauded fine-dining room Per Se (see p147), lacks ambience, and the menu (soups, tartines, salads, sandwiches) is basic. But prices are much more palatable – a dry-cured ham and emmenthal baguette is around a tenner. The baked goods, including Keller's takes on American classics like Oreo cookies, are the real highlights.

Boulud Sud

20 W 64th Street, between Broadway & Central Park West (1-212 595 1313, www.danielnyc.com). Subway 1 to 66th Street-Lincoln Center. **Open** 11.30am-11pm Mon-Sat; 11.30am-10pm Sun. **$$$. Mediterranean. Map** p132 B5 **㉙**

At his most international restaurant yet, superchef Daniel Boulud highlights the new French cuisine of melting-pot cities like Marseille and Nice. With his executive chef, Travis Swikard, he casts a wide net – looking to Egypt, Turkey and Greece. Diners can build a full tapas meal from shareable snacks like octopus

a la plancha, with marcona almonds and arugula. Heartier dishes combine Gallic finesse with polyglot flavours: sweet-spicy chicken tagine with harira soup borrows from Morocco. Desserts – such as grapefruit givré stuffed with sorbet, sesame mousse and rose-scented nuggets of Turkish delight – take the exotic mix to even loftier heights.

Ding Dong Lounge

929 Columbus Avenue, between 105th & 106th Street (Duke Ellington Boulevard) (1-212 663 2600, www.dingdonglounge. com). Subway B, C to 103rd Street. **Open** 4pm-4am daily. **Bar. Map** p134 B5 **㉚**

Goth chandeliers and kick-ass music mark this dark dive as punk – with broadened horizons. The tap pulls, dispensing Stella Artois, Guinness and Bass, are sawn-off guitar necks, and the walls are covered with vintage concert posters. The affable local clientele and mood-lit conversation nooks make it surprisingly accessible.

Hungarian Pastry Shop

1030 Amsterdam Avenue, between 110th & 111th Streets (1-212 866 4230). Subway 1 to 110th Street-Cathedral Parkway. **Open** 7.30am-11.30pm Mon-Fri; 8.30am-11.30pm Sat; 8.30am-10.30pm Sun. **$. Café. Map** p134 B4 **㉛**

So many theses have been dreamed up, procrastinated over or tossed aside in the Hungarian Pastry Shop since it opened more than five decades ago that the Columbia University neighbourhood institution merits its own dissertation. The java is strong enough to make up for the erratic array of pastries, and the Euro feel is enhanced by the view of St John the Divine cathedral from outdoor tables.

Jacob's Pickles

NEW *509 Amsterdam Avenue, between 84th and 85th Streets (212 470 5566, www.jacobspickles.com). Subway 1 to 86th Street.* **Open** 11am-2am Mon-Thur; 11am-4am Fri; 9am-4am Sat; 9am-2am Sun. **Bar. Map** p132 B2 **㉜**

This gastropub shoehorns a grab bag of tippling memes – craft beer, Dixieland grub, house-made bitters, local wines on tap – into one rustic barroom. More than two dozen taps offer an all-domestic lineup. The list is broken down by state, with a stable of Empire State breweries (Barrier, Radiant Pig, SingleCut) complemented by a constantly rotating roster of cross-country favourites. If you're feeling peckish, go for the namesake pickles or the biscuits in sausage gravy.

Manhattan Cricket Club

NEW *226 W 79th Street, between Amsterdam Avenue & Broadway (1-646 823 9252, www.burkeandwills ny.com). Subway 1 to 79th Street.* **Open** 6pm-midnight Mon-Thur; 6pm-2am Fri, Sat. **Bar. Map** p132 B3 ⑬

Upstairs from Australian bistro Burke & Wills, this gold-brocaded, cricket-inspired cocktail parlour is a polished upgrade from the shrimp-on-the-barbie kitsch that often plagues Aussie efforts. Summit Bar founder Greg Seider offers pricey but potent quaffs inspired by cricket hubs like India and South Africa. The I'll Have Another jolts a dark-and-stormy base of sweet rum and shaved ginger with the spice-heavy bite of garam masala-infused agave.

Ouest

2315 Broadway, between 83rd & 84th Streets (1-212 580 8700, www.ouestny. com). Subway 1 to 86th Street. **Open** 5.30-9.30pm Mon, Tue; 5.30-10pm Wed, Thur; 5.30-11pm Fri; 5-11pm Sat; 11am-2pm, 5-9pm Sun. **$$$. American. Map** p132 B3 ㉞

A well-heeled local clientele calls chef Tom Valenti's uptown fixture its local canteen. The friendly servers ferry pitch-perfect cocktails and rich, Italian-inflected cuisine from the open kitchen to immensely comfortable round red booths. Valenti adds some unexpected flourishes to the soothing formula: salmon gravadlax is served with a chickpea pancake topped with caviar and potent mustard oil, while the house-smoked sturgeon presides over frisée, lardons and a poached egg.

Per Se

4th Floor, Time Warner Center, 10 Columbus Circle, at Broadway (1-212 823 9335, www.perseny.com). Subway A, B, C, D, 1 to 59th Street-Columbus Circle. **Open** 5.30-10pm Mon-Thur; 11.30am-1.30pm, 5.30-10pm Fri-Sun. **$$$$. French. Map** p132 C5 ㉟

Expectations are high at this celebrated fine-dining room – and that goes both ways. You're expected to wear the right clothes (jackets for men), pay a non-negotiable service charge, and pretend you aren't eating in a shopping mall. The restaurant is expected to deliver one hell of a tasting menu for $310. And it does. Dish after dish is flawless, beginning with Thomas Keller's signature Oysters and Pearls (a sabayon of pearl tapioca with oysters and caviar).

Shake Shack

366 Columbus Avenue, at 77th Street (1-646 747 8770, www.shakeshack nyccom). Subway B, C to 81st Street-Museum of Natural History; 1 to 79th Street. **Open** 10.45am-11pm daily. **$. American. Map** p132 B3 ㊱

The spacious offspring of Danny Meyer's wildly popular Madison Square Park concession stand is now one of several locations across the city. Shake Shack gets several local critics' votes for New York's best burger. Patties are made from fresh-ground, all-natural Angus beef, and the franks are served Chicago-style on potato buns and topped with Rick's Picks Shack relish. Frozen-custard shakes hit the spot, and there's beer and wine too.

Shopping

Alexis Bittar

410 Columbus Avenue, at 80th Street (1-646 590 4142, www.alexisbittar.com). Subway B, C to 81st Street-Museum of Natural History. **Open** 11am-7pm

NEW YORK BY AREA

Mon-Thur; 11am-8pm Fri, Sat; noon-6pm Sun. **Map** p132 B3 ③⑦

Alexis Bittar started out selling his jewellery from a humble Soho street stall, but now the designer has four shops in which to show off his flamboyant pieces, such as sculptural Lucite cuffs and oversized crystal-encrusted earrings. This uptown boutique is twice the size of the West Village, Upper East Side and Soho locations, and is meant to resemble a 1940s powder room, with silk wallpaper and art deco-style lights.

Levain Bakery

167 W 74th Street, between Columbus & Amsterdam Avenues (1-212 874 6080, www.levainbakery.com). Subway 1 to 79th Street. **Open** 8am-7pm Mon-Sat; 9am-7pm Sun. **Map** p132 B3 ③⑧

Levain sells breads, muffins, brioche and other delectable baked goods, but we're crazy about the cookies. A full 6oz each, the massive mounds stay gooey in the middle. The lush, brownie-like double-chocolate variety, made with extra-dark French cocoa and semi-sweet chocolate chips, is a truly decadent treat.

Magpie

488 Amsterdam Avenue, between 83rd & 84th Streets (1-646 998 3002, www. magpienewyork.com). Subway 1 to 86th Street. **Open** 11am-7pm Mon-Sat; 11am-6pm Sun. **Map** p132 B3 ③⑨

Decorated with bamboo shelving and Hudson River driftwood, this eco-friendly boutique stocks locally made, handcrafted, sustainable items. Finds include vintage quilts, recycled-resin cuff bracelets, and handmade Meow Meow Tweet soaps and candles.

Shops at Columbus Circle

Time Warner Center, 10 Columbus Circle, at 59th Street (1-212 823 6300, www.shops atcolumbuscircle.com). Subway A, B, C, D, 1 to 59th Street-Columbus Circle. **Open** 10am-9pm Mon-Sat; 11am-7pm Sun (hrs vary for some businesses). **Map** p132 C5 ④⓪

Classier than your average mall, the 2.8 million-sq-ft Time Warner Center features upscale stores such as Coach, Cole Haan and LK Bennett for accessories and shoes, London shirtmaker Thomas Pink, fancy kitchenware purveyor Williams-Sonoma, as well as shopping centre staples J.Crew, Aveda, and organic grocer Whole Foods. Some of the city's top restaurants (including Thomas Keller's gourmet destination Per Se, see p147) have made it a dining destination that transcends the stigma of eating at a mall.

Zabar's

2245 Broadway, at 80th Street (1-212 787 2000, www.zabars.com). Subway 1 to 79th Street. **Open** 8am-7.30pm Mon-Fri; 8am-8pm Sat; 9am-6pm Sun. **Map** p132 B3 ④①

Zabar's is more than just a market – it's a New York City landmark. It began in 1934 as a tiny storefront specialising in Jewish 'appetising' delicacies and has gradually expanded to take over half a block of prime Upper West Side real estate. Prices remain surprisingly reasonable. Besides the famous smoked fish and rafts of delicacies, Zabar's has fabulous bread, cheese, olives and coffee.

Nightlife

Beacon Theatre

2124 Broadway, between 74th & 75th Streets (1-212 465 6500, www.beacon theatrenyc.com). Subway 1, 2, 3 to 72nd Street. **Map** p132 B3 ④②

This spacious former vaudeville theatre hosts a variety of popular acts, from Aziz Ansari to ZZ Top. While the vastness can be daunting, the gilded interior and uptown location make you feel as though you're having a real night out on the town.

Jazz at Lincoln Center

Frederick P Rose Hall, Broadway, at 60th Street (1-212 258 9800, www.jalc.org). Subway A, B, C, D, 1 to 59th Street-Columbus Circle. **Map** p132 C5 ④③

The jazz arm of Lincoln Center is located several blocks away from the main campus, high atop the Time

Warner Center. It includes three rooms: the Rose Theater is a traditional mid-size space, but the crown jewels are the Allen Room and the smaller Dizzy's Club Coca-Cola, with stages that are framed by enormous windows looking on to Columbus Circle and Central Park. The venues feel like a Hollywood cinematographer's vision of a Manhattan jazz club. Some of the best players in the business regularly grace the spot; among them is Wynton Marsalis, Jazz at Lincoln Center's famed artistic director.

Arts & leisure

Lincoln Center
Columbus Avenue, between 62nd & 65th Streets (1-212 546 2656, www. lincolncenter.org). Subway 1 to 66th Street-Lincoln Center. **Map** p132 B5 **㊹**
Built in the early 1960s, this massive complex is the nexus of Manhattan's performing arts scene. The campus has undergone a major revamp, providing new performance facilities as well as more inviting public gathering spaces and restaurants. There is now a central box office selling discounted tickets to same-day performances at the David Rubenstein Atrium (between 62nd & 63rd Streets, Broadway & Columbus Avenue). This visitor centre also stages free concerts and is the starting point for guided tours of the complex (1-212 875 5350, $18, $15 reductions). In addition to the concert halls, Lincoln Center contains notable artworks, including Henry Moore's *Reclining Figure* in the plaza near the theatre, and two massive music-themed paintings by Marc Chagall in the lobby of the Metropolitan Opera House.

Alice Tully Hall *1-212 875 5050.*
An 18-month renovation turned the cosy home of the Chamber Music Society of Lincoln Center (www.chamber musicsociety.org) into a world-class, 1,096-seat theatre. A new contemporary foyer is immediately striking, but, more importantly, the revamp brought some dramatic acoustical improvements.

Avery Fisher Hall *1-212 875 5030.*
This handsome, comfortable 2,700-seat hall is the headquarters of the New York Philharmonic (1-212 875 5656, www.nyphil.org), the country's oldest symphony orchestra (founded in 1842) – and one of its finest. A future renovation is planned, though the date hasn't been set. The ongoing Great Performers series – which also takes place at Alice Tully Hall and other Lincoln Center venues – features top international soloists and ensembles.

David H Koch Theater
1-212 870 5570.
The neoclassical New York City Ballet headlines at this opulent theatre, which Philip Johnson designed to resemble a jewellery box. During its spring, autumn and winter seasons, ballets by George Balanchine are performed by a wonderful crop of young dancers; there are also works by Jerome Robbins, Peter Martins (the company's ballet master in chief) and former resident choreographer Christopher Wheeldon. The popular *Nutcracker* runs from the end of November into the new year. In the early spring, look for performances by the revered Paul Taylor Dance Company.

Lincoln Center Theater *Telecharge 1-212 239 6200, www.lct.org.*
The majestic and prestigious Lincoln Center Theater complex has a pair of amphitheatre-style drama venues. The Broadway house, the 1,080-seat Vivian Beaumont Theater, is home to star-studded and elegant major productions. Downstairs is the 299-seat Mitzi E Newhouse Theater, an Off Broadway space devoted to new work by the upper layer of American playwrights. In an effort to shake off its reputation for stodginess, Lincoln Center launched LCT3, which presents the work of emerging playwrights in the new Claire Tow Theater, built on top of the Beaumont.

Metropolitan Opera House *1-212 362 6000, www.metoperafamily.org.*
The grandest of the Lincoln Center buildings, the Met is a spectacular place to see and hear opera. It hosts the Metropolitan

Opera from September to May, with major visiting companies appearing in summer. Audiences are fiercely devoted, with subscriptions remaining in families for generations. Opera's biggest stars appear here regularly, and music director James Levine has turned the orchestra into a true symphonic force.

The Met had already started becoming more inclusive before current impresario Peter Gelb took the reins in 2006. Now, the company is placing a priority on creating novel theatrical experiences with visionary directors (Robert Lepage, Bartlett Sher, Michael Grandage, David McVicar) and assembling a new company of physically graceful, telegenic stars (Anna Netrebko, Danielle de Niese, Jonas Kaufmann, Erwin Schrott). Although most tickets are expensive, 200 prime seats are sold for a mere $20 apiece from Monday to Thursday, two hours before curtain up.

Film Society of Lincoln Center
1-212 875 5600, www.filmlinc.com.
Founded in 1969, the FSLC hosts the prestigious New York Film Festival, among other annual fests, in addition to presenting diverse programming throughout the year. Series are usually thematic, with an international perspective or focused on a single auteur. The $40-million Elinor Bunin Munroe Film Center houses two plush cinemas that host frequent post-screening Q&As. Between these state-of-the-art screens and the Walter Reade Theater across the street, a small multiplex has been born. The Bunin also houses a café, Indie Food and Wine.

Symphony Space
2537 Broadway, at 95th Street (1-212 864 5400, www.symphonyspace.org). Subway 1, 2, 3 to 96th Street. **Map** p132 B1 **45**
Despite the name, programming at Symphony Space is anything but orchestra-centric: recent seasons have featured sax quartets, Indian classical music, a cappella ensembles and HD opera simulcasts from Europe. The annual Wall to Wall marathons (usually held in spring) provide a full day of music free of charge, all focused on a particular theme. The multidisciplinary performing arts centre also houses a cinema and stages works by contemporary choreographers and traditional dancers from around the globe.

Harlem & beyond

Extending north from the top of Central Park at 110th Street as far as 155th Street, Harlem is the cultural capital of black America – the legacy of the Harlem Renaissance. By the 1920s, it had become the country's most populous African-American community, attracting some of black America's greatest artists: writers such as Langston Hughes and musicians like Duke Ellington and Louis Armstrong.

On 125th Street, Harlem's main artery, street preachers and mix-tape hawkers vie for the attentions of the human parade. Although new apartment buildings, boutiques, restaurants and cafés are scattered around the neighbourhood, especially on Frederick Douglass Boulevard (Eighth Avenue) between 110th and 125th Streets, Harlem has retained much of its 19th- and early 20th-century architecture because redevelopers shunned it for so long.

East of Fifth Avenue above 96th Street is **East Harlem**, better known to its primarily Puerto Rican residents as El Barrio. (For **El Museo del Barrio**, see p138.)

From 155th Street to Dyckman (200th) Street is **Washington Heights**, which contains a handful of attractions and, near the top of Manhattan, picturesque riverside **Fort Tryon Park**.

Sights & museums

The Cloisters
Fort Tryon Park, Fort Washington Avenue, at Margaret Corbin Plaza (1-212 923 3700, www.metmuseum.org).

Subway A to 190th Street, then M4 bus or 10min walk. **Open** *Mar-Oct* 10am-5.15pm daily. *Nov-Feb* 10am-4.45pm daily. **Admission** suggested donation (incl same-day admission to Metropolitan Museum of Art) $25; free-$17 reductions. Set in a lovely park overlooking the Hudson River, the Cloisters houses the Metropolitan Museum's medieval art and architecture collections. A path winds through the peaceful grounds to a castle that seems to date from the Middle Ages; in fact it was built in the 1930s using pieces from five medieval French cloisters. Highlights include the 12th-century Fuentidueña Chapel, the Unicorn Tapestries and the *Annunciation* triptych by Robert Campin.

Studio Museum in Harlem

144 W 125th Street, between Malcolm X Boulevard (Lenox Avenue) & Adam Clayton Powell Jr Boulevard (Seventh Avenue) (1-212 864 4500, www.studio museum.org). Subway 2, 3 to 125th Street. **Open** noon-9pm Thur, Fri; 10am-6pm Sat; noon-6pm Sun. **Admission** suggested donation $7; free-$3 reductions; free Sun. No credit cards. **Map** p134 C4 ④⑥

The first black fine arts museum in the country when it opened in 1968, the Studio Museum is an important player in the art scene of the African diaspora. Under the leadership of director and chief curator Thelma Golden, this vibrant institution, housed in a stripped-down, three-level space, presents shows in a variety of media by black artists from around the world.

Eating & drinking

Amy Ruth's

113 W 116th Street, between Malcolm X Boulevard (Lenox Avenue) & Adam Clayton Powell Jr Boulevard (Seventh Avenue) (1-212 280 8779, www.amy ruthsharlem.com). Subway 2, 3 to 116th Street. **Open** 11.30am-11pm Mon; 8.30am-11pm Tue-Thur; 8.30am-5.30am Fri; 7.30am-5.30am Sat; 7.30am-11pm Sun. $. **American regional. Map** p134 C4 ④⑦

This popular no-reservations spot is the place for soul food. Delicately fried okra is delivered with no hint of slime; mac and cheese is gooey inside and crunchy-brown on top. Dishes take their names from notable African-Americans – vote for the President Barack Obama (fried, smothered, baked or barbecued chicken).

The Cecil

NEW *210 W 118th Street, between Adam Clayton Powell Jr Boulevard (Seventh Avenue) & St Nicholas Avenue (1-212 866 1262, www.thececilharlem.com). Subway B, C to 116th Street.* **Open** 5pm-midnight Mon-Thur; 5pm-1am Fri, Sat; 11am-11pm Sun. $$. **Eclectic. Map** p134 C4 ④⑧

See box p152.

Ginny's Supper Club

310 Malcolm X Boulevard (Lenox Avenue), between 125th & 126th Streets (1-212 421 3821, www.ginnyssupperclub. com). Subway 2, 3 to 125th Street. **Open** 6-10pm Mon-Wed; 7pm-2am Thur; 6pm-3am Fri, Sat; 10am & 12.30pm brunch seatings, 6-10pm Sun. **Bar. Map** p134 C3 ④⑨

See box p152.

Grange Bar & Eatery

NEW *1635 Amsterdam Avenue at 141st St (1-212 491 1635, www. thegrangebarnyc.com). Subway A, B, C, D to 145th Street; 1 to 137th Street-City College.* **Open** 11.30am-4am Mon-Fri; 10.30am-4am Sat, Sun. $$. **American. Map** p134 B1 ⑤⓪

Harlem goes back to its rural roots at this locavore bistro and bar, outfitted with Mason jars, white-oak floors and chandeliers. Aric Sassi oversees a comfort-food menu rooted in seasonal produce; having scoured nearby farms, the chef dispatches dishes such as seared crab cakes with celery-parsnip slaw and a roast-beet salad with lime yoghurt, almonds and goat-cheese croutons. At the 40ft-long butcher-block bar, cocktails designed by Dead Rabbit head bartender Jack McGarry include

Harlem gets its groove back

The neighbourhood is hopping with hot eateries and nightspots.

The Cecil

Nearly a century after its famed cultural surge, Harlem is experiencing another renaissance, this time of the culinary variety. Frederick Douglass Boulevard has become a de facto Restaurant Row, with buzzy eateries popping up along Eighth Avenue and throughout the area. Marcus Samuelsson helped to pioneer the movement in 2011 when he opened his comfort-food sensation, **Red Rooster** (see p153), named after a legendary Harlem speakeasy once located at 138th Street and Seventh Avenue. The Ethiopian-born, Swedish-raised chef – himself a Harlem resident – created a destination as cool as any downtown spot, but with a distinctly uptown flavour, raking in critical acclaim for his refined soul food that honours both the nabe's history (fried chicken and waffles) and its multicultural residents (Dominican oxtail stew, Jamaican jerk chicken). A year later, Samuelsson expanded his Harlem holdings with **Ginny's Supper Club** (see p151), a jazzy ode to the swinging speakeasies and live-music lounges of the 1920s.

In autumn 2013, Richard Parsons and Alexander Smalls paid tribute to Harlem cuisine and music with two notable openings. Inside the historic Cecil Hotel space, the twosome revived Minton's Playhouse, the 1930s jazz lounge where Thelonious Monk served as house pianist and Dizzy Gillespie invented bebop. The new supper club, **Minton's** (see p153), tips a hat to this musical past – a 1948 mural of Hot Lips Page anchors the stage where jazz bands play most nights. Next door, The **Cecil** (see p151) braids together the far-reaching flavours of the African diaspora (citrus jerk bass, roasted poussin yassa) in a polished, gold-accented dining room. Coming soon: a new jazz club in the fabled Lenox Lounge, a 1939 art deco bar where Billie Holiday and John Coltrane once performed, and Mr Henry's Bakery, a New Orleans-style café from baker-turned-actor Dwight Henry (*Beasts of the Southern Wild*, *12 Years a Slave*).

the Grange Collins (gin, pomegranate liqueur, basil, lemon juice and soda).

Minton's

NEW *206 W 118th Street, between Adam Clayton Powell Jr Boulevard & St Nicholas Avenue (1-212 243 2222, www. mintonsharlem.com). Subway B, C to 116th Street.* **Open** 6-11pm Tue-Thur; 6pm-midnight Fri, Sat; 5-10pm Sun. **$$$**. **American**. Map p134 C4 ❺❶
See box p152.

New Leaf Restaurant & Bar

Fort Tryon Park, 1 Margaret Corbin Drive (1-212 568 5323, www.newleaf restaurant.com). Subway A to 190th Street; 1 to 191st Street. **Open** noon-4pm Mon; noon-9pm Tue-Thur; noon-10pm Fri; 11am-3.30pm, 6-10pm Sat; 11am-3.30pm, 6-9pm Sun. **$$**. **American**.
At this seasonal American restaurant in lush Fort Tryon Park you can have brunch on the patio in the warmer months. Dinner in the 1930s former concessions building sees dishes such as house-made pappardelle with jumbo shrimp. Profits go to the New York Restoration Project, dedicated to the greening of the city.

Red Rooster Harlem

310 Malcolm X Boulevard (Lenox Avenue), between 125th & 126th Streets (1-212 792 9001, www.redroosterharlem.com). Subway 2, 3 to 125th Street. **Open** 11.30am-3pm, 5.30-10.30pm Mon-Thur; 11.30am-3pm, 5.30-11.30pm Fri; 10am-3pm, 5-11.30pm Sat; 10am-3pm, 5-10pm Sun. **$$**. **Eclectic**. Map p134 C3 ❺❷
See box p152.

Shrine

2271 Adam Clayton Powell Jr Boulevard (Seventh Avenue), between 133rd & 134th Streets (1-212 690 7807, www. shrinenyc.com). Subway B, C, 2, 3 to 135th Street. **Open** 4pm-4am daily. No credit cards. **Bar**. Map p134 C2 ❺❸
Playfully adapting a sign left over from previous tenants (the Black United Foundation), the Shrine deems itself a

'Black United Fun Plaza'. The interior is tricked out with African art and vintage album covers (the actual vinyl adorns the ceiling). Nightly concerts might feature indie rock, jazz, reggae or DJ sets. The cocktail menu aspires to similar diversity with wittily named tipples like the rum-based Afro Trip.

Shopping

Trunk Show Designer Consignment

275-277 W 113th Street, between Adam Clayton Powell Jr Boulevard (Seventh Avenue) & Frederick Douglass Boulevard (Eighth Avenue) (1-212 662 0009, www. trunkshowconsignment.com). Subway B, C to 110th Street-Cathedral Parkway. **Open** 1-8.30pm Tue-Fri; 1-7.30pm Sat; noon-6.30pm Sun. Map p134 C4 ❺❹
Modelling agent Heather Jones went from hosting pop-up trunk shows to co-opening this small Harlem storefront. Men's and women's threads and accessories range from edgier brands (Margiela, Rick Owens) to Madison Avenue labels (Gucci, Chanel, Céline), marked down between 20% and 70%. The shop sometimes keeps erratic hours, so call before making a special trip.

Nightlife

Apollo Theater

253 W 125th Street, between Adam Clayton Powell Jr Boulevard (Seventh Avenue) & Frederick Douglass Boulevard (Eighth Avenue) (1-212 531 5300, www. apollotheater.org). Subway A, B, C, D, 1 to 125th Street. Map p134 C3 ❺❺
This 100-year-old former burlesque theatre has been a hub for African-American artists for decades, and launched the careers of Ella Fitzgerald and D'Angelo, among many others. The now-legendary Amateur Night showcase has been running since 1934. The venue, known for jazz, R&B and soul music, mixes veteran talents such as Dianne Reeves with younger artists like John Legend.

Yankee Stadium

Outer Boroughs

NEW YORK BY AREA

Unified in 1898, NYC's five boroughs are more integrated than ever. As non-millionaires have increasingly migrated from Manhattan, the outer boroughs have developed dining, shopping and cultural scenes to rival those on the island, and they hold ample attractions for visitors. Even the most isolated borough, Staten Island, is tipped as the site of construction of the world's tallest ferris wheel, which should be complete by 2016.

The Bronx

The Bronx seems remote to most visitors, partly due to memories of urban strife in the 1970s. While some areas still have an edgy feel, the Bronx is worth visiting for its attractions, the art deco architecture of the Grand Concourse, and the borough's own Little Italy, centred on Arthur Avenue in Belmont.

Sights & museums

Bronx Museum of the Arts

1040 Grand Concourse, at 165th Street (1-718 681 6000, www.bronx museum.org). Subway B, D to 167th Street; 4 to 161st Street-Yankee Stadium. **Open** 11am-6pm Thur, Sat, Sun; 11am-8pm Fri. **Admission** free.
Featuring more than 1,000 works, this multicultural art museum shines a spotlight on 20th- and 21st-century artists who are either Bronx-based or of African, Asian or Latino ancestry.

Bronx Zoo/Wildlife Conservation Society

Bronx River Parkway, at Fordham Road (1-718 367 1010, www.bronxzoo.com). Subway 2, 5 to E Tremont/W Farms Square, then walk to the zoo's Asia entrance; or Metro-North (Harlem Line local) from Grand Central Terminal to Fordham, then Bx9 bus to 183rd Street and Southern Boulevard. **Open** *Apr-Oct* 10am-5pm Mon-Fri; 10am-5.30pm Sat,

Sun. *Nov-Mar* 10am-4.30pm daily.
Admission $17; $13-$15 reductions;
pay what you wish Wed. Some rides
& exhibitions cost extra.

The Bronx Zoo shuns cages in favour
of indoor and outdoor environments
that mimic natural habitats. There
are more than 60,000 creatures and
more than 600 species here. Monkeys,
leopards and tapirs live inside the lush,
steamy Jungle World, a re-creation of
an Asian rainforest inside a 37,000sq
ft building, while lions, giraffes, zebras
and other animals roam the African
Plains. The popular Congo Gorilla
Forest has turned 6.5 acres into a dramatic central African rainforest hab-
itat. A glass-enclosed tunnel winds
through the forest, allowing visitors to
get close to the dozens of primate families in residence. Tiger Mountain is
populated by Siberian tigers, while the
Himalayan Highlands features snow
leopards and red pandas.

New York Botanical Garden

*Bronx River Parkway, at Fordham
Road (1-718 817 8700, www.nybg.org).
Subway B, D, 4 to Bedford Park Boulevard,
then Bx26 bus to the garden's Mosholu
Gate; or Metro-North (Harlem Line local)
from Grand Central Terminal to Botanical
Garden.* **Open** *Jan, Feb* 10am-5pm
Tue-Sun. *Mar-Dec* 10am-6pm Tue-Sun.
Admission $20-$25; $8-$22 reductions.
Grounds only $13; $3-$6 reductions;
grounds free Wed, 9-10am Sat.

The serene 250 acres comprise 50
gardens and plant collections, including the Rockefeller Rose Garden, the
Everett Children's Adventure Garden
and the last 50 original acres of a
forest that once covered the whole
city area. In spring, clusters of lilac,
cherry, magnolia and crab apple
trees burst into bloom; in autumn
you'll see vivid foliage in the oak and
maple groves. The Azalea Garden features around 3,000 vivid azaleas and
rhododendrons. The Enid A Haupt
Conservatory – the nation's largest

greenhouse, built in 1902 – contains
the World of Plants, a series of environmental galleries that take you on
an eco-tour through tropical rainfor-
ests, deserts and a palm tree oasis.

Eating & drinking

Bronx Beer Hall

NEW *2344 Arthur Avenue, between
Crescent Avenue & E 186th Street
(1-347 396 0555, www.thebronxbeer
hall.com). Subway B, D, 4 to Fordham
Road, then Bx12 bus to Arthur Avenue.*
Open 11am-8pm Mon-Wed, Sun;
11am-11pm Thur-Sat. **Bar**

Surrounded by the cigar makers and
meat counters of the septuagenarian
Arthur Avenue Market, patrons can sit
at BBH's rustic wooden bar and imbibe
one of five New York State choices on
draft – there's an emphasis on the borough's own Jonas Bronck's Beer Co.

Mike's Deli

*Arthur Avenue Retail Market, 2344
Arthur Avenue, between Crescent
Avenue & E 186th Street (1-718 295
5033, www.arthuravenue.com). Subway
B, D, 4 to Fordham Road, then Bx12 bus
to Arthur Avenue.* **Open** 6.30am-7pm
Mon-Wed; 6.30am-9pm Thur-Sat;
10am-7pm Sun. **$ Italian**

This venerable deli, butcher and café
may leave you paralysed with indeci-
sion: the glossy menu lists more than 50
sandwiches, plus platters, pastas, soups,
salads, stromboli (a kind of cheese turn-
over) and sides. Try the Yankee Stadium
Big Boy hero sandwich, filled with prosciutto, soppressata, mozzarella, capi-
cola, mortadella, peppers and lettuce.

Arts & leisure

Yankee Stadium

*River Avenue, at 161st Street (1-718
293 6000, www.yankees.com). Subway
B, D, 4 to 161st Street-Yankee Stadium.*
In 2009, the Yankees vacated the fabled
'House that Ruth Built' and moved into
their new $1.3-billion stadium across

the street. Monument Park, an open-air museum behind centre field that celebrates the exploits of past Yankee heroes, can be visited as part of a tour ($25, $23 reductions, $20 booked online; 1-646 977 8687), along with the New York Yankees Museum, the dug-out, and – when the Yankees are on the road – the clubhouse.

Brooklyn

Watch your back, Manhattan; Brooklyn's popularity continues to soar. New bars and restaurants still proliferate, the music scene is thriving and the borough is now a standard destination on the tour-bus itinerary. For visitors, attractions and cultural draws are concentrated in Brooklyn Heights, Dumbo and Prospect Heights, but Williamsburg, Park Slope and Red Hook are great dining and drinking territory.

Sights & museums

Brooklyn Botanic Garden

990 Washington Avenue, at Eastern Parkway, Prospect Heights (1-718 623 7200, www.bbg.org). Subway B, Q, Franklin Avenue S to Prospect Park; 2, 3 to Eastern Parkway-Brooklyn Museum. Open Mar-Oct 8am-6pm Tue-Fri; 10am-6pm Sat, Sun. Nov-Feb 8am-4.30pm Tue-Fri; 10am-4.30pm Sat, Sun. Admission $10; free-$5 reductions; free Tue, 10am-noon Sat.
This 52-acre haven of luscious greenery was founded in 1910. In spring, when Sakura Matsuri, the annual Cherry Blossom Festival, takes place, prize buds and Japanese culture are in full bloom. Linger in serene spots like the Japanese Hill-and-Pond Garden, the first Japanese-inspired garden built in the US, and the Shakespeare Garden, brimming with plants mentioned in the Bard's works. Start your stroll at the eco-friendly visitor centre (it has a green roof filled with 45,000 plants).

Brooklyn Bridge Park

Riverside, from the Manhattan Bridge, Dumbo, to Atlantic Avenue, Brooklyn Heights (www.brooklynbridgepark.org). Subway A, C to High Street; F to York Street.
The views of Manhattan from this still-evolving riverside strip are spectacular. Brooklyn Bridge Park has been undergoing a rolling redesign that includes lawns, freshwater gardens, a water fowl-attracting salt marsh and the Granite Prospect, a set of stairs fashioned from salvaged granite facing the downtown skyline. There are also cult food stands and an open-air wine bar. The restored vintage merry-go-round known as Jane's Carousel (www.janes carousel.org) occupies a Jean Nouvel-designed pavilion near the bridge.

Brooklyn Museum

200 Eastern Parkway, at Washington Avenue, Prospect Heights (1-718 638 5000, www.brooklynmuseum.org). Subway 2, 3 to Eastern Parkway-Brooklyn Museum. Open 11am-6pm Wed, Fri-Sun; 11am-10pm Thur; 11am-11pm 1st Sat of mth (except Sept). Admission suggested donation $12; free-$8 reductions; free 5-11pm 1st Sat of mth (except Sept).
Among the many assets of Brooklyn's premier institution are the third-floor Egyptian galleries. Highlights include the Mummy Chamber, an installation of 170 objects, including human and animal mummies. Also on this level, works by Cézanne, Monet and Degas, part of an impressive European art collection, are displayed in the museum's skylighted Beaux-Arts Court. The Elizabeth A Sackler Center for Feminist Art on the fourth floor is dominated by Judy Chicago's monumental mixed-media installation, *The Dinner Party*. The fifth floor is mainly devoted to American works, including Albert Bierstadt's immense *A Storm in the Rocky Mountains, Mt Rosalie*, and the Visible Storage-Study Center, where paintings, furniture and other objects are intriguingly juxtaposed.

Green-Wood Cemetery

Fifth Avenue, at 25th Street, Sunset Park (1-718 768 7300, www.green-wood.com). Subway M, R to 25th Street. **Open** varies by season; usually 8am-5pm daily. **Admission** free.

Filled with Victorian mausoleums, cherubs and gargoyles, this lush 478-acre landscape is the resting place of some half-million New Yorkers, among them Jean-Michel Basquiat, Boss Tweed, Leonard Bernstein and Horace Greeley.

New York Transit Museum

Corner of Boerum Place & Schermerhorn Street, Brooklyn Heights (1-718 694 1600, www.mta.info/mta/museum). Subway A, C, G to Hoyt-Schermerhorn; 2, 3, 4, 5 to Borough Hall. **Open** 10am-4pm Tue-Fri; 11am-5pm Sat, Sun. **Admission** $7; free-$5 reductions.

Located in a historic 1936 IND subway station, this is the largest museum in the United States devoted to urban public transport history. Exhibits explore the social and practical impact of public transport on the development of greater New York; among the highlights is an engrossing walk-through display charting the construction of the city's century-old subway system. But the best part is down another level to a real platform where you can board an exceptional collection of vintage subway and El ('Elevated') cars.

Eating & drinking

Al di là

248 Fifth Avenue, at Carroll Street, Park Slope (1-718 783 4565, www.aldila trattoria.com). Subway R to Union Street. **Open** noon-3pm, 6-10.30pm Mon-Thur; noon-3pm, 6-11pm Fri; 11am-3.30pm, 5.30-11pm Sat; 11am-3.30pm, 5-10pm Sun. **$$. Italian**

A fixture on the Slope's Fifth Avenue for more than a decade, this convivial, no-reservations restaurant is still wildly popular. Affable owner Emiliano Coppa orchestrates the inevitable wait with panache. Coppa's wife, co-owner and chef, Anna Klinger, produces northern Italian dishes with a Venetian slant. It would be hard to better her braised rabbit with black olives atop polenta, and even simple pastas, such as the house-made tagliatelle al ragù, are superb. The full menu is also served in the bar, which has a separate entrance around the corner on Carroll Street.

BrisketTown

359 Bedford Avenue, between South 4th & 5th Streets, Williamsburg (1-718 701 8909, http://delaneybbq.com). **Open** 5-11pm Mon-Fri; 11am-11pm Sat, Sun. **$$. Barbecue**

New Jersey-born Daniel Delaney – a former journalist – might not seem like an obvious poster child for purist Texan 'cue. But the Yankee is turning out some seriously crave-worthy meat. Delaney takes the traditionalist route, coating chunks of heritage beef in salt and pepper before smoking them over oak-fuelled fire for 16 hours. That deep-pink brisket, along with remarkably tender pork ribs, draws Williamsburg's jeans-and-plaid set, who tuck in while indie tunes jangle over the speakers.

Dirck the Norseman

NEW *7 North 15th Street, at Franklin Street, Greenpoint (1-718 389 2940, www.dirckthenorseman.com). Subway G to Nassau Avenue.* **Open** 5pm-2am Mon-Fri; noon-2am Sat, Sun. **Bar**

You can't throw a bottle cap without hitting a beer bar in Brooklyn, but this Greenpoint suds depot from brew guru Ed Raven – behind bottle emporium Brouwerij Lane and beer importer Ravenbrands – one-ups the competition by crafting its beers on-site. Inspired by the Scandinavian shipbuilder who first settled the neighbourhood in 1645, the mighty Germanic hall boasts a solid, selective line-up of Deutsch-proud beers (Jever, Gaffel), but the must-order is one of the nine proprietary blends cooked up by brewmaster Chris Prout under the imprint Greenpoint Beer & Ale Co.

Maison Premiere

298 Bedford Avenue, between Grand & South 1st Streets, Williamsburg (1-347 335 0446, www.maisonpremiere.com). Subway L to Bedford Avenue. **Open** 4pm-2am Mon-Wed; 4pm-4am Thur, Fri; 11am-4am Sat; 11am-2am Sun. **Bar**
Most of NYC's New Orleans-inspired watering holes choose debauched Bourbon Street as their muse, but this gorgeous salon embraces the romance found in the Crescent City's historic haunts. Belly up to the oval, marble-topped bar and get familiar with the twin pleasures of oysters and absinthe: two French Quarter staples with plenty of appeal in Brooklyn. The mythical anise-flavoured liqueur appears in more than 20 international varieties, in addition to a trim list of cerebral cocktails.

Marlow & Sons

81 Broadway, between Berry Street & Wythe Avenue, Williamsburg (1-718 384 1441, www.marlowandsons.com). Subway J, M, Z to Marcy Avenue. **Open** 8am-midnight daily. **$$.**
American creative
In this charming restaurant and café, diners wolf down market-fresh salads, succulent brick chicken and the creative crostini of the moment. In the back, an oyster shucker cracks open the catch of the day, while the bartender mixes the kind of potent drinks that helped to make successes of the owners' earlier ventures (including next-door Diner, a tricked-out 1920s dining car).

Peter Luger

178 Broadway, at Driggs Avenue, Williamsburg (1-718 387 7400, www.peterluger.com). Subway J, M, Z to Marcy Avenue. **Open** 11.45am-9.45pm Mon-Thur; 11.45am-10.45pm Fri, Sat; 12.45-9.45pm Sun. No credit cards. **$$$.**
Steakhouse

At Luger's old-school steakhouse, the choice is limited, but the porterhouse is justly famed. Choose from various sizes, from a small single steak to 'steak for four'. Although a slew of Luger copycats have prospered in the last several years, none has captured the elusive charm of this stucco-walled, beer hall-style eaterie, with worn wooden floors and tables, and waiters in waistcoats and bow ties.

Pok Pok NY

117 Columbia Street, at Kane Street, Cobble Hill (1-718 923 9322, www.pokpokny.com). Subway F, G to Bergen Street. **Open** 5.30-10.30pm Mon-Sat; noon-10.30pm Sat, Sun. **$. Thai**
James Beard Award-winning chef Andy Ricker's restaurant replicates the dives of Chiang Mai, a tented outdoor space with colourful oil-cloths on the tables and second-hand seats. But what separates Pok Pok from other cultish Thai restaurants is the curatorial role of its minutiae-mad chef. Ricker highlights a host of surprisingly mild northern-Thai dishes, including a sweet-and-sour Burmese-inflected pork curry, *kaeng hung leh*. His *khao soi*, the beloved meal-in-a-bowl from Chiang Mai – chicken noodle soup delicately spiced with yellow curry and topped with fried noodles for crunch – is accompanied here by raw shallots and pickled mustard greens. While away the inevitable wait for a table over drinks and snacks at Whiskey Soda Lounge NY (www.whiskeysodalounge-ny.com) across the street.

Roberta's

261 Moore Street, between Bogart & White Streets, Bushwick (1-718 417 1118, www.robertaspizza.com). Subway L to Morgan Avenue. **Open** 11am-midnight Mon-Fri; 10am-midnight Sat, Sun. **$$. Italian**
This sprawling hangout has become the unofficial meeting place for Brooklyn's sustainable-food movement. Opened in

Dirck the Norseman p157

2008 by a trio of friends, Roberta's has its own on-site garden that provides some of the ingredients for its locally sourced dishes. The pizzas – like the Cheeses Christ, topped with mozzarella, taleggio, parmesan, black pepper and cream – are among Brooklyn's finest. The team recently opened Blanca, a sleek spot in the back, to showcase chef Carlo Mirarchi's acclaimed tasting menu (6-9pm Wed-Fri, 5-8pm Sat, $195).

Sunny's Bar

253 Conover Street, between Beard & Reed Streets, Red Hook (1-718 625 8211, www.sunnysredhook.com). Subway F, G to Smith-9th Streets, then B61 bus. **Open** *8pm-4am Wed-Fri; 4pm-4am Sat; 4pm-11pm Sun (extended hrs in summer). No credit cards.* **Bar**

Restored after 2012's Hurricane Sandy dealt it a devastating blow, this unassuming wharfside tavern, which has been passed down in the Balzano family since 1890, is back in business. The bar buzzes with middle-aged and new-generation bohemians. Despite the nautical feel, you're more likely to hear bossa nova or bluegrass than sea shanties from the speakers.

Tørst

NEW *615 Manhattan Avenue, between Driggs & Nassau Avenues, Greenpoint (1-718 389 6034, www.torstnyc.com). Subway G to Nassau Avenue.* **Open** *noon-midnight Mon-Wed, Sun; noon-2am Thur; noon-3am Fri, Sat.* **Bar**

Danish for 'thirst', Tørst is helmed by legendary 'gypsy brewer' Jeppe Jarnit-Bjergsø and chef Daniel Burns, formerly of Noma in Copenhagen. These warriors are laying waste to tired ideas of what a great taproom should be, with a minimalist space that looks like a modernist log cabin, and rare brews from throughout Europe and North America. The ever-changing, 21-tap draft menu can move faster than a Swedish vallhund, but usually includes selections from Jarnit-Bjergsø's own

Evil Twin Brewing. More than 100 bottled beers are also available. Luksus, the restaurant hidden away in the back room, offers a tasting menu for $95 from Tuesday through Sunday (seatings 6.30-9.30pm).

Union Hall

702 Union Street, between Fifth & Sixth Avenues, Park Slope (1-718 638 4400, www.unionhallny.com). Subway R to Union Street. **Open** *4pm-4am Mon-Fri; 1pm-4am Sat, Sun.* **Bar**

Upstairs, customers chomp on mini burgers and sip microbrews in the gentlemen's club-style anteroom (decorated with Soviet-era globes, paintings of fez-capped men, fireplaces) – before battling it out on the clay bocce courts. Downstairs, in the taxidermy-filled basement, the stage hosts bands, comedians and offbeat events.

Vinegar Hill House

72 Hudson Avenue, between Front & Water Streets, Dumbo (1-718 522 1018, www.vinegarhillhouse.com). Subway A, C to High Street; F to York Street. **Open** *6-11pm Mon-Thur; 6-11.30pm Fri; 10.30am-3.30pm, 6-11.30pm Sat; 10.30am-3.30pm, 5.30-11pm Sun.* **$$. American**

As it's tucked away in a residential street in the forgotten namesake neighbourhood (now essentially part of Dumbo), tracking down Vinegar Hill House engenders a treasure-hunt thrill. The daily-changing menu in the cosy, tavern-like space focuses on seasonal comfort foods. In the warmer months, try to snag a table in the secluded back garden.

Shopping

By Brooklyn

261 Smith Street, between DeGraw & Douglass Streets, Carroll Gardens (1-718 643 0606, www.bybrooklyn.com). Subway F, G to Carroll Street. **Open** *11am-7pm Mon-Wed, Sun; 11am-8pm Thur-Sat.*

Gaia DiLoreto's modern-day general store offers an array of New York-made goods, including pickles, soaps, T-shirts, jewellery, housewares, accessories and cookbooks by Brooklyn authors. Look out for Maptote borough-specific bags and Brooklyn Slate Co's burlap-wrapped reclaimed slate cheese boards.

Grand Street Bakery

602 Grand Street, between Leonard & Lorimer Streets, Williamsburg, Brooklyn (1-718 387 2390, www.grandstbakery. com). **Open** noon-8pm daily.
Despite the signage, this storefront doesn't sell baked goods but clothing and accessories from the '60s to the '90s that were almost exclusively made in the US. Many of the original bakery fixtures – including metal baking racks that hold stacks of Levi's 501s – remain intact. Former Urban Outfitters vintage buyer Neal Mello and his girlfriend, Cyd Mullen, scour the country for classic Americana garb, such as ladies' fisherman knit sweaters and denim overalls. Guys' buys include Pendleton plaid wool shirts and denim jackets.

Modern Anthology

68 Jay Street, between Front & Water Streets, Dumbo (1-718 522 3020, www. modernanthology.com). Subway A, C to High Street; F to York Street. **Open** 11am-7pm Mon-Sat; noon-6pm Sun.
Owners Becka Citron and John Marsala – the creative force behind the *Man Caves* TV series – have created a one-stop lifestyle shop that brings together vintage and contemporary homewares, alongside clothing, accessories and grooming products. Understatedly stylish dudes can update their wardrobes with classic shirts and sweaters by New York designers Ernest Alexander and Todd Snyder and USA-crafted footwear by Oak Street Bootmakers, among other labels. And what hip bachelor pad is complete without a stack of vintage issues of *Playboy* and barware?

Rough Trade

NEW *64 North 9th Street, between Kent & Wythe Avenues, Williamsburg (1-718 388 4111, www.roughtrade.com). Subway L to Bedford Avenue.* **Open** 11am-11pm Mon-Sat; 11am-9pm Sun.
See box p162.

Nightlife

Barbès

376 9th Street, between Sixth & Seventh Avenues, Park Slope (1-347 422 0248, www.barbesbrooklyn.com). Subway F to Seventh Avenue. **Open** 5pm-2am Mon-Thur; 5pm-4am Fri, Sat; 2pm-2am Sun.
Show up early if you want to get into Park Slope's global-bohemian club – it's tiny. Run by musically inclined French expats, this venue brings in traditional swing and jazz of more daring stripes – depending on the night, you could catch African, French, Brazilian or Colombian music or acts that often defy categorisation.

Music Hall of Williamsburg

66 North 6th Street, between Kent & Wythe Avenues, Williamsburg (1-718 486 5400, www.musichallofwilliamsburg. com). Subway L to Bedford Avenue.
When, in 2007, the local promoter Bowery Presents found itself in need of a Williamsburg outpost, it gave the former Northsix a facelift and took over the bookings. It's basically a Bowery Ballroom (see p75) in Brooklyn – and bands such as Bear in Heaven and Delta Spirit headline, often on the day after they've played Bowery Ballroom or Terminal 5.

Output

74 Wythe Avenue, at North 12th Street, Williamsburg (no phone, www.outputclub.com). Subway L to Bedford Avenue. **Open** varies.
With the opening of Output in 2013, New York nightlife's centre of gravity continues its eastward push into Brooklyn. Akin in ethos to such underground-music headquarters as

On the record

Go on a crate-digging crawl of Williamsburg and Greenpoint.

Rough Trade

In late 2013, revered UK indie retailer **Rough Trade** (see p161) opened its first US outpost in a 15,000-square-foot Williamsburg warehouse, complete with in-house café. In addition to tens of thousands of all-new titles – roughly half of them vinyl and half CDs – the megastore sells music books, magazines and equipment, and hosts gigs (ticketed and free) from the likes of Television, Sky Ferreira and Sondre Lerche. Rough Trade joins old timers like **Earwax** (167 North 9th Street, between Bedford & Driggs Avenues, 1-718 486 3771, www.earwaxrecords.net), but it's former the Polish stronghold Greenpoint, just a few blocks north, which has emerged as a crate-digging hotspot. **Academy Record Annex** (85 Oak Street, between Franklin & West Streets, 1-718 218 8200, www.academyannex.tumblr. com) recently moved from its long-time home in Williamsburg to sunny digs by the Greenpoint waterfront. Expect serious buyers, reasonable prices and a massive collection of punk, rock & roll, jazz, soul and experimental records. Another local standby is the welcoming

Permanent Records (181 Franklin Street, between Green & Huron Streets, 1-718 383 4083, www. permanentrecords.info), with thousands of (mostly used) records and CDs, some of which go for as little as a dollar. Nearby is **Co-Op 87 Records** (87 Guernsey Street, between Nassau & Norman Avenues, 1-347 463 9997, www.coop87 records.tumblr.com), launched by the folks behind the Kemado and Mexican Summer labels. The diminutive shop packs a punch with meticulously curated collector pieces, bootlegs and other rarities, from avant-garde electronica to classic rock. Trendsetting label **Captured Tracks** (195 Calyer Street, between Manhattan Avenue & Leonard Street, 1-718 609 0871, www.capturedtracks.com) also has its eponymous flagship in the 'hood; in addition to vinyl, there are art books, cassettes, vintage recording equipment and curation booths from local musicians. Don't be surprised to find yourself browsing alongside artists from the top-shelf Captured Tracks roster, such as DIIV's Zachary Cole Smith and Canadian troubadour Mac DeMarco.

Berlin's Berghain/Panorama Bar complex or London's Fabric, the club boasts a warehouse-party vibe and a killer sound system. Top-shelf DJs (both international hotshots and local heroes) spin the kind of left-field house, techno and bass music you rarely hear in more commercially oriented spots. If the weather's nice, head to the rooftop bar – the view of the Manhattan skyline is a stunner.

Pete's Candy Store

709 Lorimer Street, between Frost & Richardson Streets, Williamsburg (1-718 302 3770, www.petescandystore. com). Subway L to Lorimer Street.
An overlooked gem tucked away in an old candy shop, Pete's is beautifully ramshackle, tiny and almost always free. The performers are generally unknown and crowds can be thin, but it can be a charming place to catch a singer-songwriter.

Verboten

NEW *54 North 11th Street, between Kent & Wythe Avenues (1-347 223 4732, www.verbotennewyork.com). Subway L to Bedford Avenue.* **Open** varies.
After more than a decade of hosting top-shelf one-offs around the city, the Verboten crew opened this long-awaited 750-person-capacity club for house, techno and bass music, plus live gigs. The modern-industrial main room features an expansive dance floor and Martin Audio sound system, while the side room serves as a restaurant and lounge. Trouble & Bass, Bespoke Musik, Push the Night and PopGun all join Verboten in curatorial duties, and Carl Craig, Guy Gerber, Matthew Dear, Davide Squillace, Ida Engberg, Matt Tolfrey and Lee Curtiss are among the notables claiming residencies.

Arts & leisure

Barclays Center

620 Atlantic Avenue, at Flatbush Avenue, Prospect Heights (1-917 618 6700,
www.barclayscenter.com). Subway B, D, N, Q, R, 2, 3, 4, 5 to Atlantic Avenue-Bardays Center.
The city's newest arena, home of the rechristened Brooklyn Nets basketball team, opened in autumn 2012 with a series of concerts by native son and Nets investor Jay-Z. Though its mere existence remains a point of contention for some Brooklynites, the arena has already been a success. The staff is efficient and amiable, the acoustics are excellent, and there's a top-notch view from nearly every one of the 19,000 seats. And since it opened, it has attracted an unexpectedly cool list of acts, with local luminaries like Vampire Weekend, Yeah Yeah Yeahs and MGMT gracing its stage.

Bargemusic

Fulton Ferry Landing, between Old Fulton & Water Streets, Dumbo (1-718 624 4924, www.bargemusic.org). Subway A, C to High Street; F to York Street; 2, 3 to Clark Street.
This former coffee-bean barge usually presents four chamber concerts a week set against a panoramic view of lower Manhattan. It's a magical experience (and the programming has recently grown more ambitious), but be sure to dress warmly in the winter. In less chilly months, enjoy a drink on the upper deck during the interval.

Brooklyn Academy of Music

Peter Jay Sharp Building *30 Lafayette Avenue, between Ashland Place & St Felix Street, Fort Greene. Subway B, D, N, Q, 2, 3, 4, 5 to Atlantic Avenue-Bardays Center; C to Lafayette Avenue; G to Fulton Street.*
BAM Harvey Theater *651 Fulton Street, at Rockwell Place, Fort Greene. Subway B, Q, R to DeKalb Avenue; C to Lafayette Avenue; G to Fulton Street; 2, 3, 4, 5 to Nevins Street.*
BAM Richard B Fisher Building *321 Ashland Place, between Hanson Place & Lafayette Avenue, Fort Greene.*

NEW YORK BY AREA

B, D, N, Q, 2, 3, 4, 5 to Atlantic Avenue-Barclays Center; C to Lafayette Avenue; G to Fulton Street.
All *1-718 636 4100, www.bam.org.*
America's oldest performing-arts academy continues to present some of the freshest programming in the city. Every year in autumn and winter, the Next Wave Festival provides avant-garde music, dance and theatre in its grand old opera house in the Peter Jay Sharp Building and the smaller BAM Harvey Theater. The newest facility, BAM Fisher, houses an intimate performance space and studios. BAM Rose Cinemas (in the Peter Jay Sharp building) does double duty as a rep house for well-programmed classics on 35mm and a first-run multiplex for indie films.

Brooklyn Bowl
61 Wythe Avenue, between North 11th & 12th Streets, Williamsburg (1-718 963 3369, www.brooklynbowl.com). Subway L to Bedford Avenue. **Open** (over-21s only except noon-6pm Sat) 6pm-midnight Mon-Wed; 6pm-2am Thur, Fri; noon-2am Sat; noon-midnight Sun.
Brooklyn Bowl turns bowling into a complete night out, with a menu from popular local eaterie Blue Ribbon and a full-size concert venue. The block-long former ironworks foundry takes its design cues from the Coney Island of the 1930s and '40s, with reproductions of old freak-show posters and carnival-game relics. All the beer – by Sixpoint, Kelso and next-door Brooklyn Brewery – is made in the borough.

Coney Island
Luna Park & Cyclone *1000 Surf Avenue, at W 10th Street (1-718 373 5862, www.lunaparknyc.com).*
Deno's Wonder Wheel Amusement Park *1025 Boardwalk, at W 12th Street (1-718 372 2592, www.wonderwheel. com).*
Both *Subway D, F, N, Q to Coney Island-Stillwell Avenue.* **Open** Apr-Oct; hrs vary (see websites).

In its heyday, from the turn of the century to World War II, Coney Island was New York City's playground. Years of neglect followed, but the arrival of the new Luna Park amusement hub, which now has more than 20 rides, including the Thunderbolt – Coney Island's first custom-built rollercoaster since the Cyclone opened in 1927 – is drawing a new generation of pleasure seekers. The latter whiplash-inducing ride is still going strong, along with the 1918 Deno's Wonder Wheel – both are protected landmarks. Coney Island USA (1208 Surf Avenue, at 12th Street, 1-718 372 5159, www.coney island.com) stages seasonal sideshow and burlesque diversions.

Nitehawk Cinema
136 Metropolitan Avenue, between Berry Street & Wythe Avenue, Williamsburg (1-718 384 3980, www.nitehawkcinema. com). Subway L to Bedford Avenue.
At this cinema-restaurant-bar hybrid, you can have dinner and a movie at the same time. Seats are arranged in pairs with tables, and viewers order from a menu created by Michelin-starred chef Saul Bolton. Just write down your order at any point during the movie on a piece of paper for a server to pick up. The comfort-food grub includes a tasty burger, but the real highlights are the chef's variations on concession-stand staples, like popcorn tossed with parmesan, black pepper and garlic butter. Best of all, you can sip cocktails, beer or wine in your seat.

Polonsky Shakespeare Center
NEW *262 Ashland Place, between Fulton Street & Lafayette Avenue, Fort Greene (Ovationtix 1-866 811 4111, www.tfana. org). Subway B, D, N, Q, R, 2, 3, 4, 5 to Atlantic Avenue-Barclays Center; C to Lafayette Avenue; G to Fulton Street.*
Founded in 1979, Theatre for a New Audience has evolved into New York's most prominent classical-theatre company. Now it finally has a home of its

own in Brooklyn's cultural district. A flashy, glass-fronted 299-seat venue, designed by Hugh Hardy, the Polonsky Shakespeare Center opened its doors in 2013 with Julie Taymor's production of *A Midsummer Night's Dream*.

Queens

The borough of Queens hasn't traditionally been on most tourists' must-see list. Now, however, cultural institutions are drawing both out-of-towners and Manhattanites across the Ed Koch Queensboro Bridge. Queens is also an increasingly popular gastronomic destination. The city's largest borough is the country's most diverse urban area, with almost half its 2.3 million residents hailing from nearly 150 nations, and Flushing has the city's second largest Chinatown.

Sights & museums

MoMA PS1

22-25 Jackson Avenue, at 46th Avenue, Long Island City (1-718 784 2084, www. momaps1.org). Subway E, M to Court Square-23rd Street; G to 21st Street; 7 to 45th Road-Court House Square. **Open** noon-6pm Mon, Thur-Sun. **Admission** suggested donation $10; $5 reductions.

Housed in a Romanesque Revival former public school, MoMA PS1 mounts cutting-edge shows and hosts an acclaimed international studio programme. The contemporary art centre became an affiliate of MoMA in 1999, and the two institutions sometimes stage collaborative exhibitions. The museum's DJed summer Warm Up parties are an unmissable fixture of the city's dance-music scene, and its eatery, M Wells Dinette, is a foodie destination.

Museum of the Moving Image

36-01 35th Avenue, at 36th Street, Astoria (1-718 777 6888, www. movingimage.us). Subway M, R to *Steinway Street; N, Q to 36th Avenue.* **Open** *Galleries* 10.30am-5pm Wed, Thur; 10.30am-8pm Fri; 11.30am-7pm Sat, Sun. **Admission** $12; free-$9 reductions; free 4-8pm Fri. No pushchairs/strollers.

The Museum of the Moving Image reopened in 2011 after a major renovation that doubled its size and made it one of the foremost museums in the world dedicated to TV, film and video. The collection and state-of-the-art screening facilities are housed in the Astoria Studios complex, which was once the New York production headquarters of Paramount Pictures. The upgraded core exhibition, 'Behind the Screen', on the second and third floors, contains approximately 1,400 artefacts (including the super creepy stunt doll used in *The Exorcist*, with full head-rotating capabilities, and a miniature skyscraper from *Bladerunner*) and interactive displays. A new gallery devoted to *Muppets* creator Jim Henson is expected to open in early 2015.

Noguchi Museum

9-01 33rd Road, between Vernon Boulevard & 10th Street, Long Island City (1-718 204 7088, www.noguchi.org). Subway N, Q to Broadway, then 15min walk or Q104 bus to 11th Street; 7 to Vernon Boulevard-Jackson Avenue, then Q103 bus to 10th Street. **Open** 10am-5pm Wed-Fri; 11am-6pm Sat, Sun. **Admission** $10; free-$5 reductions; pay what you wish 1st Fri of mth. No pushchairs/strollers.

When Japanese-American sculptor and designer Isamu Noguchi (1904-88) opened his Queens museum in 1985, he became the first living artist in the US to establish such an institution. The Noguchi Museum occupies a former photo-engraving plant across the street from the studio he had occupied since the 1960s; its location allowed him to be close to stone and metal suppliers along Vernon Boulevard. Noguchi designed the entire building to be a meditative oasis amid its gritty, industrial setting. Eleven galleries – spread over two floors – and an outdoor space are filled with his sculptures, as well as drawn, painted and collaged studies, architectural models, and stage and furniture designs.

Queens Museum

New York City Building, park entrance on 49th Avenue, at 111th Street, Flushing Meadows Corona Park (1-718 592 9700, www.queensmuseum.org). Subway 7 to Mets-Willets Point, then 15min walk. **Open** noon-6pm Wed-Sun. **Admission** suggested donation $8; free-$4 reductions.

Facing the Unisphere, the 140ft stainless steel globe created for the 1964 World's Fair, in Flushing Meadows Corona Park, the Queens Museum occupies the former New York City Building, a Gotham-themed pavilion built for the earlier World's Fair in 1939. In the 1940s, the structure was the first home of the United Nations. During the 1964 World's Fair, the New York City Building showcased the Panorama of the City of New York, a 9,335sq ft scale model of the city dreamed up by powerful urban planner Robert Moses. Still on display in the museum, it includes every one of the 895,000 buildings constructed before 1992.

Eating & drinking

Bohemian Hall & Beer Garden

29-19 24th Avenue, between 29th & 31st Streets, Astoria (1-718 274 4925, www.bohemianhall.com). Subway N, Q to Astoria Boulevard. **Open** 5pm-1am Mon-Thur; 5pm-3am Fri; noon-3am Sat; noon-1am Sun. **Bar**

This authentic Czech beer garden features plenty of mingle-friendly picnic tables, where you can sample cheap, robust platters of sausage and 16 mainly European draughts. Though the huge, tree-canopied garden is

open year-round (in winter, the area is tented and heated), summer is prime time to visit.

Dutch Kills

27-24 Jackson Avenue, at Dutch Kills Street, Long Island City (1-718 383 2724, www.dutchkillsbar.com). Subway E, M, R to Queens Plaza. **Open** 5pm-2am Mon-Thur, Sun; 5pm-3am Fri, Sat. **Bar**

What separates Dutch Kills from other mixology temples modelled after vintage saloons is the abundance of elbow room. Settle into one of the deep, dark-wood booths in the front, or perch at the bar. Another bonus: the cocktails – mostly riffs on the classics – come with slightly lower prices than in similar establishments in Manhattan.

M Wells Steakhouse

NEW *43-15 Crescent Street, between 43rd Avenue & 44th Drive, Long Island City (1-718 786 9060, www. magasinwells.com). Subway N, Q, 7 to Queensboro Plaza.* **Open** 5.30-11.30pm Mon, Wed-Sat; 5.30-10.30pm Sun. **$$-$$$. Eclectic**

Just after we got hooked on the eccentric, carnivorous fare and penchant for excess at the original M Wells, the renegade LIC diner gave up its lease, and one of the most exciting restaurants New York had seen in years disappeared. Quirk power couple Hugue Dufour and Sarah Obraitis opened MoMA PS1's lunchtime cafeteria, M Wells Dinette in 2012. But M Wells Steakhouse is their full-fledged return. Housed in a former auto-body shop, the spot splices class with irreverence; black-tie waiters and a besuited sommelier dart around a room where trout swim in a concrete tank and Canadian-lumberjack movies are projected on to the wall. The likes of dry-aged Nebraska côte de boeuf for two recall the gluttonous communal spirit of the first M Wells, while other dishes capture the madcap opulence that made it special.

The Queens Kickshaw

40-17 Broadway, between Steinway & 41st Streets, Astoria (1-718 777 0913, www.thequeenskickshaw.com). Subway M, R to Steinway Street. **Open** 7.30am-1am Mon-Fri; 9am-1am Sat, Sun. **$. Café**

Serious java draws caffeine fiends to this airy café, which also specialises in grilled cheese sandwiches. While the pedigreed beans – from Counter Culture Coffee – are brewed with Hario V60 drip cones and a La Marzocco Strada espresso machine, there's no coffee-snob attitude here. Fancy grilled cheese choices include a weekend-morning offering of soft egg folded with ricotta, a gruyère crisp and maple hot sauce between thick, buttery slices of brioche.

Spicy & Tasty

39-07 Prince Street, between Roosevelt & 39th Avenues, Flushing (1-718 359 1601, www.spicyandtasty.com). Subway 7 to Flushing-Main Street. **Open** 11.30am-10.30pm Mon-Thur, Sun; 11.30am-11pm Fri, Sat. No credit cards. **$. Chinese**.

Any southern trip to Flushing for spicy Szechuan food should begin here. Revered by in-the-know regulars, this brightly lit eatery serves plates of peppercorn-laden pork and lamb swimming in a chilli sauce that's sure to set even the most seasoned palate aflame. Stock up on cold-bar options, like zesty sesame noodles, crunchy chopped cucumbers and smooth, delicate tofu – you'll need the relief. Service is speedy and mercifully attentive to water requests.

Sweet Afton

30-09 34th Street, at 30th Avenue, Astoria (1-718 777 2570, www.sweet aftonbar.com). Subway N, Q to 30th Avenue. **Open** 4pm-4am Mon-Thur; 3pm-4m Fri; 10.30am-4am Sat, Sun. **Bar**

The Sweet Afton gastropub combines an industrial feel – lots of concrete and massive beams – with the dim, dark-wood cosiness of an Irish pub. The bar's smartly curated array of reasonably priced suds includes strong selections from craft breweries like Ommegang, Sixpoint and Captain Lawrence, but the bartender will just as happily mix a cocktail. The satisfying food menu is highlighted by the beer-battered McClure's pickles – an epic bar snack.

Nightlife

Creek & the Cave

10-93 Jackson Avenue, at 11th Street, Long Island City (1-718 706 8783, www.creeklic.com). Subway 7 to Vernon Boulevard-Jackson Avenue.

This hardworking venue offers all the things comedians and their fans need to survive: multiple performance spaces, convivial environs, a fully stocked bar, cheap Mexican food and a patio on which to rant and laugh late into the night. As if this weren't enough, owner Rebecca Trent also shows her appreciation for all who make the trek to Queens by making nearly every show free.

Arts & leisure

Chocolate Factory Theater

5-49 49th Avenue, at Vernon Boulevard, Long Island City (1-718 482 7069, www.chocolatefactorytheater.org). Subway G to 21st Street; 7 to Vernon Boulevard-Jackson Avenue.

Brian Rogers and Sheila Lewandowski founded this 5,000sq ft performance venue in 2005, converting a one-time hardware store into two spaces: a low-ceilinged downstairs room and a loftier, brighter upstairs white box that caters to the interdisciplinary and the avant-garde. Past choreographers include Beth Gill, Jillian Peña, Big Dance Theater and Tere O'Connor. Rogers, an artist in his own right, also presents work here.

Essentials

The Broome

Hotels

New York's hotel business is booming, with a room-count increase of nearly 25 per cent over the past five years. And despite an average rate of more than $300 a night in the autumn high season, most of them are full year-round. There is now more boutique choice in popular areas like Chelsea, Greenwich Village and the Lower East Side with the arrival of the **High Line Hotel** (see p176), the **Marlton** (see p175) and the **Ludlow** (see p173). But perhaps the strongest indication of the economic recovery is a cluster of development on, or around, midtown's West 57th Street, including the glamorous **Viceroy New York** (see p180). Touristy Times Square is also seeing an influx of more stylish options, and it's worth looking to the outer boroughs for competitive pricing – Brooklyn is an increasingly desirable place to stay.

Prices & information

Accommodation in this chapter has been designated a price band to give you an idea of what you can expect to pay at a given hotel, but note that rates can vary wildly according to the season or room category. As a guide, you can expect to pay $500 or more per night in the deluxe category (**$$$$**), $300-$500 for expensive hotels (**$$$**), $150-$300 for moderate properties (**$$**) and under $150 for budget lodgings (**$**). Don't forget to factor in 14.75 per cent tax, plus an extra $3.50 per night for most rooms.

Downtown

Financial District

Andaz Wall Street

75 Wall Street, at Water Street (1-212 590 1234, www.wallstreetandaz.com). Subway 2, 3, 4, 5 to Wall Street. **$$$.**

The New York outpost of this Hyatt subsidiary occupies the first 17 floors of a former Barclays Bank building. Inside, the vibe is anything but corporate: upon entering the spacious bamboo-panelled lobby-lounge, you're greeted by a free-range 'host', who acts as a combination check-in clerk and concierge. Chic, loft-style rooms are equally casual and user-friendly, with free non-alcoholic drinks and snacks. The restaurant (Wall & Water), bar and spa are welcome attributes in an area with little action at weekends.

Conrad New York

102 North End Avenue, at Vesey Street (1-212 945 0100, www.conradnewyork. com). Subway A, C to Chambers Street; 1, 2, 3 to Chambers Street; E to World Trade Center; R to Cortlandt Street; 2, 3 to Park Place. **$$$**.

This Hilton offshoot fronts Battery Park City's riverside park. West-facing rooms have Hudson views, but there's also plenty to see within the art-rich property. Sol LeWitt's vivid 100ft by 80ft painting *Loopy Doopy (Blue and Purple)* graces the dramatic 15-storey, glass-ceilinged, granite-floored lobby, and coolly understated guestrooms are adorned with pieces by the likes of Elizabeth Peyton and Mary Heilmann. Nespresso machines and marble bathrooms with Aromatherapy Associates products are indulgent touches. The rooftop bar (open May-Oct) offers Statue of Liberty views.

Tribeca & Soho

The Broome

NEW *431 Broome Street, between Broadway & Crosby Street (1-212 431 2929, www.thebroomenyc.com). Subway 6 to Spring Street.* **$$$**.

The Broome takes the boutique concept to new bijou levels. Set in a five-storey 1825 building and co-owned by four long-time local restaurateurs, it has just 14 rooms, furnished with residential pieces from chic interior stores

SHORTLIST

Best new
- The Broome (left)
- citizenM New York (p178)
- The Marlton (p175)
- Viceroy New York (p180)

Best budget chic
- 414 Hotel (p178)
- Bowery House (p172)
- The Jane (p175)
- New York Loft Hostel (p182)
- Pod 39 (p177)

Rooms with a view
- Conrad New York (left)
- The Standard (p175)
- Z NYC Hotel (p182)

Best spas
- Greenwich Hotel (p172)
- The Surrey (p180)

Best restaurants
- Ace Hotel New York(p176)
- Chambers Hotel (p180)
- The Ludlow (p173)
- NoMad Hotel (p177)

Contemporary cool
- Hôtel Americano (p176)
- Wythe Hotel (p182)

Best pools
- Gansevoort Meatpacking NYC (p175)
- McCarren Hotel & Pool (p182)
- Greenwich Hotel (p172)

Best (neo) classics
- Hotel Elysée (p180)
- High Line Hotel (p176)
- NoMad Hotel (p177)
- The Surrey (p180)

Best art
- Carlton Arms Hotel (p177)
- Gramercy Park Hotel (p177)
- James New York (p172)

ESSENTIALS

like Mitchell Gold & Bob Williams and Design Within Reach. Many quarters overlook the open-air interior courtyard, where Moroccan tiles, flower boxes, and classic French café tables create a tranquil setting for the complimentary continental breakfast in warm weather. With a one-to-one staff-to-room ratio, you can expect personal attention and nice touches like lavender-and-bergamot-infused sheets, free local calls and movies.

Crosby Street Hotel

79 Crosby Street, between Prince & Spring Streets (1-212 226 6400, www.firmdalehotels.com). Subway N, R to Prince Street; 6 to Spring Street. **$$$$**.

In 2009, Britain's hospitality power couple, Tim and Kit Kemp, brought their super-successful Firmdale formula across the Atlantic with the warehouse-style Crosby Street Hotel. Design director Kit's signature style – a fresh, contemporary take on classic English decor characterised by an often audacious mix of patterns, bold colours and judiciously chosen antiques – is instantly recognisable. Other Firmdale imports include a carefully selected art collection, a guests-only drawing room as well as a public restaurant and bar, a slick, 99-seat screening room and a private garden.

Duane Street Hotel

130 Duane Street, at Church Street (1-212 964 4600, www.duanestreethotel.com). Subway A, C, 1, 2, 3 to Chambers Street. **$$**.

Opened on a quiet Tribeca street in 2007, this boutique property takes its cues from its well-heeled residential neighbourhood, offering loft-inspired rooms with high ceilings, oversized triple-glazed windows, hardwood floors and a chic, monochrome colour scheme. Free Wi-Fi, Ren products in the slate-tiled bathrooms and complimentary passes to the nearby swanky Equinox gym cement the value-for-money package – a rare commodity in this part of town.

Greenwich Hotel

377 Greenwich Street, between Franklin & North Moore Streets (1-212 941 8900, www.thegreenwichhotel.com). Subway 1 to Franklin Street. **$$$$**.

The design inspiration at this Tribeca retreat, co-owned by Robert De Niro, is as international as the jet-set clientele. Individually decorated rooms combine custom-made English leather seating, Tibetan rugs and gorgeous Moroccan or Carrara-marble-tiled bathrooms, most outfitted with capacious tubs that fill up in a minute flat (bath salts from Nolita spa Red Flower are provided). In the tranquil subterranean spa, the pool is beneath the frame of a 250-year-old Kyoto farmhouse. For dinner, there's no need to rub shoulders with the masses at the always-mobbed house restaurant, Locanda Verde – have your meal delivered to the cloistered courtyard.

James New York

27 Grand Street, at Thompson Street (1-212 465 2000, www.jameshotels.com). Subway A, C, E to Canal Street. **$$$**.

Hotel art displays are usually limited to eye-catching lobby installations or forgettable in-room prints. Not so at the James, where the corridor of each guest floor is dedicated to the work of an individual artist, selected by a house curator. Although compact, bedrooms make the most of the available space with high ceilings and wall-spanning windows. Natural materials warm up the clean contemporary lines, and bathroom products are courtesy of Intelligent Nutrients. A two-level 'urban garden' (open May-Oct) houses an outdoor bar and eatery. The rooftop bar, Jimmy, opens on to the (tiny) pool.

Chinatown, Little Italy & Nolita

Bowery House

220 Bowery, between Prince & Spring Streets (1-212 837 2373, www.thebowery house.com). Subway J, Z to Bowery. **$**.

Ludlow

Two young real-estate developers transformed a 1927 Bowery flophouse into this stylish take on a hostel. Corridors with original wainscotting lead to cubicles (singles are a cosy 35sq ft) with latticework ceilings to allow air circulation. It might not be the best bet for light sleepers, but the place is hopping with pretty young things attracted to the hip aesthetic and the location. Quarters are decorated with vintage prints and historical photographs, and towels and robes are courtesy of Ralph Lauren. The (gender-segregated) communal bathrooms have rain showerheads and products from local spa Red Flower, while the guest lounge is outfitted with chesterfield sofas and a huge LCD TV.

Nolitan

30 Kenmare Street, at Elizabeth Street (1-212 925 2555, www.nolitanhotel. com). Subway J, Z to Bowery; 6 to Spring Street. **$$$**.
The 55 airy rooms of this boutique hotel feature floor-to-ceiling windows, wooden floors, custom-made walnut beds and Red Flower toiletries. The emphasis on keeping it local is reflected in numerous guest perks: the luxuriously laid-back property lends out bikes and lays on free local calls and discounts at neighbouring boutiques. Admire views of Nolita and beyond from the 2,400sq ft roof deck, or your private perch – more than half the guest quarters have balconies.

Sohotel

341 Broome Street, between Bowery & Elizabeth Street (1-212 226 1482, www. thesohotel.com). Subway J, Z to Bowery; 6 to Spring Street. **$$**.
Established as an inn in 1805, but altered considerably since then, this is the oldest hotel in the city. But it's no period piece; a recent renovation put a contemporary spin on the original character with exposed-brick walls, ceiling beams, hardwood floors and subway-tiled showers. The hotel offers perks that place it a rung above similarly priced establishments, including bathroom products courtesy of CO Bigelow, complimentary morning tea and coffee served in the lobby, free in-room Wi-Fi, and a on-site craft-brew emporium, Randolph Beer.

Lower East Side

The Ludlow

NEW *180 Ludlow Street, between Houston & Stanton Streets (1-212 432 1818, www.ludlowhotel.com). Subway F to Lower East Side-Second Avenue.* **$$$**.

ESSENTIALS

Hot on the heels of Sean MacPherson's affordable Village lodging, the Marlton (see p175), comes this collaboration with co-owners of the Greenwich Hotel and Pod 39. The newly built red-brick property has an artfully aged interior, but the design is eclectic. An oak-panelled lobby leads to a sprawling living room with a salvaged limestone fireplace and a bar that spills out on to an ivy-clad patio. Rooms mix classic and contemporary elements: big factory-style windows, rustic ceiling beams, Indo-Portuguese four-poster beds and petrified-wood nightstands. Bathrooms are fitted with brass rain showers or soaking tubs and Martin Margiela robes. The restaurant, Dirty French, due to open as we went to press, is the first foray into Gallic cuisine for the team behind Carbone (see p88).

East Village

Bowery Hotel

335 Bowery, at 3rd Street (1-212 505 9100, www.theboweryhotel.com). Subway B, D, F, M to Broadway-Lafayette Street; 6 to Bleecker Street. **$$$$**.
This fanciful boutique property from prominent hoteliers Eric Goode and Sean MacPherson is the capstone in the gentrification of the Bowery. Shunning minimalism, they created plush rooms that pair old-world touches (oriental rugs, wood-beamed ceilings, marble washstands) with modern amenities (flatscreen TVs, Wi-Fi).

East Village Bed & Coffee

110 Avenue C, between 7th & 8th Streets (1-917 816 0071, www.bedandcoffee. com). Subway F to Lower East Side-Second Avenue; L to First Avenue. **$**.
This East Village B&B (minus the breakfast) embodies quirky downtown culture. Each of the guest rooms has a unique theme, for example, the Black and White Room or the Treehouse (not as outlandish as it sounds; it has an ivory and olive colour scheme, and animal-print linens). Guests have the run of three loft-like living spaces and fully equipped kitchens. When the weather's nice, sip your complimentary morning java in the private garden.

Greenwich Village

Jade Hotel

52 W 13th Street, between Fifth & Sixth Avenues (1-212 375 1300, www.the jadenyc.com). Subway F, M, 1, 2, 3 to

The Marlton

14th Street; L to Sixth Avenue; L, N, Q, R, 4, 5, 6 to 14th Street-Union Square. **$$$**.

With its Georgian-style portico and decorative brickwork, this recently constructed hotel is indistinguishable from the surrounding pre-war apartment buildings. The rooms, designed by Andres Escobar in an art deco style, feature marble-inlaid Macassar ebony desks, chrome period lamps and champagne satin poufs – to preserve the period illusion, the TV is hidden behind a decorative cabinet. The classic black-and-white tiled bathrooms are stocked with toiletries from venerable Village pharmacy CO Bigelow.

The Marlton

NEW *5 W 8th Street, between Fifth & Sixth Avenues(1-212 321 0100, www. marltonhotel.com). Subway A, B, C, D, E, F, M to W 4th Street; N, R to 8th Street-NYU.* **$$**.

Hip hotelier Sean MacPherson has transformed a former low-rent lodging into an affordable boutique hotel. The 1900 building has plenty of local history – Beat icon Jack Kerouac wrote a couple of novellas there, and the place put up would-be Andy Warhol assassin Valerie Solanas – but the lobby's deceptively lived-in-looking interior, with broken-in leather armchairs and a coffee bar, has largely been created from scratch. Measuring a mere 150sq ft each, the bedrooms are mini versions of a Paris grand hotel, with gilt-edged velvet headboards, crown mouldings and petite marble sinks, and Côté Bastide products in the bathrooms.

West Village & Meatpacking District

Gansevoort Meatpacking NYC

18 Ninth Avenue, at 13th Street (1-212 206 6700, www.hotelgansevoort.com). Subway A, C, E to 14th Street; L to Eighth Avenue. **$$$**.

This Meatpacking District pioneer is known for its rooftop-pool-lounge playgrounds at two NYC locations (the other is on Park Avenue). By day, you can soak up the sun, and the Hudson River panorama, on a lounger by the 45ft heated open-air pool. After dark, the wraparound terrace bar becomes a DJed outdoor party with a glittering Manhattan backdrop. The guest quarters feature Studio 54-inspired photography that plays on the hotel's reputation as a party hub, and plush feather-bed layers atop excellent mattresses and marble bathrooms amp up the luxury. The Exhale spa is a dimly lit subterranean sanctuary.

The Jane

113 Jane Street, at West Street (1-212 924 6700, www.thejanenyc.com). Subway A, C, E to 14th Street; L to Eighth Avenue. **$-$$**.

Opened in 1907 as the American Seaman's Friend Society Sailors Home, the six-storey landmark was a residential hotel when hoteliers Eric Goode and Sean MacPherson took it over. The Jane's wood-panelled, 50sq ft rooms were inspired by vintage train sleeper compartments: there's a single or bunk bed with built-in storage and brass hooks for hanging up your clothes – but also iPod docks and wall-mounted flatscreen TVs. Alternatively, opt for a more spacious, wainscotted Captain's Cabin with private facilities – many have terraces or Hudson River views. If entering the hotel feels like stepping on to a film set, there's good reason. Inspiration came from various celluloid sources, including *Barton Fink*'s Hotel Earle for the lobby.

The Standard

848 Washington Street, at 13th Street (1-212 645 4646, www.standardhotels. com). Subway A, C, E to 14th Street; L to Eighth Avenue. **$$$**.

André Balazs's lauded West Coast mini-chain arrived in New York in 2009. Straddling the High Line, the

ESSENTIALS

retro 18-storey structure has been configured to give each room an exhilarating view, either of the river or a midtown cityscape. Quarters are compact (from 230sq ft) but the combination of floor-to-ceiling windows, curving tambour wood panelling and 'peekaboo' bathrooms (with Japanese-style tubs or huge showerheads) give a sense of space. Eating and drinking options include a chop house, a beer garden and an exclusive top-floor bar with a massive jacuzzi and 180-degree vistas.

Midtown

Chelsea

High Line Hotel

180 Tenth Avenue, at 20th Street (1-212 929 3888, www.thehighlinehotel.com). Subway C, E to 23rd Street. **$$$**.

The railway line-turned-park lends its name to this boutique hotel in the old guest wing of the General Theological Seminary, an imposing 1895 neo-Gothic landmark. Exuding an old-fashioned residential vibe, the 60 rooms feature antique Persian rugs, custom-designed wallpaper and a mix of vintage furnishings and reproductions of pieces sourced by the hotel's design firm, Roman and Williams. Many rooms retain original fireplaces – though these days the eco-friendly property is heated by a geothermal system. Rewired 1930s rotary phones may seem like an antidote to the digital age, but there's also free Wi-Fi, and you can connect your iPod to the retro Tivoli radio by the bed.

Hôtel Americano

518 W 27th Street, between Tenth & Eleventh Avenues (1-212 216 0000, www.hotel-americano.com). Subway C, E to 23rd Street. **$$$**.

You won't find any Talavera tiles in Grupo Habita's first property outside Mexico. Mexican architect Enrique Norten's sleek, mesh-encased structure stands alongside the High Line.

The minimalist rooms have Japanese-style platform beds, iPads and, in one of several subtle nods to US culture, super-soft denim bathrobes. After a day of gallery-hopping, get an elevated view of the neighbourhood from the rooftop bar and grill, where a petite pool does double duty as a hot tub in winter.

Inn on 23rd

131 W 23rd Street, between Sixth & Seventh Avenues (1-212 463 0330, www.innon23rd.com). Subway F, M, 1 to 23rd Street. **$$**.

This renovated 19th-century townhouse offers the charm of a traditional B&B with enhanced amenities (an elevator, pillow-top mattresses, private bathrooms, white-noise machines). Owners Annette and Barry Fisherman have styled each bedroom with a unique theme, such as the Asian-inspired Bamboo and the 1940s room, furnished with vintage Heywood-Wakefield pieces. The 'library', a cosy jumble of tables and chairs, is open 24/7 to guests for coffee and tea, and hosts wine and cheese receptions on Friday and Saturday evenings.

Flatiron District & Union Square

Ace Hotel New York

20 W 29th Street, at Broadway (1-212 679 2222, www.acehotel.com). Subway N, R to 28th Street. **$$$**.

Founded in Seattle by a pair of DJs, this cool chainlet has expanded beyond the States to London and Panama. In its New York digs, the musical influence is clear: select rooms in the 1904 building have functioning turntables, stacks of vinyl and gleaming Gibson guitars. And while you'll pay a hefty amount for the sprawling loft spaces, there are options for those on a smaller budget, fitted with vintage furniture and original art. In the buzzing lobby, the bar is set within a panelled library salvaged from a Madison Avenue apartment. Guests can score a table at chef April Bloomfield's popular Breslin Bar & Dining Room (see p107) and the John Dory Oyster Bar (see p108). There's even an outpost of Opening Ceremony (see p65) if you haven't a thing to wear.

NoMad Hotel

1170 Broadway, at 28th Street (1-212 796 1500, www.thenomadhotel.com). Subway N, R to 28th Street. **$$$**.
Like nearby hipster hub the Ace Hotel, the NoMad (which shares a developer) is also a self-contained microcosm encompassing destination dining – courtesy of Daniel Humm and Will Guidara, of the Michelin-three-starred Eleven Madison Park (see p107) – and the first stateside outpost of Parisian concept store Maison Kitsuné. Jacques Garcia, designer of Paris celeb hangout Hôtel Costes, transformed the interior of a 1903 New York office building into this convincing facsimile of a grand hotel. The chic rooms, furnished with vintage Heriz rugs and distressed-leather armchairs, are more personal – Garcia based the design on his old Paris apartment. Many feature old-fashioned claw-foot tubs for a scented soak in Côté Bastide bath salts.

Gramercy Park & Murray Hill

Carlton Arms Hotel

160 E 25th Street, at Third Avenue (1-212 679 0680, www.carltonarms. com). Subway 6 to 23rd Street. **$**.
The Carlton Arms Art Project started in the late 1970s, when a small group of creative types brought fresh paint and new ideas to a run-down shelter. Today, the site is a bohemian backpackers' paradise and a live-in gallery – every room, bathroom and hallway is festooned with outré artwork, including a couple of early stairwells by Banksy. Eye-popping themed quarters include the Money Room and a tribute to the traditional English cottage; new works are introduced regularly and artists return

to restore their creations. Roughly half of the rooms have shared bathrooms.

Gramercy Park Hotel

2 Lexington Avenue, at 21st Street (1-212 920 3300, www.gramercyparkhotel.com). Subway 6 to 23rd Street. **$$$$**.
Many NYC hotels have exclusive terraces or gardens, but only one boasts access to the city's most storied private outdoor space: Gramercy Park. The hotel's interior resembles a baronial manor occupied by a rock star, with rustic wooden beams and a roaring fire in the lobby; a $65 million art collection, including works by Richard Prince, Damien Hirst and Andy Warhol; and studded velvet headboards and mahogany drink cabinets in the bedrooms. Get a taste of the Eternal City in Maialino, Danny Meyer's tribute to Roman trattorias.

Pod 39

145 E 39th Street, between Lexington & Third Avenues (1-212 865 5700, www. thepodhotel.com). Subway S, 4, 5, 6, 7 to 42nd Street-Grand Central. **$**.
The city's second Pod occupies a 1918 residential hotel for single men – you can hang out by the fire or play ping-pong in the redesigned gents' sitting room. As the name suggests, rooms are snug, but not oppressively so; some have queen-size beds, others stainless-steel bunk beds with individual TVs and bedside shelves inspired by airplane storage. But you should probably know your roommate well since the utilitarian, subway-tiled bathrooms are partitioned off with sliding frosted-glass doors. April Bloomfield's on-site eaterie Salvation Taco (see p114) supplies the margaritas at the seasonal rooftop bar.

Herald Square & Garment District

Refinery Hotel

63 W 38th Street, between Fifth & Sixth Avenues (1-646 664 0310, www. refineryhotelnewyork.com). Subway B,

ESSENTIALS

D, F, M, N, Q, R to 34th Street-Herald Square; B, D, F, M to Bryant Park; 7 to Fifth Avenue. **$$$**.

The Garment District finally has a fittingly fashionable hotel. Stonehill & Taylor Architects, the firm behind this 1912 neo-Gothic building's conversion and design, took inspiration from its former life as a hat-making hub. In the guest rooms, furnishings subtly reference the garment industry. Super-soft bed throws mimic burlap, coffee tables are modelled on factory carts, and desks are reproductions of vintage Singer sewing-machine tables. Luxurious touches like Frette linens and walk-in showers with room for two offset the industrial elements. Eating and drinking options include Winnie's Lobby Bar (which takes its name from the owner of a ladies' tearoom in the building in the early 20th century) and a sprawling indoor-outdoor roof bar.

Theater District & Hell's Kitchen

414 Hotel

414 W 46th Street, between Ninth & Tenth Avenues (1-212 399 0006, www.414hotel.com). Subway A, C, E to 42nd Street-Port Authority. **$$**.

Tucked into a residential yet central neighbourhood, this budget boutique hotel is a real find. The place is twice as big as it looks, as it consists of two walk-up buildings separated by a leafy courtyard, which in warmer months is a lovely place to eat your complimentary breakfast. Rooms are simple yet chic, with a modern colour scheme that pairs grey headboards and red accents, and equipped with fridges, flatscreen TVs and iPod docks.

citizenM New York

NEW *218 W 50th Street, between Broadway & Eighth Avenue (1-212 461 3638, www.citizenm.com). Subway C, E to 50th Street; N, Q, R to 49th St; 1 to 50th Street.* **$$**.

See box p179.

The Out NYC

510 W 42nd Street, between Tenth & Eleventh Avenues (1-212 947 2999, www.theoutnyc.com). Subway A, C, E to 42nd Street-Port Authority. **$-$$**.

This all-gay (but 'straight-friendly') megacomplex is located just a few blocks from Times Square and the Theater District, and in convenient proximity to the Hell's Kitchen strip of gay bars. But there's actually no need to leave – the Out also houses BPM nightclub and the unremarkble but serviceable KTCHN restaurant, as well as a spa, gym and the Rosebud NYC cocktail bar. Despite a few style statements, the monochrome room decor is on the spare side. The quad rooms, with four curtained cubby-bunks that are reminiscent of sleeper compartments – upgraded with double beds and TVs – are a budget option for groups.

Row NYC

NEW *700 Eighth Avenue, between 44th & 45th Streets (1-212 869 3600). Subway A, C, E to 42nd Street-Port Authority; N, Q, R, S, 1, 2, 3, 7 to 42nd Street-Times Square.* **$$**.

See box p179.

Yotel New York

570 Tenth Avenue, at 42nd Street (1-646 449 7700, www.yotel.com). Subway A, C, E to 42nd Street-Port Authority. **$$**.

The British team behind this futuristic hotel is known for airport-based capsule accommodation that gives travellers just enough space to get horizontal between flights. Yotel New York has ditched the 75sq ft cubbies in favour of 'premium cabins' more than twice the size. Adaptable furnishings (such as beds that fold up futon-style) maximise space, and the bathroom has streamlined luxuries such as a heated towel rail and monsoon shower. If you want to unload excess baggage, the 20ft tall robot (or Yobot, in the hotel's playful lingo) will

Hip to be square

'Stylish Times Square hotel' isn't necessarily an oxymoron.

citizenM New

Most New Yorkers avoid tourist-clogged Times Square, but a crop of stylish hotels is luring locals looking for a lunchtime or after-work destination as well as visitors.

The fast-growing **citizenM** (see p178) brand aims to democratise the luxury-hotel experience. With rates starting at less than $200 a night, guests can can kick back on a $10,000 Vitra armchair in the eclectic lobby and admire the 26-foot-tall installation *Walking in Times Square* by Julian Opie. Catering to a time-zone-crossing, tech-savvy clientele (the M stands for 'mobile'), the Amsterdam-based company has devised a new model informed by its founders' travel frustrations, cutting high-overhead amenities like room service in the process. The 24-hour canteenM dispenses cocktails, coffee, all-day breakfast and other dishes. The compact rooms focus on the essentials: an extra-large king-size bed and a powerful rain shower (in a cool cubicle with coloured ceiling lights). You can control the hue, and everything else in the room – from the blinds to the digital wall art – using a Samsung tablet.

Row NYC (see p178) is a transformation of the corporate behemoth Milford Plaza into a trendier beast. Now the 1,331-room hotel has funky light installations and an 'internet lounge' with eight guests' iMacs, rooms jazzed up with vivid accent walls, platform beds and clean-lined, contemporary bathrooms, plus City Kitchen, a food market featuring such NYC vendors as Luke's Lobster and Dough.

For a more upscale experience, **The Knickerbocker** (6 Times Square, at 42nd Street, 1-855 865 6425, www.theknickerbocker.com), an overhauled 1906 landmark, opens around time of publication of this guide. While some rooms have close-up views of Times Square's dazzling displays, inside all is calm and understated, with oak veneer furnishings and white marble bathroom vanities. The rooftop bar, with a menu devised by Aureole's Charlie Palmer, who also helms two other on-site eateries, provides ringside seats to the biggest show in town on New Year's Eve.

stash it for you in a lobby locker. In contrast with the compact quarters, the sprawling public spaces include a wraparound terrace so large it's serviced by two bars.

Fifth Avenue & around

Chambers Hotel

15 W 56 Street, between Fifth & Sixth Avenues (1-212 974 5656, www.chambershotel.com). Subway E, M to Fifth Avenue-53rd Street. **$$$**.

Room design at this small boutique hotel takes its cue from upscale New York loft apartments, combining designer furniture with raw concrete ceilings, exposed pipes, floor-to-ceiling windows and polished walnut floorboards or Tibetan wool carpeting. Guest quarters also feature some of the 500-piece art collection. Everything is designed to make you feel at home, from the soft terrycloth slippers in bright colours to the architect's desks stocked with a roll of paper and coloured pencils should creative inspiration hit. There's no need to leave the hotel for meals, since David Chang's Má Pêche and an outpost of his Milk Bar are on site.

Viceroy New York

NEW *120 W 57th Street, between Sixth & Seventh Avenues (1-212 830 8000, www.viceroyhotelsandresorts.com/newyork). Subway F, N, Q, R to 57th Street.* **$$$**.

Designed by Roman and Williams, Viceroy New York has a cool midcentury vibe. In the snug standard quarters, custom-made iroko-wood cabinets flanking the bed evoke a first-class cabin back when ocean liners were glamorous. You'll find an Illy espresso maker tucked behind one of the tambour doors, while on the nightstand is a Beats by Dr Dre Beatbox Portable sound system that blows away standard iPod docks. The on-site American eaterie, Kingside, is helmed by Landmarc chef Marc Murphy.

Midtown East

Hotel Elysée

60 E 54th Street, between Madison & Park Avenues (1-212 753 1066, www.elyseehotel.com). Subway E, M to Lexington Avenue-53rd Street; 6 to 51st Street. **$$$**.

The former home of Tennessee Williams and Tallulah Bankhead, this small 1926 property is like a scaled-down grand hotel: rooms are furnished with antiques, gilt-framed paintings and old prints, and most of the marble-tiled bathrooms have tubs. Many suites are decked out with (non-functioning) fireplaces and crystal chandeliers. Stop by the sedate second-floor lounge for complimentary wine and cheese, served every evening, on your way to dinner at the exclusive Monkey Bar (see p129) – a few tables are set aside for guests every night.

Upper East Side

The Surrey

20 E 76th Street, between Fifth & Madison Avenues (1-212 288 3700, 1-800 978 7739). Subway 6 to 77th Street. **$$$$**.

Occupying an elegant 1920s building that has been given a $60 million overhaul, the Surrey updates the grand hotel model. The coolly elegant limestone and marble lobby showcases museum-quality contemporary art, and guestrooms are dressed in a refined palette of cream, grey and beige, with the addition of luxurious white marble bathrooms. But the centrepiece is undoubtedly the incredibly comfortable DUX by Duxiana bed, swathed in sumptuous Sferra linens. The hotel is flanked by top chef Daniel Boulud's Café Boulud and his chic cocktail destination, Bar Pleiades (see p139); there's also a luxurious spa (see p142).

ESSENTIALS

Upper West Side

Hotel Belleclaire

250 W 77th Street, at Broadway (1-212 362 7700, www.hotelbelleclaire.com). Subway 1 to 79th Street. **$$**.

This centegenarian landmark debuted a major renovation in 2013. The grand panelled lobby, which retains its original skylight and mosaic-tiled floor, now has a stylish coffee bar. Guest quarters feature wooden floors and details such as padded headboards, Frette linens and iHome iPod docks. Snacks from gourmet grocer Dean & Deluca and bath products courtesy of iconic East Village chemist CO Bigelow are further perks. Parents, in particular, will appreciate the refrigerators in every room and the 'media lounge' housing two arcade-game stations and three free-to-use iMacs.

NYLO New York City

NEW *2178 Broadway, at 77th Street (1-212 362 1100, www.nylohotels.com/nyc). Subway 1 to 79th Street.* **$$**.

Launched by former W honcho Michael Mueller, NYLO is short for New York Loft and the airy guest quarters have stacked-plywood furnishings, original art and 'brick' wallpaper that playfully reference the loft-living archetype. The functional style doesn't skimp on comfort, though: beds have a cushy, custom-made pillow-top mattress, and in-room amenities include free Wi-Fi and a Keurig coffeemaker to brew your free Wolfgang Puck joe. Deluxe rooms on the top three floors open on to terraces, some with views of the Hudson River or Central Park. In addition to a sprawling bar, the uptown arm of contemporary Chinese restaurant RedFarm (see p94) is on site.

Harlem

Harlem Flophouse

242 W 123rd Street, between Adam Clayton Powell Jr Boulevard (Seventh Avenue) & Frederick Douglass Boulevard (Eighth Avenue) (1-917 720 3707, www.harlemflophouse.com). Subway A, B, C, D to 125th Street. **$**.

The dark-wood interior, moody lighting and lilting jazz make musician Rene Calvo's Harlem inn feel more like a 1930s speakeasy than a 21st-century B&B. The airy suites have restored tin ceilings, a quirky mix of junk-store furnishings and period knick-knacks, and working sinks in antique cabinets. There are just two suites per floor; each pair shares a bathroom.

Wythe Hotel p182

Brooklyn

McCarren Hotel & Pool

160 North 12th Street, between Bedford Avenue & Berry Street, Williamsburg (1-718 218 7500, www.chelseahotels. com). Subway L to Bedford Avenue. **$$$**.
Small boutique-hotel chain Chelsea Hotels, which operates an ironically retro retreat in Long Island, brings resort style to Brooklyn. In summer, the 40-foot saltwater pool opens on the secluded back patio; there's also a ninth-floor roof bar that takes in the Manhattan skyline. Guest rooms evoke midcentury minimalism with bamboo flooring, taupe leather platform beds and Carrara-marble-tiled bathrooms with toiletries from NYC's Malin + Goetz. The hotel restaurant, the Elm, is helmed by Michelin-starred chef Paul Liebrandt.

New York Loft Hostel

249 Varet Street, at Bogart Street, Bushwick (1-718 366 1351, www.nyloft hostel.com). Subway L to Morgan Avenue. **$**.
Set in an arty enclave, this budget lodging fuses the traditional youth hostel set-up (dorm-style rooms with single beds and lockers, communal kitchen and lounging areas) with a fashionable loft aesthetic. In the former clothing warehouse, linen curtains billow in front of huge windows, and there's industrial-chic exposed brick and piping. The patio is the site of summer barbecues.

Nu Hotel

85 Smith Street, between Atlantic Avenue & State Street, Boerum Hill (1-718 852 8585, www.nuhotelbrooklyn.com). Subway A, C, F to Jay Street-Borough Hall; F, G to Bergen Street; R to Court Street; 2, 3, 4, 5 to Borough Hall. **$$**.
Conveniently placed for shops and restaurants, Nu Hotel has bundled quirky niceties into a classy, eco-friendly package. Rooms are decked out with wood flooring, organic linens and recycled teak furniture, 42in flatscreen TVs and Bluetooth-enabled iHome sound systems for wireless tunes. Standard rooms are comfortably sized, but the lofty Urban Suites are outfitted with hammocks and a padded-leather sleeping alcove.

Wythe Hotel

80 Wythe Avenue, at North 11th Street, Williamsburg (1-718 460 8000, www. wythehotel.com). Subway L to Bedford Avenue. **$$**.
A 1901 cooperage near the waterfront topped with a three-storey glass-and-aluminium addition, the Wythe perfectly captures the neighbourhood's elusive hip factor. Since the launch team includes Andrew Tarlow, the man behind local eateries Diner and Marlow & Sons, it's not surprising that the ground-floor restaurant, Reynard, was an instant hit. In many of the rooms, floor-to-ceiling windows offer a Manhattan skyline panorama. Heated concrete floors, exposed brick, reclaimed-timber beds and witty wallpaper create a rustic-industrial vibe, offset by fully plugged-in technology: a cable by the bed turns your iPhone into a surround-sound music system.

Queens

Z NYC Hotel

11-01 43rd Avenue, at 11th Street, Long Island City (1-212 319 7000, www.zhotel ny.com). Subway E, M to Court Square-23rd Street; F to 21st Street-Queensbridge; N, Q, 7 to Queensboro Plaza. **$$**.
The Z shares a gritty industrial side street with tool suppliers and flooring wholesalers, but the Queensboro Bridge-side setting and largely low-rise neighbours facilitate its most stunning feature: knock-your-socks-off midtown views through floor-to-ceiling windows. Offbeat details, such as lightbulbs encased in mason jars dangling over the bed, wall stencils of iconic New York images and black flip-flops instead of the standard white slippers, enliven the stock boutique luxury of the accommodation. The sprawling roof bar offers 360-degree panoramas.

Getting Around

Arriving and leaving

By air

John F Kennedy International
Airport *1-718 244 4444, www.panynj. gov/airports/jfk.html.*
The **subway** (see p184) is the cheapest option. The **AirTrain** ($5, www.airtrainjfk.com) links to the A train at Howard Beach or the E, J and Z trains at Sutphin Boulevard-Archer Avenue ($2.50-$2.75).

NYC Airporter buses (1-718 777 5111, www.nycairporter.com; one way $16, round trip $29) connect JFK and Manhattan, with stops near Grand Central Terminal, Penn Station and Port Authority Bus Terminal. Buses run every 30mins from 5am to 11.30pm daily.

A **yellow cab** to Manhattan will charge a flat $52.50 fare, plus toll (usually $5) and tip (15 per cent is the norm). The fare to JFK from Manhattan is not a set rate, but is usually roughly the same (see p185).

La Guardia Airport *1-718 533 3400, www.panynj.gov/airports/laguardia. html.*
Seasoned New Yorkers take the **M60 bus** ($2.50), to 106th Street at Broadway. The ride takes 40-60mins, depending on traffic, and runs 24 hrs daily. The route crosses Manhattan at 125th Street in Harlem. Get off at Lexington Avenue for the 4, 5 and 6 trains; at Malcolm X Boulevard (Lenox Avenue) for the 2 and 3; or at St Nicholas Avenue for the A, B, C and D trains.

Less time-consuming options include **NYC Airporter** buses (one way $13, round trip $23). Taxis and car services charge about $30, plus toll and tip.

Newark Liberty International
Airport *1-973 961 6000, www.panynj. gov/airports/newark-liberty.html.*
The best bet is the $12.50, half-hour trip via **New Jersey Transit** to or from Penn Station. The airport's monorail, **AirTrain Newark** (www.airtrainnewark.com), is linked to the NJ Transit and Amtrak train systems.

Bus services operated by **Coach USA** (1-877 894 9155, www.coach usa.com) run to Manhattan, stopping at Bryant Park in midtown and inside the Port Authority Bus Terminal (one way $16, round trip $28); buses leave every 15-30mins. A **car** or **taxi** will run at $60-$75, plus toll and tip.

By bus

Most out-of-town buses come and go from the **Port Authority Bus Terminal** (see below). Greyhound (1-800 231 2222, www.greyhound. com) runs long-distance travel to US destinations. The company's **BoltBus** (1-877 265 8287, www. boltbus.com), booked online, serves several East Coast cities. **New Jersey Transit** (1-973 275 5555, www.njtransit.com) runs services to most of New Jersey and parts of New York State. Finally, **Peter Pan** (1-800 343 9999, www. peterpanbus.com) runs extensive services to cities across the Northeast; its tickets are also valid on Greyhound buses.

Port Authority Bus Terminal *625 Eighth Avenue, between 40th & 42nd Streets, Garment District (1-212 564 8484, www.panynj.gov/bus-terminals/ port-authority-bus-terminal.html). Subway A, C, E to 42nd Street-Port Authority.*

By rail

Grand Central Terminal *42nd to 44th Streets, between Vanderbilt & Lexington Avenues, Midtown East. Subway S, 4, 5, 6, 7 to 42nd Street-Grand Central.* Home to Metro-North, which runs trains to more than 100 stations in New York State and Connecticut.

Penn Station *31st to 33rd Streets, between Seventh & Eighth Avenues, Garment District. Subway A, C, E, 1, 2, 3 to 34th Street-Penn Station.* Amtrak, Long Island Rail Road and New Jersey Transit trains depart from this terminal.

Public transport

Metropolitan Transportation Authority (MTA) *511 local, 1-877 690 5116 outside New York State, 1-212 878 7000 international, www.mta.info.* The MTA runs the subway and bus lines, as well as services to points outside Manhattan. News of service interruptions and MTA maps are on its website. Be warned: backpacks, handbags and large containers may be subject to random searches.

Fares & tickets

Although you can pay with exact change (no dollar bills) on buses, to enter the subway system you'll need either a single-ride ticket ($2.75, available from station vending machines only) or a **MetroCard**. You can buy MetroCards from booths or vending machines in the stations, from the Official NYC Information Center, from the New York Transit Museum in Brooklyn or Grand Central Terminal, and from many hotels.

The standard base fare across the subway and bus network on a MetroCard is $2.50. Free transfers between the subway and buses are available only with a MetroCard (for bus-to-bus transfers on cash fares, see p185). Up to four people can use a pay-per-ride MetroCard, sold in denominations from $5 to $80. If you put $5 or more on the card, you'll receive a five per cent bonus – or 25 cents for every $5 – thus reducing the cost of each ride. However, if you're planning to use the subway or buses often, an Unlimited Ride MetroCard is great value. These cards are offered in two denominations, available at station vending machines but not at booths: a seven-day pass ($30) and a 30-day pass ($112). Both are good for unlimited rides within those periods, but you can't share a card with your travel companions.

Subway

Cleaner and safer than it was 20 years ago, the subway system is one of the world's largest and cheapest. For fares and MetroCards, see above. Trains run around the clock. If you are travelling late at night, board the train from the designated off-peak waiting area, usually near the middle of the platform; this is more secure than the ends of the platform, which are often less populated in the wee hours.

Stations are most often named after the street on which they're located. Entrances are marked with a green and white globe (open 24 hours) or a red and white globe (limited hours). Many stations have separate entrances for the uptown and downtown platforms – look before you pay. Trains are identified by letters or numbers, colour-coded according to the line on which they run. Local trains stop at every station on the line; express trains stop at major stations only.

The most current Manhattan subway map is reprinted at the back of this guide; you can also ask MTA workers in service booths for a free copy, or refer to enlarged maps displayed in each subway station.

City buses

White and blue MTA buses are usually the best way to travel crosstown and a pleasant way to travel up- or downtown, as long as you're not in a hurry. They have a digital destination sign on the front, along with a route number preceded by a letter (M for Manhattan, B for Brooklyn, Bx for the Bronx, Q for Queens and S for Staten Island). Maps are posted on most buses and at all subway stops; they're also available from the Official NYC Information Center (see p189). The Manhattan bus map is printed in the back of this guide. All local buses are equipped with wheelchair lifts. The fare is payable with a MetroCard (see p184) or exact change ($2.50 in coins only; no pennies or dollar bills). MetroCards allow for an automatic transfer from bus to bus, and between bus and subway. If you pay cash, and you're travelling uptown or downtown and want to go crosstown (or vice versa), ask the driver for a transfer when you get on – you'll be given a ticket for use on the second leg of your journey, valid for two hours. MTA's express buses usually head to the outer boroughs for a $6 fare.

Rail

The following commuter trains serve NY's hinterland.

Long Island Rail Road *511 local, 1-718 217 5477 outside New York State, www.mta.info/lirr.*
Rail services from Penn Station, Brooklyn and Queens to towns throughout Long Island.

Metro-North Railroad *511 local, 1-212 532 4900 outside New York State, www.mta.info/mnr.*

Serves towns north of Manhattan, leaving from Grand Central Terminal.

New Jersey Transit *1-973 275 5555, www.njtransit.com.*
Services from Penn Station reach most of New Jersey, some points in NY State and Philadelphia.

PATH Trains *1-800 234 7284, www.panynj.gov/path.*
PATH trains run from six stations in Manhattan to various New Jersey destinations, including Hoboken, Jersey City and Newark. The 24-hour service costs $2.50.

Boat

NY Waterway (1-800 533 3779, www.nywaterway.com) runs a water-transport service that connects Manhattan to Queens, Brooklyn and some New Jersey cities. The **East River Ferry** runs between Midtown East at 34th Street and downtown Manhattan at Pier 11 via Long Island City in Queens and Greenpoint, Williamsburg and Dumbo in Brooklyn (from $4 one way, $12 day pass). On the West Side of the island, NY Waterway's **Hudson River ferries** link Pier 79 on 39th Street and Brookfield Place in lower Manhattan to destinations in New Jersey, including Hoboken and Jersey City ($7-$21.50 one-way). Visit the website for ferry routes and schedules.

Taxis

If the centre light atop the taxi is lit, the cab is available and should stop if you flag it down. Get in and then tell the driver where you're going. (New Yorkers generally give cross-streets rather than addresses.) By law, taxis cannot refuse to take you anywhere inside the five boroughs or to New York airports. Use only yellow medallion (licensed) cabs; avoid unregulated 'gypsy cabs'.

ESSENTIALS

Taxis will carry up to four passengers for the same price: $2.50 plus 50¢ per fifth of a mile or per minute idling, with an extra 50¢ charge (a new state tax), another 50¢ from 8pm to 6am and a $1 surcharge during rush hour (4-8pm Mon-Fri). The average fare for a three-mile ride is $14, but this will vary depending on the time and traffic.

If you have a problem, take down the medallion and driver's numbers, posted on the partition. Always ask for a receipt – there's a meter number on it. To complain or to trace lost property, call the Taxi & Limousine Commission (1-212 227 0700, 8.30am-5pm Mon-Fri) or visit www.nyc.gov/taxi. Tip 15-20 per cent, as in a restaurant. All taxis now accept major credit cards.

Car services are regulated by the Taxi & Limousine Commission. Unlike cabs, drivers can make only pre-arranged pickups. Don't try to hail one, and be wary of those that offer you a ride. These companies will pick you up anywhere in the city for a set fare.

Carmel *1-212 666 6666.*
Dial 7 *1-212 777 7777.*
GroundLink *1-877 227 7260.*

Driving
Car hire

You need a credit card to rent a car in the US, and usually must be at least 25 years old. Car hire is cheaper in the city's outskirts and further afield than in Manhattan. NYC companies add 19.875 per cent in taxes.

If you just want a car for a few hours, **Zipcar** (US: 1-866 494 7227, www.zipcar.com; UK: 0333 240 9000, www.zipcar.co.uk) is cost effective.

Alamo *US: 1-877 222 9075, www. alamo.com. UK: 0871 384 1086, www.alamo.co.uk.*

Avis *US: 1-800 230 4898, www.avis. com. UK: 0808 284 0014, www.avis. co.uk.*
Budget *US: 1-800 527 0700, www. budget.com. UK: 0808 284 4444, www.budget.co.uk.*
Enterprise *US: 1-800 261 7331, www.enterprise.com. UK: 0800 800 227, www.enterprise.co.uk.*
Hertz *US: 1-800 654 3131, www.hertz. com. UK: 0843 309 3099, www.hertz. co.uk.*

Parking

Make sure you read parking signs and never park within 15 feet of a fire hydrant (to avoid a $115 ticket and/or having your car towed). Parking is off-limits on most streets for at least a few hours daily. The Department of Transportation provides information on daily changes to regulations (dial 311).

If precautions fail, call 1-212 971 0771 for Manhattan towing and impoundment information; go to www.nyc.gov for phone numbers in other boroughs.

Cycling

While biking on NYC's streets is only recommended for experienced cyclists, the new **Citi Bike** system (www.citibikenyc.com, 1-855 245 3311) gives you temporary access to bikes at 600 stations in Manhattan and Brooklyn. Visitors can purchase a 24-hour ($9.95) or seven-day ($25) Access Pass at a station kiosk with a credit or debit card. You'll then receive a 'ride code' that will allow you to undock and ride for 30 minutes at a stretch. A longer trip will incur an extra fee.

Bike & Roll (1-212 260 0400, www.bikeandroll.com/newyork) is the city's biggest cycle-hire company, with 11 outposts. Rates (including helmet) start at $10 per hour.

ESSENTIALS

Resources A-Z

Accident & emergency

In an emergency only, dial 911 for an ambulance, police or the fire department, or call the operator (dial 0). The following hospitals have emergency rooms:

New York-Presbyterian/Lower Manhattan Hospital *170 William Street, between Beeckman & Spruce Streets (1-212 312 5000). Subway 1 to Chambers Street; 2, 3 to Fulton Street; 4, 5, 6 to Brooklyn Bridge-City Hall.*

Mount Sinai Hospital *Madison Avenue, at 100th Street, Upper East Side (1-212 241 6500). Subway 6 to 103rd Street.*

New York – Presbyterian Hospital/Weill Cornell Medical Center *525 E 68th Street, at York Avenue, Upper East Side (1-212 746 5454). Subway 6 to 68th Street-Hunter College.*

Mount Sinai Roosevelt Hospital *1000 Tenth Avenue, at 59th Street, Upper West Side (1-212 523 4000). Subway A, B, C, D, 1 to 59th Street-Columbus Circle.*

Customs

US Customs allows foreigners to bring in $100 worth of gifts (the limit is $800 for returning Americans) without paying duty. One carton of 200 cigarettes (or 100 cigars) and one litre of liquor (spirits) are allowed. Plants, meat and fresh produce of any kind cannot be brought into the country. You will have to fill out a form if you carry more than $10,000 in currency. You will be handed a white form on your inbound flight to fill in, confirming that you haven't exceeded any of these allowances.

If you need to bring prescription drugs with you into the US, make sure the container is clearly marked, and bring your doctor's statement or a prescription. Marijuana, cocaine and most opiate derivatives, along with a number of other drugs and chemicals, are not permitted: the possession of them is punishable by a stiff fine and/or imprisonment. Check in with the US Customs Service (www.cbp.gov) before you arrive if you're unsure.

Disabled

Under New York City law, facilities constructed after 1987 must provide complete access for the disabled – restrooms, entrances and exits included. In 1990, the Americans with Disabilities Act made the same requirement federal law. Many older buildings have added disabled-access features. There has been widespread compliance with the law, but call ahead to check facilities. For information on accessible cultural institutions, contact the Mayor's Office for People with Disabilities (1-212 788 2830, 9am-5pm Mon-Fri). All Broadway theatres are equipped with devices for the hearing-impaired; call Sound Associates (1-888 772 7686, www.soundassociates.com) for more information. For the visually impaired, HAI (1-212 284 4100, www.hainyc.org) offers live audio descriptions of selected theatre performances.

Electricity

The US uses 110-120V, 60-cycle alternating current rather than the 220-240V, 50-cycle AC used in Europe. The transformers that power or recharge newer electronic devices such as laptops are designed

ESSENTIALS

to handle either current and may need nothing more than an adaptor for the wall outlet. Other appliances may also require a power converter. Adaptors and converters can be purchased at department stores, airport shops, pharmacies and at branches of electronics chain Radio Shack (www.radioshack.com).

Embassies & consulates

Australia *1-212 351 6500.*
Canada *1-212 596 1628.*
United Kingdom *1-212 745 0200.*
Ireland *1-212 319 2555.*
New Zealand *1-212 832 4038.*

Internet

Cycle Café *250 W 49th Street, between Broadway & Eighth Avenue, Theater District (1-212 380 1204). Subway C, E, 1 to 50th Street; N, Q, R to 49th Street.* **Open** 8am-midnight daily.
A bike-rental shop and internet café rolled into one.
NYCWireless *www.nycwireless.net.* This group has established dozens of hotspots in the city for free wireless access. (For example, most parks below 59th Street are covered.) Visit the website for information and a map.
New York Public Library *1-212 592 7000, www.nypl.org.* Branches of the NYPL are great places to get online for free, offering both Wi-Fi and computers for public use. (Ask for an out-of-state card, for which you need proof of residence, or a guest pass.) The Science, Industry & Business Library (188 Madison Avenue, at 34th Street, Midtown East), part of the Public Library system, has about 70 computers. All libraries have a computer limit of 45 minutes per day.
Starbucks *www.starbucks.com.* Many branches offer free Wi-Fi; there's a search facility on the website.

Opening hours

These are general guidelines:
Banks 9am-6pm Mon-Fri; generally also Sat mornings.
Businesses 9am or 10am to 5pm or 6pm Mon-Fri.
Pubs & bars 4pm-2am Mon-Thur, Sun; noon-4am Fri, Sat (but hours vary).
Shops 9am, 10am or 11am to 7pm or 8pm Mon-Sat (some open at noon and/ or close at 9pm). Many also open on Sun, usually 11am or noon to 6pm.

Police

The NYPD stations below are in central, tourist-heavy areas of Manhattan. To find the nearest police precinct or for information about police services, call 1-646 610 5000 or visit www.nyc.gov.
Sixth Precinct *233 W 10th Street, between Bleecker & Hudson Streets, West Village (1-212 741 4811).*
Seventh Precinct *19½ Pitt Street, at Broome Street, Lower East Side (1-212 477 7311).*
Midtown North Precinct *306 W 54th Street, between Eighth & Ninth Avenues, Hell's Kitchen (1-212 767 8400).*
17th Precinct *167 E 51st Street, between Lexington & Third Avenues, Midtown East (1-212 826 3211).*
Central Park Precinct *86th Street & Transverse Road, Central Park (1-212 570 4820).*

Postal services

Post offices are usually open 9am-5pm Mon-Fri (a few open as early as 7.30am and close as late as 8.30pm); some are open Sat until 3pm or 4pm. The **James A Farley Post Office** (421 Eighth Avenue, between 31st & 33rd Streets, Garment District, 1-800 275 8777 24hr information, www.usps.com) is open 24 hours daily for automated postal services.

Smoking

The 1995 NYC Smoke-Free Air Act makes it illegal to smoke in virtually all indoor public places. Since 2011 smoking has also been prohibited in New York City parks, pedestrian plazas (such as Times Square and Herald Square) and on beaches. Violators could face a $50 fine.

Telephones

As a rule, you must dial 1 + the area code before a number, even if the place you are calling is in the same area code. The area codes for Manhattan are 212 and 646; Brooklyn, Queens, Staten Island and the Bronx are 718 and 347; 917 is now mostly for mobile phones and pagers. Numbers preceded by 800, 877 and 888 are free of charge when dialled from within the US.

To dial abroad, dial 011 followed by the country code, then the number. For the operator dial 0. Mobile phone users from other countries will need a tri-band handset. Public pay phones take coins and credit cards. The best way to make long-distance calls is with a phone card, available from the post office and chain stores such as Duane Reade and Rite Aid.

Time

New York is on Eastern Standard Time. This is five hours behind Greenwich Mean Time. Clocks are set forward one hour in early March for Daylight Saving Time (Eastern Daylight Time) and back one hour at the beginning of November. Going from east to west, Eastern Time is one hour ahead of Central Time, two hours ahead of Mountain Time and three hours ahead of Pacific Time.

Tipping

In restaurants, it's customary to tip at least 15 per cent.

Tourist information

Official NYC Information Center at Macy's Herald Square

151 W 34th Street, between Broadway & Seventh Avenue (1-212 484 1222, www.nycgo.com). Subway 1, 2, 3, A, C, E to 34th Street-Penn Station; B, D, F, M, N, Q, R to 34th Street-Herald Square. **Open** 9am-7pm Mon-Fri; 10am-7pm Sat; 11am-7pm Sun.
Other locations throughout the city.

What's on

The weekly *Time Out New York* magazine (www.timeout.com/newyork), which hits newsstands on Wednesdays, is NYC's essential arts and entertainment guide. The best source for all things gay is *Next* (www.nextmagazine.com); the monthly *Go!* (www.gomag.com) is geared towards girls.

Visas

Currently, 37 countries participate in the Visa Waiver Program (VWP; www.cbp.gov/esta) including Australia, Ireland, New Zealand and the UK. Citizens of these countries do not need a visa for stays in the US shorter than 90 days (business or pleasure) as long as they have a machine-readable passport (e-passport) valid for the full 90-day period, a return ticket, and authorisation to travel through the ESTA (Electronic System for Travel Authorization) scheme. Visitors must fill in the ESTA form at least 24 hours before travelling (72 hours is recommended) and pay a $14 fee; the form can be found at www.cbp.gov/xp/cgov/travel/id_visa/esta/).

If you do not qualify for entry under the Visa Waiver Program, you will need a visa; ensure you leave plenty of time to check before travelling.

ESSENTIALS

Index

Sights & Areas

a

American Folk Art Museum p143
American Museum of Natural History/Rose Center for Earth & Space p143
Apollo Theater p153

b

Barclays Center p163
Bronx p154
Bronx Museum of the Arts p154
Bronx Zoo/Wildlife Conservation Society p154
Brooklyn p156
Brooklyn Academy of Music 163
Brooklyn Botanic Garden p156
Brooklyn Bridge Park p156
Brooklyn Museum p156

c

Carnegie Hall p122
Cathedral Church of St John the Divine p143
Central Park p130
Chelsea p97
Chelsea Piers 105
Chinatown p66
Chrysler Building p128
Circle Line Cruises p117
City Hall p50
Cloisters, the p150
Coney Island p164
Cooper-Hewitt, National Design Museum p131, p136

d

Dover Street Market New York p114

Downtown p50
Drawing Center p61

e

East Village p77
Eldridge Street Synagogue p71
Ellis Island Immigration Museum p56
Empire State Building p124

f

Fifth Avenue p124
Financial District p50
Flatiron Building p106
Flatiron District p106
Fraunces Tavern Museum p51
Frick Collection p137

g

Garment District p115
Governors Island p51
Gramercy Park p111
Grand Central Terminal p128
Greenwich Village p86
Green-Wood Cemetery p157
Guggenheim p139

h

Harlem p150
Hell's Kitchen p117
Herald Square p115
High Line p92

i

International Center of Photography p124
Intrepid Sea, Air & Space Museum p117

j

Jewish Museum p137

l

Lincoln Center p149
Little Italy p66

Lower East Side p70
Lower East Side Tenement Museum p70

m

Madison Square Garden p116
Madison Square Park p106
Meatpacking District p92
Merchant's House Museum p77
Metropolitan Museum of Art p137
Metropolitan Opera House 149
Midtown p96
Midtown East p128
Mmuseumm p61
MoMA-PS1 p165
Morgan Library & Museum p113
Murray Hill p111
Museo del Barrio, El p138
Museum at Eldridge Street p71
Museum at FIT p97
Museum of American Finance p51
Museum of Arts & Design p145
Museum of Chinese in America p66
Museum of the City of New York p138
Museum of Mathematics p106
Museum of Modern Art (MoMA) p124
Museum of the Moving Image p165
Museum of Reclaimed Urban Space p78
Museum of Sex p107

n

National Museum of the American Indian p56